Transforming Language Teaching and Teacher Education for Equity and Justice

NEW PERSPECTIVES ON LANGUAGE AND EDUCATION

Founding Editor: Viv Edwards, *University of Reading, UK*

Series Editors: Phan Le Ha, *University of Hawaii at Manoa, USA* and Joel Windle, *Monash University, Australia.*

Two decades of research and development in language and literacy education have yielded a broad, multidisciplinary focus. Yet education systems face constant economic and technological change, with attendant issues of identity and power, community and culture. What are the implications for language education of new 'semiotic economies' and communications technologies? Of complex blendings of cultural and linguistic diversity in communities and institutions? Of new cultural, regional and national identities and practices? The New Perspectives on Language and Education series will feature critical and interpretive, disciplinary and multidisciplinary perspectives on teaching and learning, language and literacy in new times. New proposals, particularly for edited volumes, are expected to acknowledge and include perspectives from the Global South. Contributions from scholars from the Global South will be particularly sought out and welcomed, as well as those from marginalized communities within the Global North.

All books in this series are externally peer-reviewed.

Full details of all the books in this series and of all our other publications can be found on http://www.multilingual-matters.com, or by writing to Multilingual Matters, St Nicholas House, 31–34 High Street, Bristol BS1 2AW, UK.

NEW PERSPECTIVES ON LANGUAGE AND EDUCATION: 103

Transforming World Language Teaching and Teacher Education for Equity and Justice

Pushing Boundaries in US Contexts

Edited by
Beth Wassell and Cassandra Glynn

MULTILINGUAL MATTERS
Bristol • Jackson

DOI https://doi.org/10.21832/WASSEL6515
Library of Congress Cataloging in Publication Data
A catalog record for this book is available from the Library of Congress.
Names: Wassell, Beth A., editor. | Glynn, Cassandra, editor.
Title: Transforming World Language Teaching and Teacher Education for
    Equity and Justice: Pushing Boundaries in US contexts/Edited by
    Beth Wassell and Cassandra Glynn.
Description: Bristol; Jackson: Multilingual Matters, 2022. | Includes bibliographical
    references and index. | Summary: "This edited book expands the current scholarship
    on teaching world languages for social justice and equity in K-12 and postsecondary
    contexts in the US. The chapters address how world language teachers approach
    social justice in their teaching, and how teacher educators prepare teachers to teach
    for social justice in the language classroom"—Provided by publisher.
Identifiers: LCCN 2021058416 (print) | LCCN 2021058417 (ebook) | ISBN
    9781788926508 (paperback) | ISBN 9781788926515 (hardback) | ISBN
    9781788926539 (epub) | ISBN 9781788926522 (pdf)
Subjects: LCSH: Social justice and education—United States. | Language and
    languages—Study and teaching—United States. | Educational
    equalization—United States. | Language teachers—Training of—United States.
    Classification: LCC LC192.2.T75 2022 (print) | LCC LC192.2 (ebook) | DDC
    379.2/60973—dc23/eng/20220217
LC record available at https://lccn.loc.gov/2021058416
LC ebook record available at https://lccn.loc.gov/2021058417

British Library Cataloguing in Publication Data
A catalogue entry for this book is available from the British Library.

ISBN-13: 978-1-78892-651-5 (hbk)
ISBN-13: 978-1-78892-650-8 (pbk)

Multilingual Matters
UK: St Nicholas House, 31–34 High Street, Bristol BS1 2AW, UK.
USA: Ingram, Jackson, TN, USA.

Website: www.multilingual-matters.com
Twitter: Multi_Ling_Mat
Facebook: https://www.facebook.com/multilingualmatters
Blog: www.channelviewpublications.wordpress.com

The policy of Multilingual Matters/Channel View Publications is to use papers that are
natural, renewable and recyclable products, made from wood grown in sustainable
forests. In the manufacturing process of our books, and to further support our policy,
preference is given to printers that have FSC and PEFC Chain of Custody certification.
The FSC and/or PEFC logos will appear on those books where full certification has been
granted to the printer concerned.

Typeset by Nova Techset Private Limited, Bengaluru and Chennai, India.

Contents

Contributors

Anke al-Bataineh is a former secondary special needs teacher who has MAs in Teaching and Endangered Languages, and a PhD in Language Sciences. Dr al-Bataineh's doctoral research examined the maintenance of Western Armenian in the Middle East and Europe. Based on this research and her more than 15 years of teaching languages in diverse contexts, Dr al-Bataineh co-created an immersion summer camp and collocal teacher training program for Western Armenian teachers from around the world and is developing innovative project-based curriculum for endangered languages. She is also Chair of the MA in English Language Teaching at Western Governors University.

Hannah Baggett is a former high school French teacher and current associate professor in the College of Education at Auburn University. Her research interests include critical theories, race and education, and educator beliefs. She also has particular interest in qualitative and participatory methods. Her work has been published in journals such as the *American Educational Research Journal*, *Teaching and Teacher Education*, *Whiteness and Education* and *Qualitative Inquiry*.

Samuel Chakmakjian is a heritage speaker of Western Armenian, a fourth-generation Bostonian, and an alumnus and former teacher at St. Stephen's Armenian Saturday School of Greater Boston. He holds a bachelor's degree in Language and Linguistics from Brandeis University, and a master's degree in *Sciences du langage* with a concentration on Armenian from *l'Institut national des langues et civilisations orientales* (INALCO) of Paris. He is currently pursuing a doctorate in Linguistics at INALCO.

Joan Clifford, PhD, is Assistant Professor of the Practice in Spanish in the Department of Romance Studies and Director of Community-Based Language Initiatives in Duke Service-Learning at Duke University. She regularly teaches service-learning courses, has directed global education programs in Chile, Mexico and Spain, and worked with immersive co-curricular service-learning programs in Argentina, Ecuador and the US. Joan explores best practices for community-based learning for world language students in her co-authored book, *Community-Based Language Learning: A Framework for Educators* (2019).

Mary Curran is a Professor of Professional Practice and Director of Local-Global Partnerships at Rutgers Graduate School of Education. Her research focuses on community-engaged language partnerships and language teacher education.

Johanna Ennser-Kananen is a University Lecturer of English at the University of Jyväskylä in Finland. Her current work focuses on linguistically and culturally sustaining education for migrant teachers and anti-oppressive (language) pedagogies for migrant students, particularly those with refugee experience. Within those areas, she is particularly interested in legitimacy of knowledge (epistemic justice) and language practices. She is the co-editor of the *Routledge Handbook of Educational Linguistics* and has published in the *Modern Language Journal*, the *International Review of Education*, the *Encyclopedia of Applied Linguistics* and the *International Journal of Language Studies*, among others.

Cassandra Glynn is an Associate Professor at Concordia College in Moorhead, Minnesota, where she teaches foundational education and methods courses and supervises student teachers. She is also Director of the Master of Education in World Language Instruction at Concordia College in partnership with Concordia Language Villages. Her research focuses on representation in language programs and social justice approaches to teaching world languages. Prior to working in teacher education, she taught middle and high school German and French in Minnesota and North Dakota.

Krishauna Hines-Gaither is the Associate Vice President for Diversity, Equity & Inclusion and the Director of the Intercultural Engagement Center at Guilford College. She received her PhD from UNC-Greensboro in Cultural Studies. She has taught and published in the fields of Spanish, Race & Ethnicity Studies, Women and Gender Studies and (Afro)Latin American Studies. Krishauna co-founded African American Linguists. She is the past Chair of ACTFL's Educators of African American Students SIG, and the past President of the Foreign Language Association of North Carolina.

Stacey Margarita Johnson is Assistant Director at the Center for Teaching, Senior Lecturer in the Department of Spanish and Portuguese, and Affiliated Faculty in the Center for Second Language Studies at Vanderbilt University. She is also Editor of the journal *Spanish and Portuguese Review* and producer and host of the podcast, 'We Teach Languages'. Her research focuses on classroom practices, adult learning, critical pedagogy, and technology in language teaching. She is the author of the books *Hybrid Language Teaching in Practice: Perceptions, Reactions, and Results*, co-authored with Berta Carrasco (2015) and *Adult Learning in the Language Classroom* (2015).

Liz Torres Melendez was the Immigrant Student Coordinator at Guilford College from July 2018 to May 2020. Liz received her Bachelor of Arts in History from the UNC-Asheville in 2018. She recently completed her Master of Arts in Museum Studies from the University of North Carolina at Greensboro. Liz was born in Manati, Puerto Rico. She moved to North Carolina when she was four years old, and she has called central North Carolina home since then. Liz's research interests include the immigration system, the impact of internalized superiority and inferiority, and the history of movements against colonization.

Terry Osborn, PhD, is a Professor of Education at the University of South Florida. He taught secondary German for six years in Georgia and Florida prior to entering higher education. Osborn served twice as Interim Chancellor and as Vice Chancellor of Academic and Student Affairs at the University of South Florida Sarasota-Manatee. Osborn was previously Dean of the College of Education and held administrative roles on the faculties of Fordham University, Queens College of City University of New York and the University of Connecticut. Osborn researches and publishes in the areas of foreign/world language education, interdisciplinary education, and critical pedagogy.

Nina Simone Perez is an Afro Latina from Charlotte, North Carolina. Her mother is African American and her father is Puerto Rican. Her family resides in Florida, North Carolina and New York. Nina has danced her entire life, and she loves to teach contemporary dance. She graduated from Guilford College in May 2020 where she received a bachelor's degree in Business Administration, and minored in Sociology. She worked as an Ambassador in the Intercultural Engagement Center at Guilford College since her first year of college, and as an intern her senior year. Nina hopes to continue working in the diversity and inclusion field.

Dorie Conlon Perugini is a doctoral student at the University of Connecticut in the department of Literatures, Cultures and Languages concentrating on Applied Linguistics and Discourse Studies. She is also an elementary Spanish teacher in Glastonbury, Connecticut where she teaches grades 1–5 and conducts action research. Her research interests include intercultural competence, social justice, raciolinguistics and culturally sustaining pedagogies. Dorie has co-edited *Teaching Intercultural Competence Across the Age Range: From Theory to Practice*, which shares the journey of world language teachers partnering with graduate students from the University of Connecticut to help students develop intercultural competence.

Leisa Quiñones Oramas is currently a middle and high school Spanish teacher in Boston. A native of the coastal northwestern town of Puerto Rico, Leisa moved to New England after finishing her dual bachelor's degree in Comparative Literature and Hispanic Studies. There she completed a Master of Arts in Spanish Language and Cultures and a Master of Arts in Teaching in Second Language Acquisition. She also taught various levels of Spanish at local universities and colleges. For the first three years of her career as a high school teacher, she taught Spanish at a large school district, where she faced the many thrills, challenges and rewards of teaching in an urban classroom. Throughout her career, she has focused on making language learning relevant to students by fostering oral communication and the use of art and authentic resources.

L.J. Randolph Jr. is an Associate Professor of Spanish and Education and Coordinator of the World Language Teacher Education Program at the University of North Carolina Wilmington. He teaches courses in Spanish language, contemporary Latina/o/x cultures and second language teaching methods. His research focuses on a variety of critical issues in language education, including the teaching of Spanish to heritage and native speakers and the incorporation of social justice-oriented pedagogies. He is a past President of the Foreign Language Association of North Carolina and currently serves on the Board of Directors for the American Council on the Teaching of Foreign Languages (ACTFL).

Manuela Wagner is Professor of Foreign Language Education in the Department of Literatures, Cultures and Languages at the University of Connecticut. Her research interests include the development of intercultural competence in education, social justice and human rights education, advocacy for all language learners, intellectual humility and conviction, and humor. She enjoys collaborating with colleagues from and in a variety of contexts as in her most recent co-authored book *Teaching Intercultural Citizenship Across the Curriculum: The Role of Language Education* (ACTFL, 2019) which deals with the theory behind and applications of interdisciplinary intercultural units fostering intercultural citizenship.

Beth Wassell is a Professor in the Department of Language, Literacy and Sociocultural Education at Rowan University in Glassboro, NJ, where she teaches courses in language education, culturally relevant pedagogy and education research. Her research focuses on teaching and teacher education in language classrooms and on preparing educators to support linguistically diverse learners. Prior to her work in higher education, she taught high school Spanish in Florida and New Jersey and ESOL to adults in Pennsylvania.

Jennifer Wooten is the Director of Language Instruction and Senior Lecturer in the Department of Spanish and Portuguese Studies at the University of Florida. She has developed and taught beginning and intermediate language courses, advanced undergraduate courses like Spanish for Educators that focus on experiential learning in and with local Latino communities, and graduate courses to help instructors of world languages critically consider the connections of language, culture and power in the classroom and beyond. She is also the former past President of the International Society for Language Studies, an organization for scholars who explore critical perspectives on language.

Kayane Yoghoutjian has a BA in Education from Haigazian University, Lebanon, and a teaching diploma with an emphasis in teaching Armenian and Social Studies. She is currently pursuing her MA in Education at the Lebanese American University, where she also works as a research assistant in the Department of Education. Yoghoutjian is a native speaker of Western Armenian and has been involved in teaching in formal and informal contexts and formats for the past 12 years. She currently represents the Calouste Gulbenkian Foundation (Portugal) in Lebanon and coordinates school reform projects and other educational programs in Western Armenian.

Acknowledgments

It is impossible to express how much we have learned and grown by collaborating with the authors on this project. Thank you to Anke al-Bataineh, Hannah Baggett, Samuel Chakmakjian, Joan Clifford, Mary Curran, Johanna Ennser-Kananen, Krishauna Hines-Gaither, Stacey Margarita Johnson, Liz Torres Melendez, Terry Osborn, Nina Simone Perez, Dorie Conlon Perugini, Leisa M. Quiñones-Oramas, L.J. Randolph Jr., Manuela Wagner, Jennifer Wooten and Kayane Yoghoutjian. Each of these authors highlighted voices and perspectives that are typically absent in language education scholarship. Many also invited new scholars to serve as co-authors. Our goal was to provide a space in this volume to highlight the voices of those who have historically been left out of scholarship, and we are proud of the outcome. Through these actions, our colleagues are doing the work to dismantle and reimagine world language education.

We would like to convey additional thanks to Manuela Wagner, who was kind enough to provide feedback on an early draft of our introductory chapter. Thank you, also, to Pamela Wesely, who provided general feedback and *ad hoc* reviews. Two additional anonymous reviewers provided thoughtful, valuable feedback that greatly helped us to strengthen the final version of this book. We were so fortunate to have the support of Faten Baroudi and Esra Sevinc, PhD in Education students at Rowan University, who provided help with some of the least interesting aspects of academic publishing: APA formatting and general editing. A special thanks to Anna Roderick at Multilingual Matters, who eagerly supported this project and who responded to our never-ending questions with patience and kindness. We are also grateful to our colleagues at Rowan University (NJ) and Concordia College (MN), who continue to push our thinking around issues of equity and inclusion more generally. We are also so grateful to have found 'our people' at ACTFL through the Critical and Social Justice Approaches Special Interest Group (CSJA SIG) – we appreciate you, look forward to the messy and challenging work that we still have ahead, and hope to continually welcome more faces and voices into the fold. Finally, thank you to the many, many innovative teachers, administrators, professors and other educators who are enacting critical pedagogy in world language contexts, demanding justice in schools and classrooms and taking action to reimagine world language classrooms for the better. We are very fortunate to get to learn from and with such a smart and courageous group of educators.

Editors' Note

We want to begin this volume by acknowledging that we identify as white, cisgendered, middle-class, heterosexual, English-speaking women – identities that have granted us an extraordinary amount of privilege and a number of resources in both our professional and personal lives. As scholars who look closely at issues of equity, justice and human rights, we understand that the act of publishing a book such as this one perpetuates a long history of centering white, privileged voices in scholarship. Our voices inevitably shape the content and context of this book. We look forward to critique of how other perspectives, different frameworks or other interpretations could push the ideas presented in this book even further toward equitable, inclusive and just world language education.

We also want to acknowledge that some authors that we invited to contribute to this book identify as white or are privileged in other ways. These authors are engaged in pushing boundaries and transforming world language education, and we know that they also recognize the privilege they experience and how they can wield this privilege to work toward change in the face of systems that marginalize and oppress. We were also intentional about inviting scholars with a variety of experiences and backgrounds, and in our call for proposals, we encouraged authors to partner with P-12 educators, students, community members and others whose voices have been marginalized in much of the scholarship in world language education. This led to a number of first-time authors, some of whom identify as students, teachers, or community members, to join the work of writing this book. This is a first step. In reflecting more on our process and decision-making, to sufficiently correct this injustice, we recommend that scholars who continue this line of critical inquiry deliberately invite authors and contributors who identify as BIPOC, who are members of the LGBTQ community, who are speakers of languages other than English, who come from other countries that are not typically centered in knowledge production, or who may be marginalized in other ways. However, by simply inviting scholars to collaborate, submit a manuscript or co-author a chapter, we run the risk of further burdening our colleagues, many of whom have been tasked with undervalued or underpaid academic labor. Those of us with privilege must take on the responsibility to substantively support and mentor scholars who work 'at the

xvi   Transforming World Language Teaching and Teacher Education for Equity and Justice

nexus of multiple oppressions' (Navarro, 2017: 507). And finally, we need to ensure that it becomes common practice, rather than unique or extraordinary, to build authentic, sustained and truly collaborative working relationships with the students, teachers and communities we intend to benefit from our scholarship.

Reference

Navarro, T. (2017) But some of us are broke: Race, gender, and the neoliberalization of the academy. *American Anthropologist* 119 (3), 506–517.

1 Rethinking Our Introduction: Calling out Ourselves and Calling in Our Field

Cassandra Glynn and Beth Wassell

We (Cassandra and Beth) sat down together to write the introductory chapter to this edited volume back in February 2020, at a very different time in our world. We had planned to make the argument that, after over 20 years of scholarship on critical and social justice approaches in world language education,[1] this work still exists at the margins of our field – as an add-on, as a checking of a box, or as something that is only for more progressive, liberal or 'woke' educators. At that time, we couldn't have imagined what would happen over the next few months – a global pandemic in which Black and Brown Americans were dying at disproportionate rates (Kaur, 2020), the highest unemployment rates since the Great Depression (Long & Van Dam, 2020), the horrifying killings of George Floyd, Breonna Taylor and Ahmaud Arbery, and all of the complex, justice-related issues that were both overtly and implicitly connected to these events.

Throughout the months that followed the onset of the pandemic, we watched as language teachers were forced to move to a 'new normal' and were met with an avalanche of webinars and virtual meetings with strategies, tools and activities to support remote learning from our national, regional and local organizations, and from other experts in language education. We were grateful for the voices of a few of our colleagues who reminded us about emerging issues of justice and equity: learners with no access to technology; learners whose families were sick or who had a loved one pass away; learners who were now essential workers and charged with being a central earner for their families; and learners who were undocumented or experiencing the pandemic in detention centers, to name just a few. However, early in the pandemic, these voices were the minority, and their ideas and strategies were often relegated to tweets, comments or short segments of webinars. Although there were some voices drawing attention to issues of anti-racism and equity, we observed only limited evidence of social justice issues as the central, explicit focus for world language educators' professional learning. Within a year's time, we would also witness the intense efforts in many states to restrict teaching about racism and other injustices through proposed legislation banning the teaching of so-called 'divisive' concepts, such as critical race theory, anti-racist content, and even diversity and inclusion training (Stout & LeMee, 2021).

In late May 2020, after the world-wide response to the murder of George Floyd and undeniable calls for a reckoning around race in the US, we were able to reconnect and rethink this chapter. We wondered: how could we write an introductory chapter to a book on social justice and equity *without* centering these events and their implications for our field? Systemic racism, discrimination and other human rights and social justice issues have continually plagued the institution of education in the US and have trickled down to all aspects of schooling, teaching and learning. In this sense, these invisible, structural forces have shaped the way we think about, talk about, and *do* world language education, making it time for us to reconsider everything we do as stakeholders in our field.

This leads us to a moment when everything has to be on the table: curriculum, instruction, teacher education, professional development and our identities as world language teachers. To this end, in this chapter, we argue for dismantling how we think about and what we do in language teaching. We echo critical scholars in language education, but also emphasize the connectedness of key segments of our field, for example, the connections between professional outlets and current instructional approaches that have gained popularity, and theorize how, taken together, these segments contribute to oppression and injustice for our learners and do little to support their future outcomes as intercultural, justice-oriented citizens in society.

To engage in this dismantling, we start by calling out and calling in, distinguishing between the two forms of drawing attention to issues of justice and equity. The chapter begins with the work of 'calling out' our own complicity in upholding oppression and injustice for our learners. We recognize that there are times when 'calling out' is appropriate and even necessary, and we engage in 'calling out' by asking ourselves how our own actions, as teachers and as scholars, have contributed to oppression as a first step toward greater accountability (Jewell, 2020). By calling ourselves out, we are publicly drawing attention to circumstances that influenced decisions we made or actions we took and the lessons we learned from those experiences. We then critically interrogate, or 'call in,' key areas in the field of world language education in the US context: curriculum, standards and approaches, and teacher education and development. In this way, we raise issues inherent in the field as a call to action for scholars and practitioners seeking to reimagine world language education. Finally, we advocate for rebuilding our field on a foundation that centers our critical stance on justice and equity. We describe how the chapters in this volume contribute to this rebuilding process and how our colleagues have begun to engage in this paramount work.

Calling Ourselves Out

'Calling someone out,' in the context of antiracist work, serves the purpose of making oppressive and detrimental thinking or behavior visible and holding individuals or systems accountable for their thinking or actions (Jewell, 2020). In our (Beth and Cassandra's) time as educators in K-12 and college classrooms, we acknowledge that we have contributed to systemic inequities in education, perpetuating notions about what world language education should be and what it means to be a language teacher. Although we have spent a significant amount of time as teacher educators and scholars seeking to disrupt current approaches to language education and to draw attention to issues of access for minoritized students in language study, our work has also created additional problems. In the section that follows, we draw on two separate, individual narratives as a starting point to contextualize and then problematize our own work in world language education. We do this to promote the importance of first looking critically inside ourselves prior to looking outward into the field.

Cassandra's voice

More than two decades after starting my teaching career, I wonder what my students' experiences would have been like in my classroom if I had been introduced to critical pedagogy and social justice education while in my teacher education program. I started teaching in an urban middle school with a student population composed of mainly African American students, Latinx students and a mix of low-income and middle-class white students. I can say with certainty that I failed my students. I spent the first few months expecting my students to respond to education in the way that I had, in a very middle-class, white way, and I proceeded to teach language in a Eurocentric manner, buying into the classic narrative of what a world language curriculum should look like. Guess which students benefited most from my lessons? Definitely not my Black and Brown students. Even after a 7th grade African American student adamantly told me, 'It ain't cool for no Black boy to be learning French,' I still grappled unsuccessfully with the tools to examine my curriculum and my approach; I had no idea where to begin.

I recognized that there were issues and a significant opportunity gap (though at the time, we called it an achievement gap) and I launched into new ideas for reaching learners without first critically examining my own identity as a white teacher, my biases, and my relationships with students. I was sent to an urban middle school conference with three other teachers from the school where I learned about a 'school skills' curriculum for 'at risk' students. I brought this curriculum back to the middle school and found myself running an after school program for 'at risk' students in which this curriculum was implemented. The administration identified students who would benefit from the program, and they sent the students to me, most of whom were African American males. I failed to recognize that the majority of the 'at risk' students who administrators identified as problems and 'at risk' were African American, and I had not considered what it meant to be a white teacher working with minoritized students in this program. We didn't recognize, at that point, the issue with the label 'at risk,' which positions students through a deficit lens, as problems. At one point, my administration placed an 8th grade African American student with a significant Emotional Behavior Disorder in my class every quarter, having her repeat the curriculum several times, simply because my class was the only class in which she did not have outbursts. I was told that they did not care if she learned or not, they just wanted her to be quiet and behave. I was complicit, allowing her to repeat my class with the mindset that I was protecting her, when I should have been advocating for her.

Just two years after I began teaching, I moved to a large first-ring suburban school district that was actively engaged in examining issues of equity, and I took my first critical pedagogy class in graduate school. Stepping away and having the opportunity to reflect on my time in the urban school, I could clearly see that I had been perpetuating racist practices. However, what felt even worse when I looked back was that I thought that I had built trust and strong, personal relationships with my middle school students, particularly with my minoritized students. My relationships with students always came before the content, but I came to realize that no amount of relationship building could erase my ignorance and the inequitable practices I had helped to uphold in that school. At the time, I felt that I had cared deeply about my students, but this growing understanding of my privilege and positionality and of critical pedagogy caused me to realize that I hadn't demonstrated true solidarity and love; I hadn't empowered my students in the way they should have been.

Beth's voice

My narrative focuses on a much more recent point in my career: the fall of 2019. Because of administrative responsibilities I had taken on, fall 2019 was the first time in about five years that I had the opportunity to teach my department's world language teaching methods course. Coincidentally, it was also the first time I would support my students through the completion of the edTPA assessment, which was newly required by our state for teacher certification.

I began by revisiting the syllabus that I had refined over several years and started to restructure the material to span two semesters, in connection with our state's recent change to a year-long clinical practice experience. The key topics I focused on in the course were ambitious and included advocacy, standards, second language acquisition, curriculum, unit planning, lesson planning, instruction and assessment. I remembered how overwhelmed I always felt when teaching this course because of the extensive amount of content that we had 'to fit' into our content-specific teacher preparation classes. Despite this challenge, I wanted to add a stronger emphasis on teaching for and about social justice and equity into the course. However, in my beginning-of-the-semester haste, I did exactly what I regularly caution educators *not* to do. I added a component in the beginning of the semester on framing our stance and practice in culturally sustaining pedagogy, building relationships with students and affirming their identities, which I scheduled to take place over two weeks. But then, after that, I went back to several traditional readings, videos and resources to teach second language acquisition, unit and lesson planning. Although those resources provide guidance for standards-based planning and teaching, they do so with few references to the more critical issues and content that I want educators to draw on as the context for instruction.

Perhaps even worse, the two weeks at the end of the semester – when I had planned to shift back to key texts by my colleagues that emphasize critical approaches, and unit and lesson planning for social justice – was minimized when I felt pressure to focus more time on preparing for the high-stakes edTPA. Similar to the realities of many of our K-12, public school teacher colleagues, I felt I had to 'teach to the test.' By doing so, I lost the time and space to help our pre-service teachers explore the curricular and instructional choices they could make to enhance equity and to create more inclusive spaces in their classrooms. Although I advocate for the integration of social justice education into planning and instruction in my work with K-12 and postsecondary language teachers, I went back to how I was taught methods, placing the focus on the nuts and bolts of teaching and learning while neglecting the larger and more complex foundations of equity, cultural responsiveness and justice that should be centered in world language classrooms.

Calling in Our Field

We contend that the practices that we engaged in as teachers and as teacher educators had their roots in the structural and institutional elements of our field – the taken-for-granted belief systems and ways of doing things that we experienced, that we notice our colleagues doing, and the things we hear, observe and experience in our larger professional discourse. What would it sound like if we were to engage in the work of 'calling in' aspects of the field of world language education, or in other words, circling back to some of the ways that our field has implicitly contributed to issues of social justice, inclusion or equity? By calling in our field, our hope is that this will lead to engaged discussion and steps toward action rather than embarrassment or shame around practices that have long entrenched world language education. Ross (2019: para. 6) notes that calling in allows everyone to move forward and states, 'Call-ins are agreements between people who work together to consciously help each other expand their perspectives. They encourage us to recognize our requirements for growth, to admit our mistakes and to commit to doing better'.

Curriculum, standards and approaches

We (Beth and Cassandra) open up textbooks, peer into language classrooms and examine conference sessions at local, state and national levels to find a predominance of language-driven approaches that lack a critical approach to teaching languages and cultures. Certainly, approaches to language teaching have evolved, each new iteration and idea seeming to push against traditional approaches to language teaching. Gonzalez (2019) states in her interview with Rebecca Blouwolff, ACTFL's 2019 Teacher of the Year, that language teaching has shifted from learning about the language to learning to use the language in meaningful ways, heralding a focus on comprehensible input as a key method of providing students with scaffolded language that they can understand. The *World-Readiness Standards* (National Standards Collaborative Board, 2015) as well as state standards have perpetuated an emphasis on communication as the centerpiece of language learning. Communicative, contextualized language activities have been prioritized in language classes as the language teaching field recognizes the limitations of textbooks and language drills. Although this shift is significant, we still find ourselves discussing the shortcomings of a language-driven approach in developing students' critical consciousness about the world around them, causing us to wonder just how much language teaching has evolved and has it evolved in the right ways?

Almost two decades ago, Reagan and Osborn (2002) argued for a social justice approach that included a dialogic approach to teaching language, engagement in inquiry, a view of culture as dynamic, and the development of critical literacy skills; yet we still have not seen this kind of approach taken up widely in the world language field. Around that same time, Kubota (2003) elucidated the shortcomings of the ACTFL *Culture* Standards related to *Products, Practices, and Perspectives*, abbreviated as the three Ps. She noted that although they lead to exploration of 'the Self' and 'the Other,' they also pose a danger of reinforcing stereotypes and gloss over 'the political and ideological construction of knowledge about culture' (Kubota, 2003: 72); that is, elements of the three Ps that students examine may stem from political invention. Kubota (2003: 75) also interrogated the *Comparisons* Standards, underscoring the way in which they tend toward similarities and differences, promoting a binary way of thinking that translates into 'correct and incorrect' with regard to cultural ways of being. Although the original ACTFL Standards have undergone changes to become the *World-Readiness Standards*, which integrate more analysis and critical thinking, the complexity of teaching about culture and the importance of intercultural citizenship continue to be points of conversation in the world language field (see Byram & Wagner, 2018; Ennser-Kananen, 2016; Wagner *et al.*, 2019), suggesting that the *World-Readiness Standards* retain the pitfalls outlined by Kubota back in 2003. Further, the world language field, as a whole, has yet to acknowledge that 'we are still reducing culture to something light, curious, and often pleasantly amusing that barely challenges our identities and beliefs' (Ennser-Kananen, 2016: 557).

Some gains have been made in more recent years to push the field toward a balance of language and culture in the classroom and a deeper understanding of the target cultures being studied. The publication of the *NCSSFL-ACTFL Can-Do Statements for Intercultural Communication* (ACTFL, 2017) served to emphasize the inextricable link between language and culture and to provide a framework for what 'intercultural communicative interaction looks like within varied cultural and social contexts, using culturally appropriate functional language and behavior' (Van Houten & Shelton, 2018: 35). Given the goal of the *Can-Do Statements* to promote a shift in students' attitudes about other cultures and to better understand their own cultures, the groundwork for critical approaches to language teaching has been laid. However, the *Can-Do Statements* do not inherently ask students to consider issues of equity and power underlying the culture(s) and experiences of others they are studying. Social justice issues are not expressly included as an integral part of students' development of intercultural communicative competence in the *Can-Do Statements*; although they integrate language and culture, moving beyond a language-focused approach, they have only just scratched the surface.

Complicating the issue, world language textbooks remain a ubiquitous feature of the world language classroom, despite mixed perceptions from both students and teachers about the efficacy of textbooks to build students' proficiency in the language (Hadley, 2018). We would argue that textbooks can be harmful when relied on heavily in classrooms as they not only provide a superficial understanding of the target cultures, they also tend toward elitist, cisgender, heteronormative and other narrow, problematic views of language and culture that raise questions about access and equity. They rarely reflect the diversity of the target cultures, much less the diversity of our own classrooms. Novice teachers, in particular, tend to rely on textbooks, if they are part of the curriculum, in order to develop language lessons (Hadley, 2018). This may signal issues around teachers' preparedness to use the textbook for what it is – a tool – instead of a curriculum. If we re-examine the narratives above, we see that Cassandra, like many world language teachers, depended on the traditional curriculum that felt comfortable and familiar, but certainly did not feel representative of or relevant to her minoritized students. Had she been educated in critical pedagogy and other asset pedagogies prior to beginning her teaching career, perhaps she would have known that presenting students with topics about which she was not very familiar, but reflected students' lives and experiences, would have been an appropriate step to take. This would have pushed her out of her comfort zone, but armed with the ability to carry out an asset pedagogy approach, perhaps she would have known that she could learn alongside her students and co-construct knowledge about topics that were not included in the textbook curriculum.

In an effort to push back against textbooks and more traditional approaches to language teaching, teachers promoting Comprehensible Input (CI) and Teaching Proficiency through Reading and Storytelling (TPRS) seek to provide contextualized, meaningful language to students. Teacher-ready materials have been created that include short texts. One example is 'Brandon Brown dice la verdad' (Gaab, 2016), which contains a picture of a blonde boy with a European American sounding name who gets caught lying to his mother. Although engaging and comprehensible, these kinds of materials can lack cultural authenticity and ignore social justice issues; if a text contains social justice issues or problematic components like a white gaze, and these issues are not addressed, they can cause further damage by perpetuating stereotypes and elitist thinking. Although these types of TPRS texts are geared toward beginners, we argue that cultural authenticity and social justice topics should not wait until students have gained a particular proficiency level, especially if we are concerned about attracting and retaining students whose lives are regularly impacted by issues of equity and justice in their homes, schools and communities. As Johnson and Randolph (2017) explain, if the main goal is simply language acquisition, then these types of texts serve their purpose, but leave a critical exploration of the three Ps of culture and development of critical consciousness and global citizenship unchecked.

Cammarata et al. (2016) encourage the field to reconsider the goals of world language instruction, noting the potential of content-based instruction (CBI) in presenting learners not just with language, but meaningful content. Drawing from Legendre (1998), who posits that language learning should be intertwined with developing other views of the world and disrupting intolerance and racism, Cammarata et al. (2016) insist that engaging with content around themes of justice and ethics should be a vital task associated with world language curriculum. Critical content-based instruction (CCBI) (Sato *et al.*, 2017) has been used to describe an approach to teaching content that is built on the tenets of critical peda-gogy and critical literacy, disrupting dominant narratives about language and culture. However, CBI and CCBI seem to pose significant issues for traditional language teachers who feel unprepared to integrate other aca-demic content into world language classes (Troyan *et al.*, 2017), even though content around justice and ethics is inherently interdisciplinary in nature (Cammarata *et al.*, 2016) and would allow students to meet the *Making Connections* standard. As a result, CBI and CCBI are rarely observed in traditional K-12 world language programs and in lower levels of post-secondary language courses. Instead, the focus remains on lan-guage, rather than on a balance of language and meaningful content that could support students to interrogate social justice-related topics linked to the target language and cultures.

Despite strong arguments from so many well-respected scholars, some of whom have contributed to this volume, we find that we are still in a place of language-focused teaching, bringing to light several important questions: (1) Why haven't we come together as a field to acknowledge that language teaching must extend far beyond simply teaching the lan-guage and asking students to regurgitate memorized language chunks and structures? (2) Why are we still approaching culture, not as complex, dynamic, and riddled with power structures, but instead as something light and amusing? (3) How do our current curricular and instructional practices harm our most vulnerable or underrepresented students in schools and instead perpetuate a Eurocentric, cisgender, heteronormative view of the world?

Part 1 of this volume, *Disrupting Teaching Stance and Practice in the Classroom*, serves to answer some of these questions, to demonstrate what is possible in the world language classroom, and to describe how our field can strive toward educating world language students in a way that promotes critical examination of topics important in target language and home communities, is affirming of students' identities and experiences, and extends beyond language acquisition to develop lifelong skills and a critical consciousness of the world. This section begins with chapters that are theoretical in nature, providing a big picture view, and moves toward narratives of teachers enacting practices in classrooms and sharing their experiences.

We begin with Hannah Baggett, who analyzes qualitative data from in-service high school world language teachers and argues for a contin-uum of critical consciousness and in enacting critical pedagogy. The vignettes from the data she presents provide an understanding of how and the extent to which teachers navigate language, culture and power as they are asked to provide responses to three teaching tensions focused on cul-tural or religious practices, dialect, and a critical topic involving power.

Her emphasis on the notion of possibility in the language classroom suggests the potential for classrooms to become 'sites of resiliency, healing and justice' (p. 38). Baggett draws particular attention to the relationship between language and power and underscores the importance of understanding the value judgments underlying choices around dialects, vocabulary provided to students, and cultural topics being taught.

Dorie Conlon Perugini and Manuela Wagner espouse an approach to teaching languages that allows teachers to facilitate students' development as intercultural citizens. They build on Baggett's points about the value-laden nature of language and culture in the classroom, and suggest that rather than teaching students '"acceptable" or "appropriate" language or behaviors' (p. 53), teachers give students opportunities for inquiry and self-discovery, allowing them to decenter their own culture when interacting with people of backgrounds and cultures different than their own. Inherent in their work is an emphasis on authentic resources that center voices that have been systematically excluded from curriculum and instructional resources, including 'Afro-Latinx voices in Spanish, Black German voices in German curricula, and members of the LBGTQ+ communities, to name a few' (p. 54).

In the next chapter, Joan Clifford shares a model of Community-Based Language Learning (CBLL) and global health curricula. Like Conlon Perugini and Wagner, Clifford focuses on centering underrepresented voices and experiences and interrogating students' current beliefs about Western medicine and access to healthcare. She includes counter-storytelling and co-teaching by community partners, and aims to open dialogue with students to process their experiences with CBLL and engage in reflection. Clifford notes, '[t]he most valuable outcome of incorporating reflection practices into the curriculum is that students learn self-reflection strategies that they will then apply in life-long learning' (p. 81). Clifford provides a roadmap for other educators to replicate CBLL in their own programs.

Krishauna Hines-Gaither, Nina Simone Perez and Liz Torres Melendez offer Afro Latina counterstories about language learning experiences, using critical race theory (CRT) and feminist theory as frameworks for understanding these counterstories. The authors interviewed five Afro Latina students about their experiences studying Spanish in traditional language classrooms, noting that the participants often had negative experiences. Students felt that their identities were not affirmed; rather, their teachers devalued their dialects and cultures. Given the significant experiences participants shared about lack of belonging and representation, colorism and anti-Blackness in their world language programs, the authors insist that '[g]oing beyond the illusion of inclusion to deliberate representation is within our reach' (p. 101). In order to move world language teachers toward deliberate representation and affirmation of students' identities, they provide teachers with seven recommendations that can be implemented in classrooms.

In the final chapter of this section, Johanna Ennser-Kananen and Leisa M. Quiñones Oramas draw on critical race theory (CRT) and Latinx critical theory (LatCrit) frameworks to engage in counter-storytelling and examine the experience of a Latina Spanish teacher. They note that an identity as pedagogy approach runs the risk of centering the teacher's voice and experience while decentering students' identities; however, they aim to 'encourage teachers to look for and address differences in experience, belonging and identities, and guide students in making sense of them rather than minimize, reject or attack them' (p. 116). Their chapter also serves as a means of drawing attention to the racialized experiences of teachers of color (TOC) in the world language teaching profession, and the authors underscore the importance of providing spaces for TOC narratives that offer 'reflection and resistance' (p. 107).

The chapters in Part 1 push us to question the purpose of world language teaching and learning, and provide illustrations of what teachers, classrooms and students would look like if we embraced critical approaches. The interconnectedness of language and power, the role of identity and the centering of marginalized voices are key themes that span across the authors' contributions. However, the chapters also point out the ways we must restructure the field to make it more conducive to critical approaches and transformative outcomes; this work starts with rethinking world language teacher education and teacher development.

Teacher education and development

The perceived 'crisis' in teacher education (Grossman, 2008) along with reforms related to accreditation, licensure, alternative educator preparation, and required state and national assessments, have resulted in a plethora of constraints on teacher preparation programs across the US. In our roles as world language teacher educators, we (Beth and Cassandra) have observed these changes over time, including a more significant emphasis on accreditation and the emergence of edTPA as a high-stakes assessment. In response to these external forces on teacher education reform, scholars have continued to advocate for a critical approach toward teacher preparation. Kincheloe (2007: 111) underscored the need for critical teacher education that moves away from positioning teachers as 'low-level functionaries' who simply follow directives and curriculum guides. Taking a more critical stance in teacher education creates opportunities for teacher educators and their students to explore contradictions between theory and practice, to problematize assumptions about education, and to consider what it means to think and act ethically.

In the context of world language education, Reagan (2016) acknowledges that language teachers feel a push and pull between wanting to take a critical approach yet needing to teach discrete language skills. He quotes an English teacher who wrote in a student teacher's evaluation, 'I'm all for taking a critical approach, but some days you just need to teach apostrophes' (Reagan, 2016: 174). This quote illustrates the perception that critical pedagogy is at odds with teaching language functions, features or skills. However, teachers who take a critical approach can aim to meet multiple goals and objectives simultaneously; they seek to increase students' language proficiency and teach linguistic features, while also introducing complex ideas (Reagan, 2016). Returning to Beth's narrative above, this push-pull tension resulted in her artificially and problematically separating the components in her methods class into two categories: part of her course emphasized communication, proficiency and linguistic features, and another part focused on social justice education and developing culturally sustaining pedagogy.

The 'push and pull' described by Reagan is likely influenced by the strong emphasis in language teacher education on teaching methods and the methods course as the centerpiece of language teacher preparation programs. Macedo and Bartolomé (2001: 122) addressed the problematic nature of teaching methods courses, stating that they tend to reinforce the idea of a particular method having 'almost magical properties' to meet the needs of diverse learners in the classroom. However, such methods are explored and endorsed with little attention to the sociocultural, political and power structures underlying students' experiences in schools. Although they may be presented in texts and by instructors as neutral or 'value-free,' Tochon (2011: 13) argues that 'methods cannot be separated from epistemology, and always have a moral and political dimension ... The insistence on methods being apolitical is a political stand'. Our ways of thinking about teaching languages and about languages themselves also plays into how we enact language teacher education.

World language education, as a branch of applied linguistics or language education more broadly, has been slow to consider the implications of monoglossic, raciolinguistic and deficit language ideologies, particularly for language-minoritized students (e.g. de Los Ríos & Seltzer, 2017; Rosa & Flores, 2014; Seltzer, 2019) and the potential of a translanguaging approach (García & Kleyn, 2016). Moreover, Charity Hudley *et al.* (2020: 221), in a recent article about rethinking scholarship in applied linguistics, argue that '[s]cholars and students of linguistics are rarely trained to develop a critical perspective on how race and racism, as mechanisms of structural inequality, shape and harm both our research and our discipline'. To what extent has this lack of focus in applied linguistics graduate programs trickled down to the ways language teacher educators approach their programs and courses?

Perhaps our focus on 'methods' in language teacher education is leading us to miss something more important about becoming a teacher. Ladson-Billings (2006) argues that successful teaching for students who have historically been marginalized is primarily about 'what to do.' She suggests that the problem is rooted in how we think – about the social contexts, about the students, about the curriculum, and about instruction, rather than the methods that we use. To what extent, then, are we, as teacher educators, preparing new language teachers to firmly adopt a stance toward social justice and equity? Are we providing them with the opportunities and skills to critically examine and understand their own identities as language educators, perhaps as a means to preempt some of the issues that Cassandra faced in her first teaching experience? Are our students developing dispositions toward disrupting issues of justice in classrooms and schools and toward centering asset-based pedagogies, or are we contributing to more of the same by emphasizing methods, skills and practices? Are we preparing teachers to reject the traditional world language syllabus that focuses heavily on communication or grammar but deemphasizes intercultural competence and culturally sustaining pedagogy? For Beth, part of the issue was that she felt she had to work against her students' more traditional conceptualizations of language teaching as highly grammar-based and decontextualized; thus, she spent a significant portion of the semester with her students on developing a communicative approach. She missed the opportunity to ensure that her pre-service teachers were first seeing all learners, their families and communities through an asset lens and fully drawing on their cultural capital.

What should a re-imagined world language methods course look like, or an entire teacher preparation program? And in the contexts where teacher educators are resisting or reimagining traditional world language teacher preparation, what are the institutional structures and resources that are making this possible? The authors in Part 2 provide several examples of how they are destabilizing traditional approaches to world language teacher education and suggesting innovative and responsive alternatives. The section begins with a conceptual chapter by Terry Osborn, who along with colleague Timothy Reagan, is considered a trailblazer of social justice in world language education (e.g. Osborn, 2005; Reagan & Osborn, 2002). Osborn argues for a radical shift in focus for language teacher preparation that includes a critical awareness of colonialism, empire, capitalism and globalization. He joins the growing number of scholars in language education more broadly (e.g. Rosa & Burdick, 2017) who are questioning the taken-for-granted objectivity of language and language use in connection to power, authenticity and other mediating and contextual factors. Osborn reminds us that, from the outset, novice teachers need to understand that the value placed on one language form or forms is inherently ideological. This points to the need for teacher educators to rethink the readings, lessons and activities we use in programs, particularly at the beginning when we are helping new teachers to examine and grow their personal belief systems about languages, how we 'language' in different contexts and how this informs language teaching and learning.

The second chapter in this section extends Osborn's concepts into a context that has been underexamined in the scholarly literature: endangered heritage languages. Anka al-Bataineh, Kayane Yoghoutjian and Samuel Chakmakjian's chapter provides an account of an innovative teacher preparation program in Western Armenian, an endangered language. They provide extensive detail about the tensions between social justice pedagogy and heritage language pedagogy. Despite these tensions, the authors provide refreshing examples of how a decolonizing approach can be enacted despite the extensive challenges that occur in heritage, indigenous or endangered languages and language programs.

Mary Curran's chapter provides another program-level case that started with the rich linguistic and cultural diversity and resources of their communities. She explains her institution's reform efforts over two years to center social justice education and culturally sustaining pedagogy. She describes program-wide requirements and specific assignments within courses that help students engage authentically with issues of culture, equity and justice throughout the span of their pre-service development. Curran also describes innovative clinical and field experiences that are responsive to the larger community's needs in out-of-school settings. Her chapter illustrates how the Rutgers program has created an institutionalized approach that ensures that social justice education is embedded in essentially everything students experience during their development as beginning teachers.

Part 2 ends with Jennifer Wooten, L.J. Randolph Jr. and Stacey Margarita Johnson's course-level approach to engaging pre-service teachers in critical work. Their chapter expertly translates theory to practice, resulting in a plethora of practical ideas and activities for methods instructors. Using frameworks that connect critical pedagogy and andragogy, they consider the unique needs of adult learners as they experience personal and ideological change. They remind us that traditional language teaching methods courses see learners as 'language learning machines' (Pennycook, 2001: 127) 'rather than assisting [pre-service teachers] in developing as people and as critically engaged teachers' (this volume: 181). Their methods courses serve as a space for novice teachers to conceptualize themselves as change agents in both curriculum and instruction and engage in purposeful, impactful social justice pedagogy.

The chapters in Part 2 share a call for teacher education programs to challenge teacher candidates' beliefs about their own identities as language teachers, the act of teaching language, and ideologies surrounding language learning and teaching. They offer a glimpse into what teacher education could and should look like by demonstrating how a commitment to critical pedagogy, social justice education and decolonization can disrupt current approaches to world language teacher education programs and methods courses. Moreover, the chapters underscore the importance of sustained change at the teacher development level in order to effect change in classrooms and in students' world language experiences.

The authors featured throughout the chapters use a variety of approaches to inquiry and reflect diverse ontological, epistemological and axiological orientations. Some chapters blur the boundaries between theoretical and empirical and others call into question what many see as 'legitimate' scholarship in education and applied linguistics. In recognition that '[k]nowledges from academic and professional research-based institutions have long been valued over the organic intellectualism of those who are most affected by educational and social inequities,' (Caraballo *et al.*, 2017: 311), the authors in this volume have sought to stress the voices of individuals, students, educators and communities that are central to teaching, learning and using language(s) in K-12 and postsecondary classrooms and beyond.

Conclusion

In order to realize a 'reimagined' field of world language education, there are other structural and practical aspects of our profession that need to be examined and dismantled, including the professional learning landscape and scholarly initiatives we prioritize. The current professional learning landscape, including conferences, conventions, professional development opportunities, practitioner journals and other resources geared toward educators, includes little on social justice, equity, critical or culturally sustaining approaches that are specific to world language teaching, learning and classrooms. Our national, regional or state organizations could support this 'reimagining' by requiring proposals, sessions or papers to include how their content addresses issues of equity, justice or inclusion. Professional journals could more regularly integrate content on learner diversity, on teacher and student representation, or on critical approaches, rather than relegating them to a special issue.

We have begun to see some movement in this direction, particularly among state, regional and national organizations. For example, the Minnesota Council on the Teaching of Languages and Cultures (MCTLC) committed to including strands representing the voices of Black, indigenous, people of color (BIPOC), immigrants and heritage language teachers during their 2020 virtual conference, increasing BIPOC representation on their board and recognizing a Hmong teacher of the year. The Northeast Conference on the Teaching of Foreign Languages (NECTFL) created a 2020–21 webinar series on social justice in world languages and established the 2021 conference theme of *Finding Our Voice: World Languages for Social Justice*. And finally, ACTFL dedicated their 2020 *Assembly of Delegates*, a meeting of leaders in the field at their annual conference, to a theme of 'Words and Actions.' The four-hour session focused on examining structures that marginalize groups of educators; processes for recognizing the Teacher of the Year that impede teachers of less commonly taught languages or BIPOC teachers from being considered; and other initiatives that must be undertaken to achieve a more just and equitable organization. As advocates and activists, we must continue to hold organizations accountable for continuing to examine and change policies, practices and other institutional structures that uphold the status quo and keep us from achieving a more equitable and just field of world language education.

The field has also recognized significant disparities in who is doing scholarship and who holds positions of power in our organizations; for instance, a recent analysis suggested a disparity in 'professional mobility and visibility of scholars of color' in the American Association of Applied Linguistics (AAAL). The authors argue that 'expanding our epistemological field; and, ultimately, sustaining our vibrancy and strength as a discipline' requires highlighting issues of inequality and race (Bhattacharya *et al.*, 2020: 999). Reimagining scholarship in applied linguistics and world language education starts not only with the research questions we ask and that we see as relevant, but also the ways that established scholars, editors and funders explicitly support and privilege the work of scholars of color and of other marginalized identities or backgrounds. Similarly, we know that world language education has been a site of exclusion and marginalization for students of color (e.g. Anya, 2020), particularly beyond novice levels of language learning, yet studies that explain the policies, practices and systems that impede enrollment and retention are limited. We also know that the racial diversity of the teaching workforce does not match the demographics of students in US schools due to a variety of systemic historical factors (Carter Andrews *et al.*, 2019). Additional scholarship about the barriers to recruitment, certification and retention for teachers of color, for world languages teachers in particular, would strengthen the anecdotal accounts we share in committee meetings and in professional groups.

Returning to the start of the chapter, where we described the uncertain times in which we find ourselves, our P-12 and postsecondary students are living through one of the most divisive and unsettling times in US history. Although we have discussed the structural or systemic initiatives we need to take as a field, there is also work for us to do on an individual level. What roles will we play, as world language educators, to counter the rhetoric of hate, white supremacy and systemic racism? And how will we help students see an antiracist and justice-oriented response as a key tenet of being engaged, intercultural US citizens? What shifts could we make in world language curricula and instruction that would support these new, re-envisioned roles? How could we, through our work with the students within our care, reignite a culture of engagement, empathy, responsibility and action?

Discussion Questions

(1) If you were to call yourself out, what kind of story might you tell about your own professional experiences?

(2) In what way would you call out the field of world language education? What have you observed or experienced that should be called out in order to address issues and work toward a reimagined field of world language education?

(3) What might a reimagined world language classroom feel like, look like and sound like? What about a reimagined curriculum, or a reimagined world language conference?

Note

(1) Throughout this book, we use the term 'world language education' to focus on the issues within a subset of language education: languages other than English that are taught in US classrooms. In most states in the US, programs have shifted from using 'foreign language' to 'world language' as a means to counter the othering that the term 'foreign' suggests. Although many of the issues discussed by the authors in this book span other language contexts, such as bilingual education or TESOL in the US, or English as an Additional Language in countries where English is not the most commonly spoken language, this book focuses specifically on world language programs and classrooms within the US.

References

ACTFL (2017) NCSSFL-ACTFL Can-Do Statements for Intercultural Communication. See https://www.actfl.org/resources/ncssfl-actfl-can-do-statements

Anya, U. (2020) African Americans in world language study: The forged path and future directions. Annual Review of Applied Linguistics 40, 97–112. https://doi.org/10.1017/S0267190520000070

Bhattacharya, U., Jiang, L. and Canagarajah, S. (2020) Race, representation, and diversity in the American Association for Applied Linguistics. Applied Linguistics 41 (6), 999–1004. https://doi.org/10.1093/applin/amz003

Byram, M. and Wagner, M. (2018) Making a difference: Language teaching for intercultural and international dialogue. Foreign Language Annals 51 (1), 140–151.

Cammarata, L., Tedick, D.J. and Osborn, T.A. (2016) Content based instruction and curricular reforms: Issues and goals. In L. Cammarata (ed.) Content-based Foreign Language Teaching: Curriculum and Pedagogy for Developing Advanced Thinking and Literacy Skills (pp. 15–36). New York: Routledge.

Caraballo, L., Lozenski, B.D., Lyiscott, J.J. and Morrell, E. (2017) YPAR and critical epistemologies: Rethinking education research. Review of Research in Education 41 (1), 311–336.

Carter Andrews, D.J., Castro, E., Cho, C.L., Petchauer, E., Richmond, G. and Floden, R. (2019) Changing the narrative on diversifying the teaching workforce: A look at historical and contemporary factors that inform recruitment and retention of teachers of color. Journal of Teacher Education 70 (1), 6–12. https://doi.org/10.1177/0022487118812418

Charity Hudley, A.H., Mallinson, C. and Bucholtz, M. (2020) Toward racial justice in linguistics: Interdisciplinary insights into theorizing race in the discipline and diversifying the profession. *Language* 96 (4), 200–235. See https://languagelsa.org/index.php/language/perspectives_charity_hudley_et_al

de Los Ríos, C.V. and Seltzer, K. (2017) Translanguaging, coloniality, and English classrooms: An exploration of two bicoastal urban classrooms. *Research in the Teaching of English* 52 (1), 55–76.

Ennser-Kananen, J. (2016) A pedagogy of pain: New directions for world language education. *The Modern Language Journal* 100 (2), 556–564. https://onlinelibrary.wiley.com/doi/abs/10.1111/modl.1_12337

Gaab, C. (2016) *Brandon Brown dice la verdad*. Lewiston, ME: Fluency Matters Publishing.

García, O. and Kleyn, T. (eds) (2016) *Translanguaging with Multilingual Students: Learning From Classroom Moments*. New York: Routledge.

Gonzalez, J. (2019) How world language teaching has evolved. (Interview with Rebecca Blouwolff). *Cult of Pedagogy*, 29 September. See https://www.cultofpedagogy.com/world-language/

Grossman, P. (2008) Responding to our critics: From crisis to opportunity in research on teacher education. *Journal of Teacher Education* 59 (1), 10–23.

Hadley, G. (2018) Teacher and learner views on language textbooks. *World of Better Learning* blog, 9 March. See https://www.cambridge.org/elt/blog/2018/03/09/teacher-learner-views-language-textbooks/

Jewell, T. (2020) *This Book is Antiracist: Twenty Lessons on How to Wake up, Take Action, and Do the Work*. London: Frances Lincoln Children's Books.

Johnson, S.M. and Randolph, L.J. (2017) Social justice in the language classroom: A call to action. *Dimension*, 99–121.

Kaur, H. (2020) The coronavirus pandemic is hitting black and brown Americans especially hard on all fronts. *CNN*, 8 May. See https://edition.cnn.com/2020/05/08/us/coronavirus-pandemic-race-impact-trnd/index.html

Kincheloe, J.L. (2007) *Critical Pedagogy* (3rd edn). New York: Peter Lang.

Kubota, R. (2003) Critical teaching of Japanese culture. *Japanese Language and Literature* 37 (1), 67–87.

Ladson-Billings, G. (2006) From the achievement gap to the education debt: Understanding achievement in US schools. *Educational Researcher* 35 (7), 3–12.

Legendre, J. (1998) Explanatory memorandum to report on linguistic diversification. See http://assembly.coe.int/nw/xml/xref/xref-xml2html-en.asp?fileid=16644&lang=en

Long, H. and Van Dam, A. (2020) U.S. unemployment rate soars to 14.7 percent, the worst since the Depression era. *The Washington Post*, 8 May. See https://www.washingtonpost.com/business/2020/05/08/april-2020-jobs-report/

Macedo, D. and Bartolomé, L.I. (2001) *Dancing with Bigotry: Beyond the Politics of Tolerance*. New York: Palgrave Macmillan.

National Standards Collaborative Board (2015) *World-Readiness Standards for Learning Languages* (4th edn). Alexandria, VA: National Standards Collaborative Board.

Osborn, T. (2005) *Critical Reflection and the Foreign Language Classroom*. Charlotte, NC: IAP.

Pennycook, A. (2001) *Critical Applied Linguistics: A Critical Introduction*. Mahwah, NJ: Routledge.

Reagan, T. (2016) Language teachers in foreign territory. In L. Cammarata (ed.) *Content-based Foreign Language Teaching: Curriculum and Pedagogy for Developing Advanced Thinking and Literacy Skills* (pp. 173–191). Abingdon: Routledge.

Reagan, T. and Osborn, T. (2002) *The Foreign Language Educator in Society: Toward a Critical Pedagogy*. Mahwah, NJ: Lawrence Erlbaum.

Rosa, J. and Burdick, C. (2017) Language ideologies. In O. García, N. Flores and M. Spotti (eds) *The Oxford Handbook of Language and Society* (pp. 103–124). New York: Oxford University Press.

Rosa, J. and Flores, N. (2017) Unsettling race and language: Toward a raciolinguistic perspective. *Language in Society* 46 (5), 621–647.

Ross, L. (2019) Speaking up without tearing down. *Teaching Tolerance* 61. See https://www.tolerance.org/magazine/spring-2019/speaking-up-without-tearing-down

Sato, S., Hasegawa, A., Kumagai, Y. and Kamiyoshi, U. (2017) Content-based instruction for the social future: A recommendation for critical content-based language instruction (CCBI). *L2 Journal* 9 (3), 50–69.

Seltzer, K. (2019) Reconceptualizing 'home' and 'school' language: Taking a critical translingual approach in the English classroom. *TESOL Quarterly* 53 (4), 986–1007.

Tochon, F.V. (2011) Reflecting on the paradoxes of foreign language teacher education: A critical system analysis. *Porta Linguarum* 15, 7–24.

Troyan, F.J., Cammarata, L. and Martel, J. (2017) Integration PCK: Modeling the knowledge(s) underlying a world language teacher's implementation of CBI. *Foreign Language Annals* 50 (2), 458–476.

Van Houten, J. and Shelton, K. (2018) Leading with culture. *The Language Educator*, January/February, 34–39.

Wagner, M., Cardetti, F. and Byram, M. (2019) *Teaching Intercultural Citizenship across the Curriculum*. Alexandria, VA: ACTFL.

Part 1

Disrupting Teaching Stance and Practice in the Classroom

2 What Tension? Exploring a Pedagogy of Possibility in World Language Classrooms

Hannah Baggett

Teaching Tensions as Possibilities

World language classrooms, with their focus on cultural and language education, present unique possibilities for social justice education in that they afford the opportunity to 'teach students that we always think within a cultural context, and, therefore, that our knowledge, values, identities, and perspectives are always framed by the languages we use and the cultures that situate those languages' (Kumashiro, 2009: 97). Moreover, language classrooms provide teachers and students with opportunities to analyze the relationship between language and culture (Berman, 2002; Demuro & Gurney, 2018; Guilherme, 2002; Kubota, 2004); to 'decenter dominant ways of viewing the world' (Muirhead, 2009: 248); and to examine and trouble the power inherent in representing people, voices and cultures (Appadurai, 1988; Muirhead, 2009; Osborn, 2000). Importantly, critical pedagogies, wherein teachers and students develop critical consciousness (Freire, 1970), or understanding and intention to promote change, are central to education for social justice and examination of the ways that world languages are situated in particular sociopolitical and cultural contexts.

Given the contested nature of languages and how they operate alongside, in conjunction with, and as fundamental to privilege and oppression, critical pedagogies in language education afford educators and students opportunities to 're-examine not only the purposes of foreign language instruction, but even more, the hidden (and often not-so-hidden) biases about language, social class, power, and equity that underlie language use' (Reagan & Osborn, 2002: 30). Calls for further integration of social justice curriculum and instruction in K-12 language classrooms have steadily increased (see Ennser-Kananen, 2016; Glynn *et al.*, 2018; Osborn, 2006) and language teacher educators are likewise considering how to prepare and sustain language teachers with and in critical perspectives and pedagogies (i.e. Wooten & Cahnmann-Taylor, 2014). Scholarship on the work of language teachers has increasingly focused on language teachers' beliefs in the context of diversity and diverse students, the ways that they take up social justice in their classrooms, and the necessary supports that must be in place in order for the work of social justice to happen (Wassell *et al.*, 2019).

Often, though, teachers are conceptualized as those who either *are*, or who *are not* teaching for social justice, creating a binary, or different categories of teachers that ignore developmental frameworks integral to understanding educators' work. Teachers must consistently assume the roles and responsibility that come with teaching for social justice, engaging in a 'life-long journey of transformation' which involves identity work; critical knowledge of, and developing, relationships with students; becoming multilingual and multicultural; challenging oppression; and forming a community of 'critical friends' (Nieto, 2000). Writing specifically about race and racism, Kendi (2019), for example, has written about the ways that people never become 'racist' or 'antiracist'; instead, he writes, 'We can only strive to be one or the other' (2019: 27) through ongoing choices about expressions of belief and actions. In considering teachers' work, then, conceptualizing a *possibility* of practice as part of a continuum of development might better position teacher educators and practitioners to imagine future possibilities and how to best push forward in working towards social justice education in language classrooms. This pedagogy of possibility (Muirhead, 2009) underscores how we might think about future efforts towards social justice teaching and to emphasize the developmental nature of coming to critical consciousness and social justice work.

In this chapter, I draw on data captured from practicing public high school language teachers to argue that world language teachers are well-poised to integrate ideas about power, oppression and privilege and their relation to language and cultural practices. I draw on Muirhead's (2009) *pedagogy of possibility*, explained in the next section, to analyze the ways world language teachers responded to a series of three brief vignettes that prompted reflection about how they might (1) modify planned instruction for a student who is fasting for a religious holiday; (2) address linguistic variations in spoken modern languages; and (3) collaborate with colleagues on a unit about the influence of colonization on language development. Language teachers, in their responses, exhibited critical consciousness as they responded to these tensions and drew on ideas about responsive instruction, asset-based thinking about students and their families, and 'teachable moments' about power. These findings help us understand what we might imagine possible in language classrooms where teaching is rooted in critical pedagogies and commitments to justice and equity, which are so desperately needed in our public schools.

Pedagogy of Possibility

A first feature of a pedagogy of possibility is language teachers' critical consciousness about identities: teachers must 'recognize themselves as political and cultural beings who hold biases, perspectives, and ways of understanding the world that may run in opposition to other people's experiences' (Muirhead, 2009: 247). Further, critical consciousness about language teaching is predicated on teachers' understanding that a language is not simply a set of words to be memorized and regurgitated (Love, 2004). Languages function as cultural media and are bound up with social and political forces. White supremacist and capitalist power and market forces related to those powers (Osborn, 2003) shape which languages are deemed to be of most worth, and even which accents and vocabulary are the 'purest'. Pronunciation, subject-verb agreement, dialect, accent and vocabulary all operate within a negotiated field of power and stature; these elements of language use are axes along which speakers are marginalized and privileged. Thus, power constructs inherent in language teaching, such as the teaching of specific codes and linguistic structures as linguistic imperialism, and the problematic privileging of certain practices and norms from the target culture over others, must be examined (Kubota, 1998, 2004, 2005). A recognition of linguistic diversity and the power associated with languages is essential to developing an understanding of target languages and cultures (Kubota & Lin, 2009) and how dominant cultures and discourses inform our understanding of 'appropriate' language use.

As a next part of a pedagogy of possibility, language teachers must 'seek cultural and linguistic legitimacy,' connecting 'all of their students to the study of a second language, regardless of the language variety they speak' (Muirhead, 2009: 248). Language use, and perceptions about what is 'appropriate', are not only bound up with language speakers and identities, but with race (racism) and ethnicity (ethnocentrism). The burgeoning field of raciolinguistics, for example, seeks to examine the recursive relationships between and among language, race and power; how language shapes our understanding of race and ethnicity; and how racialized discourses operate (Alim *et al.*, 2016; Cushing-Leubner, 2017; Flores & Rosa, 2015; Rosa & Flores, 2017). Much as perceptions exist about linguistics and cultures and which types or versions of cultures and their associated world languages are 'correct,' perceptions about *who* is appropriate for second language instruction are also connected to ideas about race, ethnicity and gender. Scholars are thus increasingly focused on who has access to language study in public schools (Baggett, 2016; Finn, 1998; Glynn & Wassell, 2018; Schoener & McKenzie, 2016), with evidence suggesting that students of color have fewer opportunities to enroll in language classes as a function of racialized systems of opportunity, tracking and dominant discourses about students and ability, in addition to teachers' perceptions about the students in their classes. Furthermore, long-standing critiques of the positioning of world languages as 'elite' education (Reagan & Osborn, 2002) underscore the tensions inherent in offering world language courses to some students and not others. For example, there are power-laden contrasts in requiring language study for college admission while language teachers are also charged with teaching 'non-official languages (viewed as unimportant) in a *de facto* officially monolingual English-speaking context' (García, 1992: 19). That is, many Americans hold ethnocentric views about languages other than English as foreign, threatening and 'un-American', but may also undertake and advocate for language study when it serves them, such as when language study is a necessary mechanism for college admissions. There are also tensions in expectations for English language learners, for example, to assimilate in public schools at the expense of their own languages and cultures (e.g. Valenzuela, 2005), in contexts that simultaneously tout the benefits of learning a world language. In short, educators and stake-holders advocate for world language curricula and instruction for white, English-dominant students, while devaluing students of color who speak languages other than standard English (e.g. Love, 2019). This ideological terrain is thus where world language teachers' work is situated, and about which they must develop a critical consciousness and work to legitimize cultural and linguistic pluralism.

Finally, a pedagogy of possibility entails the ways in which language teachers cultivate development of intercultural competencies with their students. These competencies lie on a developmental continuum from ethnocentrism to ethnorelativism (i.e. Bennett, 1993) with teachers working to develop students' understandings of differences (Muirhead, 2009). This 'challenging task posed for second language professionals is to negotiate the concept of cultural difference with an understanding that it is a complex and precarious notion that can either promote or stagnate our understanding of the Self and the Other' (Kubota, 2004: 21). That is, teachers must be prepared to challenge students' static notions of culture and language since, when analyzed absent a critical lens, students may come to the understanding that 'American' culture is superior while neglecting to examine the white supremacist cisheteropatriarchal underpinnings of US American society (Osborn, 2002). This domain of a pedagogy of possibility is particularly aligned with goals for social justice education, as it focuses on students' competencies to 'view the world from multiple perspectives' (Muirhead, 2009: 250) and ultimately towards understanding and challenging inequities.

Method

Questionnaire data presented in this chapter were generated by teachers in a southeastern region of the US who were asked to respond to three brief 'teaching tensions'. These teaching tensions were constructed from my experiences as a high school French teacher, as they all happened in the context of my work in one school system over a period of five school years (see Table 2.1).

These vignettes were designed to prompt a range of ideas about possible teaching practices, rooted in critical consciousness about language, culture and power. Teachers were recruited via email blasts from state-level organizations, district-level professional development coaches, fellow practicing teachers, and from me directly. The link to the questionnaire was also shared on social media by colleagues and participants. Teachers wrote their responses to these tensions via Qualtrics, an online data collection tool.

Approximately 70 language teachers responded to the questionnaire. They represented varying modern/world languages, a majority of which were Spanish, French and German. Their teaching responsibilities spanned public K-12 classrooms and beginner to advanced language classes, including Advanced Placement and International Baccalaureate programs, but a majority were high school teachers. Teachers' pathways to teaching and licensure ranged from traditional teacher preparation programs to lateral entry and alternative certification programs, with most of the teachers reporting that they had a four-year undergraduate degree in education. In addition, teachers had varying years of experience in the field, with some teachers, for example, reporting they were in their first years as teachers, and others who were considered 'veteran' teachers; a majority of the teachers were mid-career, with between 4 and 15 years of experience. Finally, teachers reported varying ethnoracial, gender and sexual identities, and nationalities, but a majority of teachers reported that they were white/European-American, cis-hetero women.

In this study, I drew on critical explanations about structural domination, inequity and inequality; a guiding assumption for this inquiry was

Table 2.1 Teaching tensions

Teaching Tension 1	According to your curriculum pacing guide and your textbook, you are to begin a unit about 'Food and Dining Out' on Monday. One of your Muslim students has indicated that she will be fasting for Ramadan, a religious holiday, beginning on Monday. How would you resolve this tension?
Teaching Tension 2	A student in your advanced course is a heritage language speaker. The students in your class notice his/her pronunciation is distinct. How would you resolve this tension?
Teaching Tension 3	A colleague presents you with an idea of developing an additional unit about the impact of colonization on language development. She asks you to help develop and implement the project. How would you resolve this tension?

that public school language classrooms, like classrooms of other content areas, are nested in power systems that perpetuate dominant ideologies, inequity and inequality. A next assumption was that teachers must be critically conscious about those systems of power in order to work for justice and equity in education and in their teaching practice. Thus, I first read questionnaire data for evidence of teachers' critical consciousness, broadly defined as 'reflection and action upon the world in order to transform it' (Freire, 1993: 51). Using the frame of a pedagogy of possibility (Muirhead, 2009), I read teachers' responses for this awareness as it related to languages, language instruction and the dynamic interplay between and among language, culture and power; for teachers' ideas about what they would do to present varying cultures and linguistic backgrounds as legitimate; and how they might cultivate intercultural competence in their practices and scaffold students' development of this competence.

It is important to note that there were many teachers in the dataset who did not appear to be critically conscious about power, culture and language. These teachers sometimes endorsed deficit views of students and families; articulated dysconscious and evasive ideas about race, ethnicity, culture and languages; and sometimes even evidenced a blatant disregard for the issues presented. And, indeed, much scholarship has brought to the fore ways that teachers enact epistemic, emotional, racial and linguistic violence in their classrooms (i.e. Love, 2013, 2016) as they operate under educational systems governed by, for example, white supremacist (cis-hetero) patriarchy (i.e. hooks, 2004), settler colonialism (i.e. Patel, 2019) and capitalist imperialism (i.e. Giroux, 2001). In this chapter, however, I choose to emphasize the voices and practices of teachers who appeared to take up teaching tensions in a critically conscious way in an effort to imagine what is possible for teachers to (re)make their classrooms more equitable and just for their students.

Positioning Myself

Positioning one's self to a topic and to data generated with participants during inquiry is important in social justice work. As a high school French teacher, I wasn't sure how to 'do' social justice education in the context of instruction of a world language, as my language teaching methods courses were aimed at preparing me to teach French across K-12 contexts and had been focused on communicative and intercultural competencies. I began to integrate topics and areas of potential 'tension' that I felt comfortable speaking about (in French) with a group of novice language learners, while maintaining much of my instruction in the target language. When teaching a class of French students vocabulary about family units, for example, we looked at pictures of families I designed to disrupt ideas about heteronormative and nuclear family structures. In later classes, I showed films that took up issues of racism, ethnocentrism and anti-Semitism, which we would sometimes discuss afterwards in English,[1] exploring the tension of dominant narratives about groups and how we may actually experience people. We examined troubled narratives about what constituted an 'American' identity, and who gets to be considered a US American, conversations that were especially important for the large numbers of first-generation and often undocumented students in my classes from El Salvador, Honduras, Guatemala and Mexico. It is important to note that this analysis occurred from my location as a white, English-dominant, cis-woman and in the midst of a school context where students' ethnoracial statuses were bound up with perceptions about language learning abilities; specifically, there was pervasive deficit thinking about African American and Latinx students, who comprised almost the totality of the student body.

During my time in the school system, I tried to collaborate with other teachers to integrate and address 'tensions' in the context of language teaching, with the aim of promoting justice-oriented perspectives. Teachers expressed interest, and agreed that there was potential to do so, but were often skeptical about the time it might take to plan, fearful of straying from district-mandated pacing guides and unsure of their abilities to take on similar 'tensions'. Later, as a researcher, I wondered how teachers outside of that particular system might also approach their work as instructors not just of languages but of justice and equity-oriented ideas. My experiences as a teacher working through tensions in my classroom informed my understanding that it was possible to teach for social justice in language classrooms, and this understanding drove my inquiry. Thus, in an effort to explore the ways that language teachers might be prepared to do the work of social justice in their classrooms, I prompted teachers to read and respond to several questionnaire vignettes about potential 'tensions' in the language classroom.

In what follows, I focus on practicing/in-service language teachers' ideas about how to address possible teaching tensions and to push their own and their students' understanding of language, culture and power. I focus here on *possibility* to push back on the ways that scholarship often positions teachers via the same deficit frameworks that we refuse for our K-12 students. The idea of possibility does not originate from a paternalistic determination about what teachers should or should not be doing, but rather reflects the capabilities of and rich range of practices for language teachers in the field. I also use this term to emphasize a futurity of teachers' practice; that is, while some teachers responded to these prompts about what they were currently doing in their classrooms, most imagined what they *would* do, as indicated in the wording of the prompts. In the following sections, I highlight data from teachers in addition to interpretive commentary guided by the idea of possibility in language teachers' practice.

Findings

Language teachers featured here appeared both ready and willing to grapple with teaching tensions, underscoring their critical consciousness about students, languages and power, and possibilities for practice. These possibilities were evidenced in three primary ways: first, teachers indicated they understood a need for responsive instruction for their students, indicating a critical consciousness about differences across student identities. Next, teachers evidenced asset-based thinking about students and students' cultural backgrounds, demonstrating their knowledge of the need to seek linguistic and cultural legitimacy for students. And, lastly, teachers underscored the need to address the ways that languages and power are bound up as they developed students' intercultural competence.

Affirming and responsive instruction for students

Language teachers responded to questionnaire data in ways that evidenced critical consciousness vis-à-vis their need to be responsive to students in their classes, including those students who might be historically marginalized in US public schools. For example, when presented with the idea that a Muslim student might be fasting for Ramadan during a scheduled unit of instruction about food and dining, many teachers indicated that they would change their plans for instruction. A French teacher indicated, for example, that they should 'be flexible and change the order of [lessons] until after the student's fasting period was over.' Other teachers indicated they might plan well in advance, looking at a calendar before developing a unit schedule, stating, for example, that 'knowledge of your students allows to foresee issues like this one' and that 'I should know the student well enough to know in advance that the possibility of a conflict should exist.'

Language teachers are not immune to attempts at standardization across schools and school systems, facing pressure to abide by certain dictums related to curriculum and instruction in public schools, including which textbooks and ancillary materials should be used, curricular 'pacing guides' that articulate what and when content should be taught, and common assessments. Despite these pressures, language teachers recognized the tensions between forces that might dictate how, what and when they teach content, and the needs of the students in their classrooms.

Teachers also evidenced their potential to be responsive to the students in their classrooms when presented with a teaching tension about a heritage language speaker's accent. A French teacher, for example, recounted that it would be important to 'talk about pronunciation and how even in the United States, there are many different accents in spoken English. We could then research heritage speakers throughout the Francophone world.' Teachers also indicated their critical consciousness about the contextually situated nature of language, with one French teacher noting the need to teach 'all my students about local dialects in not only the US, but in other countries and explain how both geography and history can make for differences within the same language.'

Teachers also evidenced critical reflection about their own identities in order to be responsive to students in their classrooms. For example, a Spanish teacher wrote, 'I feel that as a non-native speaker of Spanish, I lack cultural knowledge and in order to implement more culture into the classroom, it is imperative that I continue to seek useful resources to enhance the students' cultural knowledge.' This awareness constitutes a foundational aspect of a pedagogy of possibility: that language teachers engage in continuous reflection about themselves, languages, and their 'roles as either actively resisting hegemonic forces or being complicit in the maintenance of the status quo (Guilherme, 2002; Osborn, 2000; Reagan & Osborn, 2002)' (Muirhead, 2009: 246). These examples further demonstrate the ways that teachers' knowledge of their students' identities, languages and cultures was situated in a critical consciousness about the need to advocate for students, reflecting on 'students as political and cultural beings, particularly in relation to the teacher, the school system and power' (Muirhead, 2009: 247).

Asset-based thinking about students and families

In addition to being responsive to their students, teachers also endorsed asset-based thinking about students' cultures and lived experiences. Teachers indicated, for example, that they would build off students' cultural expertise. A German teacher, responding to the teaching tension about differing accents, stated: 'I would take advantage of that situation to model different accents, pronunciations and a variety of regional vocabulary and expressions … and that [heritage speaker] could be an asset for our cultural awareness.' Another Spanish teacher responded:

> Currently I have an advanced class with Guatemalans, Hondurans, Mexicans and an Argentine. This is a great experience for them as well as the non-heritage speakers in the class to hear the differences in pronunciation. It also provides many opportunities to talk about vocabulary uses in different countries/regions. Just yesterday, we had a discussion on the different words used for 'suitcase' in different countries … We make the differences learning experiences for everyone.

Similarly, a Spanish teacher addressed differences in accents in spoken languages as an opportunity to 'talk about different dialects … and we embrace student differences in my higher-level courses by asking them to read aloud and "teach" others how to pronounce things too,' drawing on student knowledge to guide instruction. In addition, a French teacher indicated they would 'ask the heritage language speaker to be responsible for leading certain speaking activities and guiding other students … In the classroom, it is great to utilize strengths in a positive manner and then dig deeper into other areas where other students may be more positive leaders.'

Teachers further exhibited willingness to treat cultural knowledge as an asset in classrooms, rather than omitting students' experiences altogether. For example, in an effort to address a conflict with the schedule of a food unit and a student's cultural practice of fasting, a French teacher stated: 'I would use this opportunity to have the student, if they feel comfortable, to talk about Ramadan. Since there are many French speaking Muslims this would be a great time for students to learn first-hand. Last year, we had a Socratic seminar on how Francophone countries view the wearing of the hijab.' Similarly, another French teacher wrote:

> This would be a great tie-in to food and dining out! Since I teach French and there are many countries where French is spoken and Islam is a main religion, this would be a terrific opportunity for the student to share information about her culture, if she was comfortable, and about her family's home country and then tie it into Francophone countries with similar beliefs.

A Spanish teacher expressed the possibility of planning an evening meal at school in conjunction with the student and their family wherein they would invite the broader school community. Some of the possibilities highlighted here place the burden of education on the student, thus presenting an additional tension in public education, writ large, in that the work of critical consciousness development and social justice education often falls to those who embody marginalized identities. Thus, language teachers should be mindful that it is their responsibility, first and foremost, to legitimize culture(s) and language(s) vis-à-vis their curricula and instruction. Several teachers summed up this responsibility by stating, for example, that this 'is an opportunity to teach the curriculum as well as the culture of the student.'

These asset-based thinking practices resonate with the second domain of a pedagogy of possibility wherein teachers work to legitimize cultural and linguistic practices, emphasizing those 'perspectives from marginalized groups within the languages being studied' (Muirhead, 2009: 249). Efforts to legitimize cultures and linguistic variations were apparent across teachers' responses, with teachers recognizing the need to position their students' cultural and linguistic wisdom as expertise and to draw on students' perspectives to scaffold understanding of cultures and languages. Similarly, a Spanish teacher noted that:

> dialects in different regions differ, but it doesn't mean that one is better or more correct than the other. I would ask this student if it was okay to focus on their region, and perhaps make a list of certain things they say one way then compare it to another student's dialect who speaks the same language but in a different way. I would also lead them to draw

similarities about language dialects in our country, by looking at regional and geographical areas. That way they could better understand this distinction.

Most exciting from this excerpt is that it underscores thinking about languages and cultures in ways that might move students beyond binaries of right/wrong or correct/incorrect, and instead focuses on legitimization variations. Indeed, this type of response demonstrates teachers' awareness and understanding that there are no 'correct' forms of language use; instead, what is deemed to be 'correct' is a product of power and who might benefit most from a hierarchy of 'correctness.' In other words, if all variations of language are deemed equally 'correct,' language use no longer functions as a mechanism for privileging some at the expense of others. A critical analysis of which dialects have been deemed more 'correct' or 'proper' can illuminate for students the ways in which language use becomes an axis of power, privilege and marginalization.

Intersections of power and language

In addition to being responsive to students' identities and treating cultural and lived experiences as expertise on which to build classroom instruction, some teachers more directly expressed the need to address and confront linguicism, racism and ethnocentrism during language teaching. One French teacher indicated the need to disrupt linguicism that might occur when heritage language speakers use language that might sound distinct, noting that they would 'take the opportunity to discuss dialects and their differences between countries/regions where the target language is spoken and highlight that differences enhance a language, rather than create issues.' Teachers further evidenced understanding of power, oppression and privilege and their relation to language and cultural practices in their responses to prompts about developing a unit about colonization and language use. For example, one French teacher wrote that it was important to include 'lessons on why French is spoken around the world ... for students to know where languages come from and why places speak the language they do.' Another Spanish teacher indicated they were already doing the work of talking about colonization in their classroom, relaying that:

> There are many videos available about colonization, which I like to show. It gives the students a perspective on the movement of the language from Europe to the Americas. Throughout my courses we have lessons on indigenous groups of the Americas. We learn about their ... languages, as well as where some of the indigenous groups still speak [these] as their first language, and Spanish as a second language.

Here, this teacher reported that they were working to engage students in critical conversations about movement and language. Another German teacher responded that, '[Developing a unit on language and colonization] sounds like a great integration unit plan that will be cross-curricular and promote students' understandings of language and how it evolves, and how language has power.' These responses underscore an emerging understanding for teachers such that language learning is not limited to discrete bits of vocabulary and conjugations, but instead is bound up with values and dominant discourses. A Spanish teacher further underscored the relationship between power, colonization and race by asserting:

> colonization as a negative force is criminally under-discussed in all subjects, and it should especially be a part of world languages education. As someone who teaches a large majority of white upper-class families of European ancestry, this is something my students have hardly been exposed to or asked to face. For this project, I would want to get, if possible, the input and participation of someone who speaks a colonized language – ideally an indigenous language in a Spanish-speaking area – as I am a speaker of a colonizing language.

This teacher indicated that she was not only aware of the power inherent in language use, but acknowledged the ways in which language has been used as an instrument of colonialism (Crookes, 1997) and the ways that white students are often shielded from discussion about race and power.

In sum, the language teachers featured here represent the possibility of practice in thinking through nuances of culture, linguistic variation, power, and sociopolitical elements of teaching. These nuances lend themselves to the last aspect of a pedagogy of possibility involving developing students' intercultural competence. Teachers who, themselves, have developed intercultural competence 'can problematize situations that push students into viewing oppressions and injustices from multiple perspectives and then allow them to act upon this knowledge' (Muirhead, 2009: 251). A possible critical discussion of colonization, for example, might include an analysis of power and language as they are bound up with settler-colonialism and the ways in which some indigenous groups were resilient to linguicism and cultural oppression. This analysis could lead students to advocate for speakers of indigenous languages even as they learn about 'world languages' that have been used as tools during colonization and imperialism.

The teachers' thinking featured here not only indicates a possibility of movement towards enacting critical pedagogies and teaching for social justice, but also suggests that teachers are capable of rich reflective work, situating their practices in liminal spaces of what is and what could be and emphasizing the developmental nature of understanding social justice work. In the next section, I outline implications for language teacher educators, pre-service and practicing language teachers, and language teaching policymakers.

Possibilities and Implications for Teacher Education

To restate, language teachers' responses to these teaching tensions show that there is a *possibility* for social justice work in many teachers' practice. Critical awareness of identities and justice issues, however, does not always translate to practice; as educators, once we become critically aware, we must make choices to affect change. How do the practices of language teacher educators, instructional coaches and professional development, then, push this potential into practice? What would my teaching practices have been in those early years if my language teacher preparation had focused more explicitly on prompting interrogation of power, language and culture? In other words, how are language teachers best supported to enact a pedagogy of possibility?

First, these findings support the need for an interdisciplinary approach in teacher preparation. Language teachers should complete coursework rooted in critical perspectives about, for example, languages and literatures, history, nation building, colonization, imperialism and raciolinguistics to emphasize the sociopolitical and cultural contexts in which languages are situated and constantly in flux. Teacher educators should engage language teachers in critical examination of how target languages are spoken, written and deployed, and the value-laden nature of choices to teach certain dialects, vocabulary and cultural practices over others. Developing teachers' understanding that languages and cultures are fluid and recursive is integral to this work, including the nature of 'culture(s) as encompassing a range of subjectivities, and ways of being, competing for legitimacy' (Demuro & Gurney, 2018: 289). Further, language teacher educators must support the cultural and identity work that language teachers must do to investigate themselves as cultural beings even as they explore how to teach culture in the language classroom. This identity work is an integral part of teaching for social justice (Nieto, 2000) and a pedagogy of possibility, wherein teachers must recognize themselves as cultural and political beings and the ways their identities are situated in power structures (Muirhead, 2009). This *concientización* or awareness (Freire, 1970) is necessary for teachers to understand that their experiences may be different from those of their students, a first recognition of the relationship between the self and the Other (Guilherme, 2002; Muirhead, 2009).

Next, teachers must develop local contextual knowledge of the students and families they teach, considering what they need to know and be able to do in their classrooms to be responsive to students, and exploring the linguistic and cultural assets their students bring so that they may be drawn upon. Integration of, for example, ethnic studies and 'ethnic literacy' components into language teacher preparation programs might serve to facilitate development of contextualized cultural awareness. These components, rooted in rationales about demographic shifts of the US American population, serve as alternatives to assimilationist models and push language teachers towards embracing a paradigm of cultural pluralism (Zephir, 2000). Furthermore, pre-service and practicing teachers must be provided opportunities to develop culturally relevant units and lessons that integrate social justice themes (Glynn *et al.*, 2018). Language teachers should be supported in selecting texts and curricular materials (Crookes, 2010) and developing language learning activities that do not promote 'L2 communicative skills regardless of social problems and contexts,' and instead those that 'develop learners' language skills as well as cognizance of social structures' (Formato, 2018: 1121).

These responses to teaching tensions model why language teachers could benefit from professional development aimed at developing curricular materials that explicitly address issues of power, linguicism, colonization and marginalization of cultures to push them towards implementing critical pedagogies. Evidence suggests that some language teachers indicate that it is not their responsibility to address issues of identity, or they may be less inclined to represent marginalized or minoritized identities and cultures in classrooms when those identities are not present (Baggett, 2020). Thus, teachers should be scaffolded in the development of their critical consciousness about power systems and reminded that work for justice and equity must happen across classrooms and contexts, regardless of students present in their classrooms. A common misconception is that teachers need only address racism, for example, when students of color are present in their classrooms. Instead, that work must happen across classrooms, and perhaps especially in classrooms comprised of white students.

Some language teachers are no doubt making modifications to standardized curricula, instructional materials and assessments to promote social justice in their classrooms (i.e. Wassell *et al.*, 2019), and engaging students in conversations about stereotypes, and lived experiences, in ways not captured here. Many language teachers, however, featured in this chapter and across the dataset, evidenced critical awareness about the issues inherent in the teaching tensions presented in this study, but did not appear ready to address them, citing a lack of available materials to support those efforts, or fear that addressing these tensions might not coincide with expectations to cover standards and learning objectives. Finally, teachers' contexts are important drivers of the ways that they make decisions in their classrooms, and they often face expectations from stakeholders that compete with pedagogies for possibility and social justice. Thus, supporting teachers to cultivate their sense of agency to modify existing curricula (or even develop their own) to be responsive to students' needs and to address issues of language, culture and power could push more language classrooms to operate as sites of social justice education.

Moving Forward

In our current sociopolitical context, politicians and policymakers with the most power and the furthest reach continue to invoke and enact dehumanizing, discriminatory rhetoric and policy about people who are perceived to be outside of a dominant 'American' designation. And although our US society is more diverse than ever, politicians and policymakers have both stoked and laid bare the anti-Blackness, racism, sexism, xenophobia and homophobia, for example, that are woven into the fabric of the country. This sociopolitical context, of course, shapes the ways that teachers make decisions about curriculum and instruction – the what, when, how, why and who they should teach. Teachers who engage in the work of social justice in this context do so with some risk for backlash and consequences, especially given the 'US preoccupation with attempting to "sanitize" the classroom from controversial issues' (Osborn, 2006: 28). There is a great deal of tension between and among the expectations of educational stakeholders, practitioners and policymakers with regard to issues of justice and equity in public school classrooms, commonly understood as 'controversial' and now increasingly framed as politically partisan (Dunn *et al.*, 2019). Despite, or perhaps because of these tensions, proponents of social justice education are clear that teachers of all content areas in K-12 public schools must understand that society is deeply unequal, stratified along identity domains such as, for example, race, class, gender, ability and sexuality, and that this inequality is embedded into the structures and systems that govern our society (Sensoy & DiAngelo, 2017). Teachers for social justice, then, should empower and equip their students to interrogate and disrupt the status quo (Ayers *et al.*, 2009), while embracing and respecting the cultural experiences and prior knowledge that their students bring to the classroom (Nieto, 2000), adopting and adapting pedagogies and curriculum that are culturally relevant (Ladson-Billings, 1995) and culturally responsive (Gay, 2018). Teachers must teach students to examine systems of power with an eye towards interruption and disruption, understanding the ways that contemporary sociopolitical and sociocultural forces impact teaching and learning (Nieto & Bode, 2008).

Amidst these positionings, we must remember that practicing language teachers face many tensions in their classrooms already, even if they do not acknowledge them, and instead may endorse 'neutrality' in their teaching practice. Indeed, there were a group of teachers who responded to these teaching tensions who did not appear to be critically aware of identities, marginalization and power in language education, sometimes referencing ideas about neutrality. Building on a pedagogy of possibility, we must work to trouble this tendency, to investigate the discourses that promote and propagandize neutrality, alerting teachers to the ways that students suffer when we refuse to affirm their identities; learn about their lived experiences; tailor our curricula and instruction; or to advocate for them, their rights and the rights of their families and communities. Further, scholars of language teacher education should build on this framework and focus their work on and with teachers who take a critical stance in the classroom so that we might learn from their practices and envision the possibilities that exist for teachers and students in public school language classrooms.

World language classrooms in public schools have often been positioned as sites to develop students into global citizens (i.e. as put forth by the *ACTFL Guiding Principles* [ACTFL, n.d.]). What is imperative now is that we position language classrooms as spaces to develop both teachers and students into *transformative* global citizens. Language classrooms offer possibilities for us to encourage not just cultural and linguistic pluralism, but provide ready-made spaces for critical cultural analysis of the forces that underlie social injustices. Likewise, they provide possibilities to study and learn from the resilience and resistance of those who face oppressive systems. In this way, it is possible to position language classrooms as sites of resiliency, healing and justice for teachers and students alike.

Questions for Discussion

(1) What identities do you bring to your work as a teacher/teacher educator? How are those identities (in)visible to those around you? What are the risks and benefits of naming and claiming those identities?
(2) How do you work to understand your students, their lived experiences and their backgrounds? How does this relational work inform your teaching of language and culture?
(3) What types of teaching 'tensions' are present in your work? How might you address them differently, after considering issues of identity, power and oppression?

Note

(1) Although I worked to speak in French for most, if not all, of every class period during my time as a public school teacher, the use of English (or another first language) can facilitate critical consciousness and understanding (Formato, 2018; Johnson & Randolph, 2015).

References

ACTFL (American Council on the Teaching of Foreign Languages) (n.d.) *Guiding Principles*. See https://www.actfl.org/guiding-principles/opening-statement (accessed 19 December 2019).
Alim, H.S., Rickford, J.R. and Ball, A.F. (2016) Introducing raciolinguistics. In H.S. Alim, J.R. Rickford and A.F. Ball (eds) *Raciolinguistics: How Language Shapes Our Ideas about Race* (pp. 1–30). New York: Oxford University Press.
Appadurai, A. (1988) Introduction: Place and voice in anthropological theory. *Cultural Anthropology* 3 (1), 16–20.
Ayers, W., Quinn, T.M. and Stovall, D. (eds) (2009) *Handbook of Social Justice in Education*. New York: Routledge.

Baggett, H.C. (2016) Student enrollment in world languages: L'égalité des chances? *Foreign Language Annals* 49 (1), 162–179.

Baggett, H.C. (2020) Relevance, representation, and responsibility: Exploring world language teachers' critical consciousness and pedagogies. *L2 Journal* 12 (2), 34–54.

Bennett, M.J. (1993) Towards ethnorelativism: A developmental model of intercultural sensitivity. In R.M. Paige (ed.) *Education for the Intercultural Experience* (pp. 109–135). Yarmouth, ME: Intercultural Press.

Berman, R.A. (2002) Foreign languages and foreign cultures. *ADFL Bulletin* 33 (2), 5–7.

Crookes, G. (1997) What influences what and how second and foreign language teachers teach? *The Modern Language Journal* 81 (1), 67–79.

Crookes, G. (2010) The practicality and relevance of second language critical pedagogy. *Language Teaching* 43 (3), 333–348.

Cushing-Leubner, J. (2017) Accompaniment for the climb: Becoming reparational language educators of Spanish as a 'heritage' language. Doctoral dissertation, University of Minnesota. See http://hdl.handle.net/11299/199091.

Demuro, E. and Gurney, L. (2018) Mapping language, culture, ideology: Rethinking language in foreign language instruction. *Language and Intercultural Communication* 18 (3), 287–299.

Dunn, A.H., Sondel, B. and Baggett, H.C. (2019) 'I don't want to come off as pushing an agenda': How contexts shaped teachers' pedagogy in the days after the 2016 US presidential election. *American Educational Research Journal* 56 (2), 444–476.

Ennser-Kananen, J. (2016) A pedagogy of pain: New directions for world language education. *The Modern Language Journal* 100 (2), 556–564.

Finn, J.D. (1998) Taking foreign languages in high school. *Foreign Language Annals* 31 (3), 277–306.

Flores, N. and Rosa, J. (2015) Undoing appropriateness: Raciolinguistic ideologies and language diversity in education. *Harvard Educational Review* 85 (2), 149–171.

Formato, G. (2018) Instilling critical pedagogy in the Italian language classroom. *Journal of Language Teaching and Research* 9 (6), 1117–1126.

Freire, P. (1970) *Pedagogy of the Oppressed*. New York: Continuum.

Freire, P. (1993) *Pedagogy of the City*. London: Burns and Oates.

García, O. (1992) Societal multilingualism in a multicultural world in transition. In H. Byrnes (ed.) *Languages for a Multicultural World in Transition* (pp. 1–27). Lincolnwood, IL: NTC.

Gay, G. (2018) *Culturally Responsive Teaching: Theory, Research, and Practice*. New York: Teachers College Press.

Giroux, H.A. (2001) *Theory and Resistance in Education: Towards a Pedagogy for the Opposition*. Westport, CT: Greenwood Publishing Group.

Glynn, C. and Wassell, B. (2018) Who gets to play? Issues of access and social justice in world language study in the US. *Dimension: Journal of the Southern Conference on Language Teaching* 2018, 18–32.

Glynn, C., Wesely, P. and Wassell, B. (2018) *Words and Actions: Teaching Languages through the Lens of Social Justice* (2nd edn). Alexandria, VA: ACTFL.

Guilherme, M. (2002) *Critical Citizens for an Intercultural World: Foreign Language Education as Cultural Politics*. Clevedon: Multilingual Matters.

hooks, b. (2004) *The Will to Change: Men, Masculinity, and Love*. New York: Atria Books.

Johnson, S.M. and Randolph Jr., L.J. (2015) Critical pedagogy for intercultural communicative competence: Getting started. *The Language Educator* 10 (3), 36–39.

Kendi, I.X. (2019) *How to be an Antiracist*. New York: One World/Ballantine.

Kubota, R. (1998) Voices from the margin: Second and foreign language teaching approaches from minority perspectives. *Canadian Modern Language Review* 54 (3), 394–412.

Kubota, R. (2004) The politics of cultural difference in second language education. *Critical Inquiry in Language Studies: An International Journal* 1 (1), 21–39.

Kubota, R. (2005) Second language teaching for multilingualism and multiculturalism. In R. Hoosain and F. Salili (eds) *Language in Multicultural Education* (pp. 31–57). Scottsdale, AZ: Information Age Publishing.

Kubota, R. and Lin, A. (eds) (2009) *Race, Culture, and Identities in Second Language Education: Exploring Critically Engaged Practice*. New York: Routledge.

Kumashiro, K.K. (2009) *Against Common Sense: Teaching and Learning toward Social Justice*. London: Routledge.

Ladson-Billings, G. (1995) Toward a theory of culturally relevant pedagogy. *American Educational Research Journal* 32 (3), 465–491.

Love, N. (2004) Cognition and the language myth. *Language Sciences* 26 (6), 525–544.

Love, B.L. (2013) 'I see Trayvon Martin': What teachers can learn from the tragic death of a young black male. *The Urban Review* 45 (3), 1–15.

Love, B.L. (2016) Anti-Black state violence, classroom edition: The spirit murdering of Black children. *Journal of Curriculum and Pedagogy* 13 (1), 22–25.

Love, B.L. (2019) *We Want to Do More Than Survive: Abolitionist Teaching and the Pursuit of Educational Freedom*. Boston, MA: Beacon Press.

Muirhead, P. (2009) Rethinking culture: Toward a pedagogy of possibility in world language education. *Critical Inquiry in Language Studies* 6 (4), 243–268.

Nieto, S. (2000) Placing equity front and center: Some thoughts on transforming teacher education for a new century. *Journal of Teacher Education* 51 (3), 180–187.

Nieto, S. and Bode, P. (2008) *Affirming Diversity: The Sociopolitical Context of Multicultural Education*. Boston, MA: Allyn & Bacon.

Osborn, T.A. (2000) *Critical Reflection and the Foreign Language Classroom*. Westport, CT: Bergin & Garvey.

Osborn, T.A. (2003) Market ideology, Critical education studies, and the image of foreign language education. *NECTFL Review* 52, 41–46.

Osborn, T.A. (2006) *Teaching World Languages for Social Justice: A Sourcebook of Principles and Practices*. Mahwah, NJ: Lawrence Erlbaum.

Patel, L. (2019) Fugitive practices: Learning in a settler colony. *Educational Studies* 55 (3), 253–261.

Reagan T. and Osborn, T.A. (2002) *The Foreign Language Educator in Society: Toward a Critical Pedagogy*. Mahwah, NJ: Lawrence Erlbaum.

Rosa, J. and Flores, N. (2017) Unsettling race and language: Toward a raciolinguistic perspective. *Language in Society* 46 (5), 621–647.

Schoener III, H.J. and McKenzie, K.B. (2016) Equity traps redux: Inequitable access to foreign language courses for African American high school students. *Equity & Excellence in Education* 49 (3), 284–299.

Sensoy, O. and DiAngelo, R. (2017) *Is Everyone Really Equal? An Introduction to Key Concepts in Social Justice Education*. New York: Teachers College Press.

Valenzuela, A. (2005) Subtractive schooling, caring relations, and social capital in the schooling of US-Mexican youth. In L. Weis and M. Fine (eds) *Beyond Silenced Voices: Class, Race, and Gender in United States Schools* (pp. 83–94). Albany, NY: SUNY Press.

Wassell, B.A., Wesely, P. and Glynn, C. (2019) Agents of change: Reimagining curriculum and instruction in world language classrooms through social justice education. *Journal of Curriculum and Pedagogy* 16 (3), 263–84.

Wooten, J. and Cahnmann-Taylor, M. (2014) Black, white, and rainbow [of desire]: The colour of race-talk of pre-service world language educators in Boalian theatre workshops. *Pedagogies: An International Journal* 9 (3), 179–195.

Zephir, F. (2000) Ethnic studies and foreign language teacher education in the United States: A response to population shifts. *Journal of Multilingual and Multicultural Development* 21 (3), 230–246.

3 Enacting Social Justice in World Language Education through Intercultural Citizenship

Dorie Conlon Perugini and Manuela Wagner

Introduction

In our language classes, we start with the premise that as language teachers we can help our students to develop their diverse identities, to use tools to critically analyze the world around them, and to collaborate with people from different backgrounds. As articulated in other literature, this approach requires teachers to reflect on their identities and move away from the single goal of teaching our students language only (e.g. Osborn, 2006; Byram & Wagner, 2018). Here we introduce a theoretical framework comprised of approaches from critical pedagogy, intercultural competence and citizenship, raciolinguistics, translanguaging and human rights education. Specifically, we provide a rationale for and an approach to teaching languages that promotes equitable experiences for all students while also giving students opportunities to address the complex problems they face in their lives in today's interconnected world. We primarily focus on the aspects of education within our daily control: curriculum development and instructional choices. The chapter also includes practical examples of applications, critical questions educators can use to guide their implementations in their contexts, as well as a reflection guide for unit and lesson planning. These examples, critical questions and reflection guide for planning are included to provide a bridge from theory to practice to equip pre-service and in-service (world) language teachers for their journeys of developing intercultural citizenship in equitable classrooms.

Why Do We Teach Languages?

While world language programs have traditionally been designed with the primary goal of helping students become proficient in a language other than English, we envision a world where the primary focus of language education is one in which students develop intercultural competence and plurilingual identities. In fact, rather than seeing ourselves as language teachers, we describe our work as facilitators of intercultural citizenship *through* languages. In this way, our language courses are designed to accomplish the goals of social justice education through helping students learn to build and maintain relationships with communities other than their own, develop positive social identities, and investigate – and even challenge and dismantle – power structures within society.

Whereas language programs should be perfectly situated to meet such goals, we challenge the assumption that this happens naturally. Even if we decide to teach with the above goals in mind, there are a number of challenges we face. Most importantly, we could still fail to connect to students in real ways, as demonstrated by a quote from a student in a study investigating the research question, 'How might understandings of culturally sustaining pedagogies be enhanced if they were informed by teaching practices developed, implemented and refined by students themselves?':

> I want to see how what I am learning connects to that, to the larger world, to other Latinos out there, to other people out there. That's what education should be about. It should include us and help us understand and push for our place in the world. (Carmen, student researcher, quoted in Irizarry, 2017: 93)

We want to re-emphasize here that we strongly believe that the goals of language education are not limited to the development of students' linguistic proficiency. In fact, in our opinion they also go well beyond the learning of 'language and culture.' For example, one student in a beginners online German class wrote a reflection related to Conchita Wurst, the winner of the 2014 European Song Contest, an international competition among member states. Conchita is a self-proclaimed drag queen and the student tried to reflect on the importance of being seen as follows:

> My reaction to this is that people should not judge by the appearances, as Conchita Wurst, I believe each person, each single one of us has a 'virtue' that we must take into account and show it to the world if its [sic] necessary. Like Frau Wurst, I want to be a person who can be recognized by the society not only because of what I have/possess but because of the person I am. (Wagner & Tracksdorf, 2018: 153)

In another example, students from an elementary school Spanish class began to collaborate with a local lawyer and a class of high school students to petition their state lawmakers to change discriminatory state practices regarding use of accent marks on official identification forms

(Conlon Perugini & Wagner, forthcoming). While, at first, many students did not understand why accent marks mattered, when they learned that the meaning of a name of someone in their own school community changed from something they considered strong – large rock – to something they considered negative – pain/sorrow/embarrassment – several became motivated to take action.

In these examples, we see the goals of the language course included more than linguistic objectives; they also helped students reflect on their own identities and address societal problems in collaboration with people from various backgrounds. The way we have planned and implemented such aims in our curricula and in collaborative projects with colleagues locally, nationally and internationally is by combining the model of intercultural citizenship (Byram, 2008) with the goals and strategies of social justice education (e.g. Glynn *et al.*, 2018; Nieto, 2010; Osborn, 2006; Reagan & Osborn, 2002). As Byram and Wagner (2018: 147) point out:

> There are important parallels between fostering social justice and developing intercultural citizenship. Both concepts promote criticality in that educators enable students to reflect critically on language, discourse, and culture with regard to power and inequality. In both approaches, educators foster students' engagement with important societal issues…

Moreover, both approaches require teachers to be(come) aware of their own values and perceptions as well as their implicit biases. Similarly, both paradigms have the aim of helping students to become critical and active intercultural citizens. Let us now take a look at the model of intercultural citizenship (Byram, 2008) followed by a short introduction of our takes on social justice and human rights education.

Intercultural Citizenship in World Language Education

Teaching for intercultural citizenship means, in a nutshell, that students apply the knowledge, skills and attitudes of intercultural (communicative) competence (Byram, 1997) to a problem in the here and now. As can be seen in Figure 3.1, according to Byram (1997), students do not only learn the necessary linguistic knowledge and skills, but can also develop

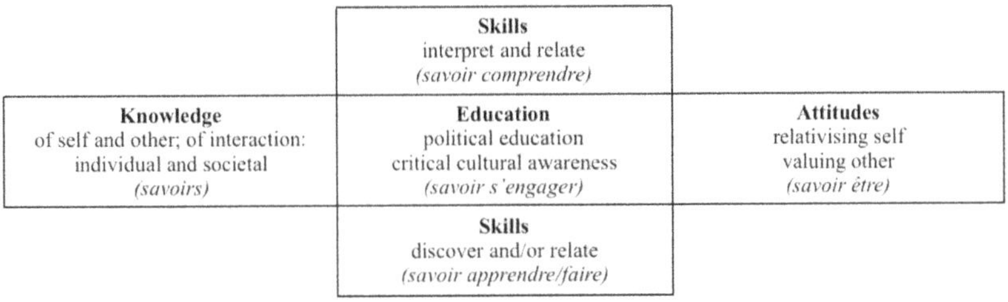

Figure 3.1 Model of intercultural competence. Adapted from Byram (1997: 34)

five distinct, but related, *savoirs*. These *savoirs* include knowledge of social groups and their products and practices in one's own and in one's interlocutor's country or region, and knowledge of the general processes of societal and individual interaction, skills of interpreting and relating and of discovering and interacting, as well as attitudes (e.g. curiosity, open-mindedness, tolerance of ambiguity) of intercultural competence that enable them to become mediators (Byram, 1997: 50). Central to Byram's model, and an area that has strong connections to the goals of social justice education, is critical cultural awareness – defined as 'an ability to evaluate critically and on the basis of explicit criteria perspectives, practices and products in one's own and other cultures and countries' (Byram, 1997: 53).

It is important to note that this approach deviates from the expectation that students should emulate the language and culture of native speakers of a language; rather, to take a step back and reflect on intercultural situations based on specific criteria, taking into account diverse perspectives. In this way, students are not expected to imitate or perform the expected behaviors found within the target culture, but to remain firmly grounded within their own culture while developing plurilingual identities (see Ladson-Billings, 2017). In other words, this approach empowers students and teachers alike, as it makes clear that students do not need to aspire to speak like or act like the ever-elusive native speaker but that they can learn the skills and knowledge to mediate between members of different communities and become intercultural speakers (see Byram, 1997; 2008; Byram & Wagner, 2018). Intercultural citizens care about social justice; believe 'in the values of humanistic thought and action'; critically evaluate a social group's beliefs and values in comparison to humanistic standards; 'promote social action in the world'; and in international projects identify with those beyond their own national borders (compare Wagner *et al.*, 2019: 24–25). Teachers who foster such an approach often ask students for input with regard to the topic or the problem they would like to address.

Wagner *et al.* (2019) provide a list of questions teachers can ask themselves when planning units for interdisciplinary intercultural citizenship: How will you ensure that your students have opportunities to:

- acquire new knowledge and understanding of 'products, perspectives and practices', as described in the *World-Readiness Standards*, related to the topic/theme?
- discover for themselves the practices of people in other regions and contexts?
- compare and contrast perspectives in different contexts on the issue in question?
- analyze and evaluate products and perspectives that influence practices and vice versa?

- take or plan informed action in their (local, national or international) community? (Wagner *et al.*, 2019: 40)

These questions help teachers and students reflect deeply not only on the products and practices of people from different backgrounds, but also what the underlying perspectives might be. The relationship between perspectives, practices and products is an important one. If we mostly analyze products and/or perspectives without considering underlying values and perspectives, we risk making superficial judgments. Trying to understand perspectives requires 'why' questions which in turn means that we need to consider an issue from another perspective. While that can be difficult and take time, it is that hard work which in our experience and that of intercultural citizenship practitioners leads to an identification beyond borders on part of the students (e.g. Byram *et al.*, 2017). These considerations bring us to how we envision social justice in the world language classroom and the connections it has with intercultural citizenship.

Social Justice in World Language Education

Defining social justice presents its own set of challenges and risks. The Conference on English Education (2009), which is now called the English Language Arts Teacher Educators, points this out in their *Beliefs about Social Justice in English Education*:

> Social justice is definitionally complex; it ignites controversy, is not neutral, and varies by person, culture, social class, gender, context, space and time. In fact, when definitions are consensus bound, a consensus definition of social justice is not likely to satisfy the most open-minded of thinkers. (2009: 2)

We acknowledge this complexity and subjectivity while at the same time recognizing the need for common understandings in order to effectively share our work and build upon the foundations already laid in teaching social justice for world languages.

Guiding our work is an understanding that social justice can mean 'members of a society sharing equitably in the benefits of that society' (Osborn, 2006) and sharing equitably in the disadvantages of that society. We also acknowledge that teaching for social justice is a political act that seeks to disrupt systems and policies that uphold inequities. As such, social justice education involves every aspect of education, including but not limited to, access, curriculum development, program offerings, hiring decisions and instructional choices.

Human Rights Education

Teaching for intercultural citizenship and social justice provides unique and exciting opportunities for our world language classrooms.

One such opportunity is the natural and organic connections this approach has with human rights education (as mentioned in Byram *et al.*, 2017; Wagner *et al.*, 2019). Human rights education was defined by the United Nations as follows:

> Human rights education can be defined as education, training and information aiming at building a universal culture of human rights through the sharing of knowledge, imparting of skills and molding of attitudes directed to
>
> (1) the strengthening of respect of human rights and fundamental freedoms;
> (2) the full development of the human personality and the sense of its dignity;
> (3) the promotion of understanding, tolerance, gender equality and friendship among all nations, indigenous peoples and racial, national, ethnic, religious and linguistic groups;
> (4) the enabling of all persons to participate effectively in a free and democratic society governed by the rule of law;
> (5) the building of maintenance of peace
> (6) the promotion of people-centered sustainable development and social justice.

Readers will notice that in human rights education, as in education for intercultural citizenship and social justice, the aim is fostering not only knowledge, but also skills and attitudes. Moreover, there clearly is overlap between human rights, social justice, and intercultural citizenship in that all approaches not only foster students' criticality, but also their participation in a democratic society. We have alluded to our interpretation of this kind of participation above. Finally, social justice is mentioned explicitly in the human rights education goals above.

Connections among Theoretical Frameworks

Before introducing how these theories can be applied in practice, we will first describe how we view these frameworks working together. Central to our approach is the overlap between social justice and intercultural citizenship education. This overlap, illustrated in Figure 3.2, forms the center for our curriculum design and instructional choices. As we will describe below in more detail, we also draw heavily from culturally sustaining pedagogies (for an overview see Paris & Alim, 2017) which we also consider through the lenses of raciolinguistics (Flores & Rosa, 2015) and translanguaging (García & Li Wei, 2014; Flores, 2016). We argue that when these theoretical approaches inform each other, we have a better chance of considering the whole student and preventing pitfalls we see in language education. In addition, human rights education informs this work and provides opportunities for students to see how language education can solve real world problems (see Figure 3.2).

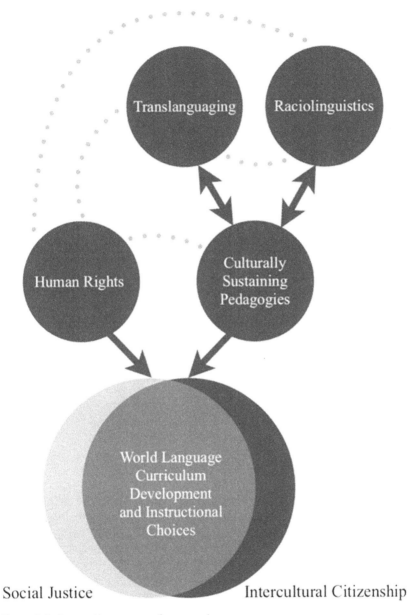

Figure 3.2 Connections among frameworks.

While evaluating our entire curriculum and each of our instructional decisions under all of the aforementioned frameworks may seem like an overwhelming task, we see them not as separate theories, but working together in unison to inform our curriculum development and instructional choices. Together, each of the frameworks in Figure 3.2 help us to consider our curricular and instructional decisions in light of a single question: Will this decision create equity or perpetuate inequity in my classroom and in society?

Finally, while we acknowledge additional complex relationships between all of these frameworks, as indicated by the dotted lines in Figure 3.2, describing these relationships in depth is beyond the scope of this chapter.

Bridging Theory to Practice

As we illustrate how we teach for intercultural citizenship and social justice, the following sections will begin first with common challenges and potential risks that often come to mind when considering this approach to language education. We then provide short examples from our own experiences of how we have navigated these challenges and risks while also providing references to examples published in different contexts and, where appropriate, practical tips and suggestions applicable to a variety of contexts. Finally, at the end of the section we provide an introduction to a reflection guide which can help teachers critically reflect on their own practice and consider what changes they can make as they work towards socially just language education for intercultural citizenship.

Target Language Use and Goals

When considering the paradigm shift from teaching languages for the sake of teaching languages to fostering intercultural citizenship and social justice education through languages, some common challenges and potential risks come to mind, especially with regard to target language use and accomplishing the language goals of our programs. First, many of us are confined to a prescribed curriculum that may limit our control of what we teach. Second, we are often tempted to have critical conversations with our classes in English given the students' limited proficiency in the target language.

While these might be common obstacles language teachers face, they might also be related to our identity as educators. Do we see ourselves as language teachers, language and culture teachers, or, as we mentioned above in our cases, teachers of intercultural citizenship, social justice and human rights through language (see also Byram & Wagner, 2018)? If it is the former two, we will be more likely to fear that students will not focus enough on linguistic aspects and/or that we will not be able to cover the prescribed aspects of the curriculum. If we, however, prioritize the development of the skills necessary for students to be empowered to acquire, analyze and communicate information in order to address problems we face in society, language is not only a necessary part of the skills, but it is also a tool through which the other goals will be achieved (see, for example, Wagner *et al.*, 2019 for a longer conversation on language educators' identities). When teaching languages for intercultural citizenship, social justice and human rights become a priority for us; we can begin to find ways through which we can help students at various levels of proficiency to interpret information and express themselves in meaningful ways about topics of interest to them. While we still might have to make certain compromises – for example, to meet the goals of a prescribed curriculum – we find that often minor adjustments go a long way in helping us achieve the goals of intercultural citizenship and social justice.

Given that it is natural and expected for students to process their reflections on complex topics in their first language (L1), we find it beneficial to provide our students with opportunities to express themselves beyond what their current second language (L2) proficiency affords. One way in which we do this is to incorporate reflective journaling in all their languages outside of the language classroom. Manuela, in the context of higher education, has asked her German students to keep a reflective journal as part of their homework, while Dorie, in the K-12 setting, has collaborated with other teachers in her building to codesign lessons and writing activities that can further the students' intercultural learning beyond the language classroom (see examples of these types of activities in Conlon Perugini, 2018; Wagner & Tracksdorf, 2018; Byram *et al.*, 2013; and Conlon Perugini & Wagner, forthcoming). These L1 reflections provide us as teachers the information and insight into our students' thinking and intercultural communicative competence progress to help us gauge how our lessons work and design or tailor subsequent lessons to our students' interests.

Readers might have noticed that we mentioned the students' L1 rather than English. We think that it is extremely important for us to foster our and our students' understanding of the varieties of home languages and cultures and to develop strategies through which we can help students develop their plurilingual and pluricultural identities. The *Common European Framework* defines plurilingual and pluricultural competences as follows: 'Plurilingual and pluricultural competence is not seen as the superposition or juxtaposition of distinct competences, but rather as the existence of a complex or even composite competence on which the user may draw' (Council of Europe, 2001: 168). This view has consequences for how we see our students' development and use of skills. Most importantly, perhaps, as in pedagogies of translingualism, we consider the whole linguistic and cultural repertoire as relevant.

In light of recommendations such as ACTFL's position that teachers use 90% or more target language in the classroom (ACTFL, 2010), we must consider the role of students' L1. While, traditionally, language teachers may draw distinct lines of separation between L1 and L2 and favor the use of L2, considering language use through a translanguaging lens requires us to reconsider both of these positions. Vogel and García

(2017: 32) provide an overview of the origin of the term translanguaging and the theories behind it, while linking translanguaging theories to views that challenge 'colonial and modernist-era language ideologies [that] created and maintained linguistic, cultural, and racial hierarchies in society'. In practice this means:

> As a pedagogical practice, translanguaging leverages the fluid languaging of learners in ways that deepen their engagement and comprehension of complex content and texts. In addition, translanguaging pedagogy develops both of the named languages that are the object of bilingual instruction precisely because it considers them in a horizontal continuum as part of the learners' linguistic repertoire, rather than as separate compartments in a hierarchical relationship. (Vogel & García, 2017: 2)

If we accept that multiple languages are not in fact 'separate compartments,' but work together in a fluid way, we can reconsider the usefulness of all linguistic resources in the classroom while still prioritizing the acquisition of a new language. In addition, when we allow the strategic and meaningful use of the students' languages, we also signal to them that all their languages are useful in any context. We would, for example, encourage conversations in class in which students can share information, stories and perspectives in their L1 and even teach some of their L1 to their classmates. This is also part of the approach of translanguaging, thereby drawing from their complete linguistic repertoire while also acknowledging their languages as part of their identities both in and out of school.

In the context of our own classrooms, we have both found meaningful ways to incorporate and encourage the use of students' full linguistic repertoire. For example, with her elementary school classes, Dorie often collaborates with classroom teachers (i.e. the students' main teacher responsible for teaching core subjects) to extend Spanish lessons beyond her allotted time. Students may learn about an issue in Spanish class and then use their new knowledge to complete an assignment during their writing block. As mentioned previously, in Manuela's university German courses she often makes use of the *NCSSFL-ACTFL Intercultural Reflection Tool* (ACTFL, 2017) to help students reflect more deeply on the topics they learn in class. In this framework, after students engage in activities in L2, they reflect more deeply on their learning outside of class, often in a blend of L1 and L2. In traditional language classrooms adhering to a strict goal of 90% target language use, these L1 activities may not take place, but in our own instruction, we believe we have a responsibility to be thoughtful in our use and encouragement of all languages and language varieties our students bring to the classroom.

Teaching Culture

Once we decide we are ready to teach intercultural citizenship through languages, we might still be presented with many challenges, especially in regard to how we incorporate culture. For example, we may be tempted to simply provide cultural facts to our students rather than enabling them to find and analyze information independently. This approach may result in presenting target cultures in ways that lead to students seeing the target culture as something exotic and 'over there.' Or, using another approach, teachers present how members of the target culture behave 'appropriately' and expect students to imitate those behaviors. In both examples, teachers may be exposing students only to dominant cultures within the target-language-speaking communities and neglecting the variety of marginalized cultures that also exist within society. As such, students may leave our classes viewing target cultures as monolithic rather than diverse.

These challenges can be exemplified in more traditional textbooks where culture is presented as an aside in the form of interesting factoids. For example, it is not hard to imagine an introductory Spanish textbook including a photo of two people greeting each other with the caption, 'Did you know in Spain it is customary for people to greet one another with a kiss on each cheek?' The teacher may then choose to guide their students in practicing this traditional greeting. While these cultural factoids can certainly provide a springboard into an investigation of culture, simply presenting consumable facts about another culture can lead students 'to other' or to romanticize the cultures which we are trying to get them to understand. And as seen in this example, the dominant culture presented as an accepted fact ignores the reality that certain cultural groups in Spain do not greet one another in this way.

In our own classrooms we had occasionally used the approaches described above and, in many ways, we are still adjusting our teaching practices to avoid these pitfalls. In order to do this, we turn to intercultural citizenship and social justice as frameworks to guide us. As we saw earlier in Byram's (1997) model, while knowledge of culture is one aspect, we now design our curriculum with essential questions that lead to an *investigation* of, rather than a presentation of, culture. In this way students are able to hone skills of discovery and interaction, develop attitudes of open-mindedness and curiosity, and build a tolerance for ambiguity. In addition, social justice frameworks help us choose essential questions that will lead to a critical investigation of what may be considered cultural 'facts,' such as the custom of greeting with kisses.

In the context of a language classroom, skills of interpreting, relating, discovery and interaction help students gain, analyze, evaluate and interpret information from a variety of sources. Wagner *et al.* (2019) provide unit plans that can be used as samples of how students can develop such skills in interdisciplinary intercultural citizenship units. This inclusion of knowledge, skills and attitudes does not happen in a vacuum, but is always linked to themes that are of interest to the students, ideally ones about which they care deeply, such as human rights violations. For example, students explore natural disasters and measures of preparedness for natural disasters in their own contexts. They use skills and knowledge about housing, weather and other related topics from their world languages curriculum, but also from social studies and sciences, while applying their prior general knowledge about the topic. Teachers provide articles, videos and other resources with information and statistics about recent natural disasters and students compare consequences as well as strategies for coping with natural disasters by comparing numbers and statistics, thereby using their mathematical knowledge and skills.

Another opportunity for the meaningful inclusion of students' general knowledge as well as knowledge from other school subjects are historical events, specifically anniversaries of historical events as is illustrated in the following example: Porto and Yulita (2018) taught a unit on the Malvinas/Falklands War during the 30-year anniversary of the conflict to a group of students in Argentina and the UK. In another chapter in the same book, Yulita and Porto (2018) combine human rights education and intercultural citizenship education by covering the 1978 Football World Cup in Argentina during a military dictatorship. Another way to integrate human rights in intercultural citizenship projects is the Global Peace Path project, an initiative by Dr Petra Rauschert and Claudia Owczarek at the University of Munich (LMU). It started in 2018 'and involved collaboration between LMU students and participants with refugee status (or applying for refugee status) from Munich and the surrounding area' (Global Peace Path, n.d.: para. 1–2). It is through these connections to human rights education that we find local and global applications for the work our students engage in through languages. For teachers hoping to incorporate human rights education or other fields with which they might feel less familiar, we recommend collaborating with experts within the field, including those within their own buildings.

In addition to the danger of presenting simple 'cultural facts' we want to be especially careful not to create the notion that 'the culture of the target language' is something that happens only in 'other' places or 'over there.' It is often assumed that language educators introduce students to internationalist perspectives by virtue of teaching languages that are connected to different countries. We want to move away from a nation-culture view. One of the dangers of considering culture related to a nation is that we miss the diversity of many languages that are spoken in different parts of the world and give preference to representation of the language in certain parts of the world based on preconceived notions. Secondly, as was pointed out previously (e.g. Osborn, 2006), a number of languages we teach are also languages of communities within which we are teaching locally and nationally. And even if the language we teach is not spoken in our immediate community, it is still beneficial to include members from our local communities who speak the same L1 as our students but have different cultural backgrounds. This requires a more complex understanding of what cultures consist of and how languages and cultures are related to identities.

Part of a more nuanced reflection on culture and language consists of the question of preconceived notions of appropriate or standard representations of language and culture. We take issue with the expectation of appropriateness on several grounds. As Flores and Rosa (2015) argued in a different context:

> Placing an emphasis on the white speaking *and* listening subject illustrates the limits to appropriateness-based models of language education. Specifically, while appropriateness-based models advocate teaching language-minoritized students to enact the linguistic practices of the white speaking subject when appropriate, the white listening subject often continues to hear linguistic markedness and deviancy regardless of how well language-minoritized students model themselves after the white speaking subject. Thus, notions such as 'standard language' or 'academic language' and the discourse of appropriateness in which they both are embedded must be conceptualized as racialized ideological perceptions rather than objective linguistic categories. (2015: 152)

To bring this to the world language context, we must ask ourselves if the examples of L2 language and culture we hold up as models for our students are objectively 'appropriate' or if we are selecting what we believe to be appropriate based on the practices of the dominant culture of the target language. If this is the case, our minoritized students may never achieve the goal of being seen as linguistically and culturally appropriate as members of the dominant culture and may still view their behavior as deviating from the norm based on their minoritized status.

An additional reason for us to shy away from simplistic activities telling students to behave a certain way is that we do not want to tell students how to be someone else, but rather help them reflect on similarities and differences and some reasons (perspectives) behind certain practices and products. That is where we see the potential for students to become mediators between representatives of different backgrounds rather than imitators of behaviors deemed to be representative of a 'culture.' Finally, we fear that telling students what to do and how to behave is especially problematic with minoritized students as it feeds into the general message that their background is not standard and that they need to assimilate in order to succeed in both school and society.

Rather than requiring students to rehearse and perform certain 'acceptable' or 'appropriate' language or behaviors, we prefer to provide students with opportunities for discovery and interaction so that they may hone abilities to defamiliarize and decenter within their own culture when interacting with members from other cultures. In order to learn to defamiliarize and decenter, students must examine how their own culture and socialization influence their understanding of an interaction and consider how their understandings may change when viewed from another cultural perspective. One way to help students practice this ability is through interpreting and relating authentic resources, as discussed in the following section.

Choosing Resources

One way we can help our students develop the skills of interpreting and relating, included in intercultural communicative competence, is by guiding them to interpret authentic resources. Commonly, and problematically, defined as resources created by and for native speakers, authentic resources allow teachers to bring into their classrooms a variety of voices and perspectives from target language communities. Authentic resources include songs, poetry, newspaper articles, stories, legends but can also include artwork and social media posts. As these multimodal examples of communication often introduce everyday language, when scaffolded appropriately for language learners, these resources can help students acquire the target language while simultaneously exposing them to samples of cultural products and practices. Teachers can then provide opportunities to investigate perspectives behind the products and practices. From a social justice perspective, we view authentic resources as opportunities to center voices that have been historically and systematically excluded from language teaching materials and curricula, such as Afro-Latinx voices in Spanish, Black German voices in German curricula, and members of the LBGTQ+ communities, to name a few. Using authentic resources in this way can serve to create windows, mirrors and sliding glass doors:

> Books are sometimes windows, offering views of worlds that may be real or imagined, familiar or strange. These windows are also sliding glass doors, and readers have only to walk through in imagination to become part of whatever world has been created and recreated by the author. When lighting conditions are just right, however, a window can also be a mirror. Literature transforms human experience and reflects it back to us, and in that reflection, we can see our own lives and experiences as part of the larger human experience. Reading, then, becomes a means of self-affirmation, and readers often seek their mirrors in books. (Sims Bishop, 1990: ix)

When choosing resources, we should keep in mind how they may serve as the windows, mirrors and sliding glass doors Sims Bishop describes, while also taking time to examine each text critically.

Though the move to using authentic resources may seem like a simple solution for diversifying world language curriculum, we argue that no resource should be introduced in the classroom without critical reflection. We must use the same skills of interpreting and relating that we want our students to develop in order to critically analyze resources for ethnocentric perspectives and bias. To highlight an example of the importance of this critical reflection and analysis and the dangers of proceeding without it, we look at the Netflix original series *Siempre Bruja*, an adaptation of the novel *Yo, Bruja* by Isadora Chacón. *Siempre Bruja* tells the story of an Afro-Latina witch named Carmen Eguiluz, played by Black actress Angely

Gaviria, from 17th-century Colombia who travels in time to present-day Colombia in order to save her lover – who is also the son of Carmen's master. While Carmen is the most prominent Black character in the series, the show also includes other recurring Black characters playing minor roles.

At first glance, this show seems to provide a window and sliding glass door into the life of a young Afro-Colombian woman and her adventures in adjusting to a new time period. However, although the main characters and a few others are Afro-Colombian, neither the author of the original book nor the majority of the production team of the Netflix series identify as Black and do not present as Black phenotypically. Analyzing this series for potential ethnocentric perspectives and identifying its bias shows how problematic this resource is if presented to students as 'authentic.' For example, throughout the series there is a denial of current racial tension within Colombia as well as a lack of understanding of how a legacy of slavery has shaped modern-day life for Afro-Colombians. Citing the racist trope of a slave falling in love with her master, Casamayor-Cisneros (2019: 5) writes:

> This is not the tale of an Afro-Colombian woman but the story of the white characters dictating her actions. *Always a Witch* does nothing but follow a tradition, long before deconstructed by Toni Morrison, of the fabrication of black characters by white artists as a means to talk about themselves.

That is not to say the cultural perspectives found within *Siempre Bruja* are inaccurate or inauthentic, but rather they represent the cultural perspectives of a predominantly non-Afro-Latinx group while positioning itself as a show about a Black woman and her experiences.

We therefore warn that using shows that appear inclusive of diverse representations at first glance as an attempt to be inclusive of diverse experiences can easily result in exactly the opposite outcome: a continuation of the legacy of American education that centers dominant perspectives. Of course, teachers could potentially use this resource to help students analyze cultural perspectives, just as we have done here. Students can reflect on whose perspectives are being portrayed and whose are being marginalized. They could then look for examples from their own culture which could lead to developing critical cultural awareness. What we want to emphasize here is that in choosing resources in the language classroom, we see a need to adopt a model that recognizes the spectrum and complexity of resources that exist in the world. In this model, teachers consider the communicative intent of the resource and whose cultural perspectives are presented through which characters/people. In order to critically analyze potential resources, teachers may consider the following questions.

To help determine the resource's communicative intent, teachers can ask themselves:

- For what purpose was this resource created?
- Who is the intended audience?

- Was the resource intended to entertain, inform or persuade the audience?
- Was the resource created to help the user practice grammar or language development?
- In what settings and in what ways would monolingual, bilingual and plurilingual users of the language use this resource?

To help determine whose cultural perspectives are being portrayed, teachers can ask themselves:

- Who is the author/creator?
- What do you know about the author/creator's identity? Which cultures, societies and social groups do they identify with?
- Who is the intended audience?
- What cultural products, practices and perspectives are found within the work? Are they accurate? What criteria are you using to determine the work's authenticity?
- Who benefits from this resource? Who does not?
- Whose voices and perspectives are being centered? Whose voices and perspectives are being marginalized?
- How is this work received by the community the work portrays? (e.g. if the work portrays the experience of an Afro-Latinx woman, how are Afro-Latinx women responding to this work?)

In addition to the questions above, we have found the *Reading Diversely* (Teaching Tolerance, 2016) tool helpful in considering the linguistic complexity and cultural diversity found within the resources we are considering. These tools may be found at https://www.tolerance.org/magazine/publications/reading-diversity.

Teaching Equitably and Dismantling Systems of Oppression

After we have settled on the goals we have for teaching culture, we must examine how our classroom practices either increase equity or uphold oppression. Some concerns we have regarding our teaching practices include:

- Teaching for social justice and intercultural citizenship can be seen as political and/or partisan which can conflict with ideas that education should be neutral. We encourage students not to engage in activism without careful consideration on how this can impact marginalized communities (leading to white saviorism).
- We fail to examine our own implicit bias and can potentially evaluate or perceive students differently based on race, ethnicity or other identities.
- We unknowingly uphold aspects of white supremacy or systems of oppression due to lack of our own critical self-examination.

- We knowingly uphold aspects of white supremacy or systems of oppression due to the fear of repercussions from speaking out or acting out.
- We think an activity was a success without considering the consequences for all our students.
- We fail to consider what stereotypes we have internalized regarding our own culture, and how they have influenced how we view target cultures.

Although the first challenge is important because it is the reason why many educators shy away from this approach to teaching, we refer readers to previous extensive work in this area. We add our voices to the many educators who acknowledge that all teaching is political (e.g. Freire, 2018; Randolph & Johnson, 2017; Norton & Toohey, 2004; Osborn, 2006). The question is whether we examine what views we knowingly or unknowingly perpetuate. Therefore, we consider it crucial to examine our own biases and to ensure we truly offer students access to a variety of perspectives. The important difference between this view of 'politics' and the view that is often seen as 'partisan politics' is that being political means that we have a concern for public life. Or as Michael Byram shares in Wagner *et al.* (2019), 'Learners being or becoming political – develop their own ideas, beliefs and commitments – become involved in public life – "practice politics" – challenge authority [or at any level – family, school, sports club, national and international government' (Byram, cited in Wagner *et al.*, 2019: 125). In other words, what we refer to is enabling students to find their place in the world by taking actions in matters they deem important.

What is often misunderstood by teachers and pre-service teachers is that providing the tools for students to develop their own beliefs and analyze problems in order to find solutions – and possibly implement them – does not mean that teachers are attempting to further their own political agenda. It is understandable, however, that teachers feel that they have to be careful as there are ethical considerations involved.

Teaching for social justice and intercultural citizenship is rewarding. However, it is also complex. As with many theories we apply in practice, we need to understand what theoretical concepts can look like in reality, how we can prepare students to understand and apply these concepts, and how we can assess them and help students assess them. It is therefore not surprising that applications of intercultural citizenship might fail to include a deep interrogation of issues of power, systems of oppression and how our own biases play a role in our teaching. As such, teachers looking to develop intercultural citizenship and social justice goals for their programs should consider if their desired outcomes and teaching practices are truly appropriate for all students or if they continue in the 'fallacy of measuring ourselves and the young people in our communities solely against white middle-class norms of knowing and being that continue to dominate notions of educational achievement' (Paris & Alim, 2017: 2).

For language education this can be found in holding up 'Standard American English' or the 'native speaker' as ideal models rather than understanding those terms in 'relation to racialized perceptions through which racially unmarked subjects' language practices are positioned as inherently legitimate and racialized subjects' practices are perceived as inherently deficient' (Rosa & Flores, 2017: 632). In a similar way, education for intercultural communicative competence must consider if the model 'intercultural speaker' we envision is a standard truly inclusive of all regardless of race, language and identity or if it is inherently biased to favor white ideals. While theories of social justice and intercultural citizenship already contain much useful information to teach languages for all students, we also find the use of culturally responsive (Ladson-Billings, 1995) and culturally sustaining pedagogies (CSP) (Paris & Alim, 2017) helpful in our teaching.

Continuing in the work of culturally responsive pedagogies, CSP is a framework for teaching that 'seeks to perpetuate and foster – to sustain – linguistic, literate, and cultural pluralism as part of schooling for positive social transformation' (Paris & Alim, 2017: 1). In stark opposition to the US's long history of educational systems that demand assimilation to white norms for academic success, CSP seeks to disrupt 'a schooling system centered on ideologies of white, middle-class, monolingual, cisheteropatriarchal, able-bodied superiority' (Paris & Alim, 2017: 13). As such, CSP views cultural competence as an essential part of education, especially for minoritized students to develop fluency in the culture of dominance, with the caveat that students remain firmly grounded in their cultures of origin (Ladson-Billings, 2017). In order for teachers to ensure racialized and marginalized students are not expected to assimilate into dominant cultures as they develop cultural competence, Ladson-Billings (2017) emphasizes the importance that teachers, especially teachers who are members of the dominant culture, increase their understanding of their own culture. She goes on to describe her experiences working primarily with white teachers who struggle to identify their own culture and analogizes those teachers to fish who have trouble seeing the water that they swim in. She attributes this perception of a lack of culture to social power dynamics that define whiteness as the unmarked, invisible norm (2017: 13). In other words, Ladson-Billings calls for the same decentering and critical cultural awareness Byram (1997) suggests students develop as part of their language learning experiences. In the context of teaching for intercultural communicative competence, the ability for teachers to critically examine their own culture and decenter their experiences has profound effects on the way in which world language teachers teach and assess intercultural competence in their classrooms.

As mentioned in the list of challenges, oftentimes we may fail to examine our own implicit bias and can potentially evaluate or perceive students differently based on race, ethnicity or other identities. To make a serious attempt to be more inclusive of minoritized students would require teachers to consider their own raciolinguistic ideologies and complicity in upholding systems of oppression. In the world language classroom, raciolinguistic ideologies can show up as teachers evaluating similar linguistic performances as different based on a student's race or perceived racialized identity. Similarly, Rosa and Flores (2017: 628) state that 'racialized subjects are perpetually perceived as linguistically deficient even when engaging in language practices that would likely be legitimized or even prized were they produced by white speaking subjects'. There is the potential for teachers to perceive racialized students as deficient in intercultural competence even when those students are engaging in intercultural practices that would likely be legitimized or prized when produced by white students.

To imagine what this might look like in a language classroom, let's consider a recent study in the hospitality industry that found service providers who are Black have to perform more *emotional labor* ('an employee's emotional display [e.g. a smile with customers] that conforms to the work role as well as the effortful strategies [e.g. frequently faking a good mood] to achieve that display' (Grandey *et al.*, 2018: 2164) in order to be evaluated on par with their white counterparts even when their work performance is objectively the same. In other words, with all else being equal, Black service providers are perceived as less interpersonally warm as their white counterparts and must 'fake it' to be rated on par with white service providers. Considerations for this type of implicit bias have important implications for teachers looking to assess the intercultural competence of their students. For example, while Byram's (1997) model of intercultural communicative competence values curiosity, is it possible for curious behavior exhibited by one student to be seen as acting interculturally competent while the same behavior from a student of another race be seen as disruptive or even threatening? Could Black students in world language classrooms have to perform more emotional labor in order to be seen as interculturally competent as their white peers even when their behavior and attitudes are otherwise objectively the same? In the context of intercultural communicative competence, we cannot assume that teachers adding intercultural communicative competence to the curriculum are immune from this kind of racist thinking; they must therefore critically reflect on their own practices in order to ensure how their teaching and assessment of intercultural communicative competence may be affected by their unexamined implicit biases and complicity in systems of oppression.

To help ourselves move towards teaching more equitably and dismantling systems of oppression, we must engage in critical self-reflection. Unlike reflecting on our pedagogy, the questions we must ask ourselves here are more difficult because they are more personal. Some of the questions we ask ourselves frequently include: In what ways might I be privileged? How does that privilege impact how I make sense of the world and how I teach? What do I do to understand my own cultural background on a deeper level? What am I doing to continuously uncover my own implicit biases? Who are the people I interact with the most? In what ways can I diversify that group of people? How might I be complicit in upholding systems of oppression? How can I use my privilege to accomplish the goals of equitable teaching and dismantling systems of oppression? We suggest asking yourselves these kinds of questions frequently and in a variety of contexts as the answers may change depending on a variety of factors. You may also want to consider journaling and finding an accountability partner or group so you can monitor your own progress.

In this chapter we introduced a variety of frameworks to help teachers think critically about the choices they make in their classrooms. In an effort to assist teachers to systematically incorporate critical self-reflection into their process of curriculum design and making instructional choices, we have created a guide to thinking critically about world language education (Appendix A). This guide is not a checklist nor a comprehensive list of considerations for equitable language teaching. Rather, teachers can use this lesson planning template to begin to reflect critically about the goals, resources and pedagogy of a specific lesson or unit in order to apply the approach outlined in this chapter to their own contexts.

Closing Thoughts

As we look back at the chapter, we realize that we have left readers with more questions than answers. This is connected to our strong conviction that educators looking to design world language education for intercultural citizenship and social justice must be concerned with their process more than their final product. While we did provide some examples that have worked in our own classrooms in order to provide a glimpse into the bridge between theory and practice, we acknowledge that this type of education will look vastly different depending on individual context. We agree with the notion that '[t]eaching world languages for social justice begins with a teacher who is concerned about social justice and holds a belief in students' humanity' (Osborn, 2006: 28) and hope the reflection questions guide teachers to consider their own concerns for social justice and the full humanity of their students.

We are also aware that we introduced several frameworks. It might be overwhelming even to think about including so many aspects in our language education curriculum. These resources can help us teach all our students the knowledge, skills and attitudes they need to engage actively in the world around them. We have highlighted the importance of teaching in just and equitable ways as we help our students foster their own plurilinguistic and pluricultural identities in the process and the necessity of teachers continuously engaging in their own critical self-reflection.

Therefore, we would like to end this chapter by sharing our own reflections and vulnerabilities. We know that no single unit we create will address everything we wish to consider. We are painfully aware that we often fall short of creating units that lead to intercultural citizenship, that give students the tools and especially the time to critically examine their environment and apply their knowledge, skills and attitudes to problems in their local, national, international communities. We shudder at the thought of missed opportunities with regard to fostering all our students' identities. However, and perhaps more importantly, we pledge that our shortcomings will not prevent us from trying every single day to do our best. For us, this means to keep wrapping our minds around these fascinating and complex topics, applying theory to practice, learning alongside and even from our students, and sharing our examples with our communities of practice. We hope we have inspired readers to do the same.

Discussion Questions

After engaging in teacher reflection in Appendix A, answer the following questions:

(1) What kinds of key takeaways about your own teaching, identity and biases do you have? What steps will you take to address equity in your teaching, the intersectionality of your identity with your students' identities, and your own biases?
(2) What did you learn about your content and communication goals? What did the reflection affirm for you and what kinds of changes do you anticipate making to your curriculum?
(3) What steps will you take to critically examine your resources going forward? Which resources currently being used in your classroom may need to be discarded in favor of locating new resources? How will you locate resources that provide windows, mirrors and sliding glass doors? If materials are required by your department, how do you plan to find a way to engage your students with the material in a critical way?

Appendix A

Reflection Questions	Teacher Reflections
Critical Self-Reflection and Pedagogy: • How will my own bias influence the way I teach this unit? • With whom can I have open, honest and respectful conversations about my own biases? • How can I help foster my students' identities through the unit? • How can I work to ensure equitable teaching and evaluation practices throughout the unit?	

Content Goals:
- In what ways do my content goals align with Intercultural Citizenship and Social Justice education?
- How will my various students see themselves reflected in the content?
- How will the content help students invest in their language learning?

Communication Goals:
- What language will my students need in order to accomplish the content goals of this unit?
- How does the language in this unit support the goals of Intercultural Citizenship and Social Justice education?

Resources:
- How will I consider my own bias in choosing and evaluating the resources I bring into my classroom?
- How will I give my students opportunities to identify and reflect upon their own bias in their interactions with classroom resources?

In what ways do these resources create windows, mirrors and sliding glass doors for my students?

References

ACTFL (2010) Use of the target language in the classroom. 22 May. See https://www.actfl.org/news/position-statements/use-the-target-language-the-classroom

ACTFL (2017) *Intercultural Reflection Tool.* See https://www.actfl.org/resources/ncssfl-actfl-can-do-statements.

Byram, M. (1997) *Teaching and Assessing Intercultural Communicative Competence.* Clevedon: Multilingual Matters.

Byram, M. (2008) *From Foreign Language Education to Education for Intercultural Citizenship: Essays and Reflections.* Clevedon: Multilingual Matters.

Byram, M. and Wagner, M. (2018) Making a difference: Language teaching for intercultural and international dialogue. *Foreign Language Annals* 51 (1), 140–151.

Byram, M., Golubeva, I., Hui, H. and Wagner, M. (eds) (2017) *From Principles to Practice in Education for Intercultural Citizenship.* Bristol: Multilingual Matters.

Byram, M., Conlon Perugini, D. and Wagner, M. (2013) The development of intercultural citizenship in the elementary school Spanish classroom. *Learning Languages* 18 (2), 16–31.

Casamayor-Cisneros, O. (2019) The real failure of 'Always a Witch' (*Siempre Bruja*). *Cite Black Women* (blog), 22 February. See https://www.citeblackwomencollective.org/our-blog/the-real-failure-of-always-a-witch-siempre-bruja.

Conference on English Education Commission on Social Justice (2009) *CEE Position Statement: Beliefs about Social Justice in English Education.* First Biennial CEE Conference. Chicago: CEE. See https://cdn.ncte.org/nctefiles/groups/cee/beliefs_about_social_justice_ee.pdf

Conlon Perugini, D. (2018) Discovering modes of transportation. In M. Wagner, D. Conlon Perugini and M. Byram (eds) *Teaching Intercultural Competence Across the Age Range: From Theory to Practice* (pp. 42–59). Bristol: Multilingual Matters.

Conlon Perugini, D. and Wagner, M. (forthcoming) 'It's who I am': Exploring equity in the elementary setting through our names.

Council of Europe. Council for Cultural Co-operation. Education Committee. Modern Languages Division (2001) *Common European Framework of Reference for Languages: Learning, Teaching, Assessment*. Cambridge: Cambridge University Press.

Flores, N. (2016) Combatting marginalized spaces in education through language architecture. *Perspectives in Urban Education* 13 (1), 1–3.

Flores, N. and Rosa, J. (2015) Undoing appropriateness: Raciolinguistic ideologies and language diversity in education. *Harvard Educational Review* 85 (2), 149–171.

Freire, P., with Ramos, M.B., Shor, I. and Macedo, D.P. (2018) *Pedagogy of the Oppressed: 50th Anniversary Edition*. New York: Bloomsbury Academic.

García, O. and Li Wei (2014) *Translanguaging: Language, Bilingualism and Education*. Basingstoke: Palgrave Macmillan.

Global Peace Path (n.d.) *Global Peace Path: Visions, Words and Actions*. See https://www.tefl.anglistik.uni-muenchen.de/projects-events/globalpeacepath/index.html.

Glynn, C., Wesely, P.M. and Wassell, B. (2018) *Words and Actions: Teaching Language through the Lens of Social Justice* (2nd edn). Alexandria, VA: American Council on the Teaching of Foreign Languages.

Grandey, A.A., Houston, L. and Avery, D.R. (2018) Fake it to make it? Emotional labor reduces the racial disparity in service performance judgments. *Journal of Management* 45 (5), 2163–2192. https://doi.org/10.1177/0149206318757019

Irizarry, J.G. (2017) For us, by us: A vision for culturally sustaining pedagogies forwarded by Latinx youth. In D. Paris and H.S. Alim (eds) *Culturally Sustaining Pedagogies: Teaching and Learning for Justice in a Changing World* (pp. 83–98). New York: Teachers College.

Ladson-Billings, G. (1995) Toward a theory of culturally relevant pedagogy. *American Educational Research Journal* 32 (3), 465–491. https://doi.org/10.3102/00028312032003465

Ladson-Billings, G. (2017) The (r)evolution will not be standardized: Teacher education, hip hop pedagogy, and culturally relevant pedagogy 2.0. In D. Paris and H.S. Alim (eds) *Culturally Sustaining Pedagogies: Teaching and Learning for Justice in a Changing World* (pp. 141–156). New York: Teachers College Press.

Nieto, S. (2010) *Language, Culture, and Teaching: Critical Perspectives*. New York: Routledge.

Norton, B. and Toohey, K. (2004) *Critical Pedagogies and Language Learning*. Cambridge: Cambridge University Press.

Osborn, T.A. (2006) *Teaching World Languages for Social Justice: A Sourcebook of Principles and Practices*. Mahwah, NJ: Lawrence Erlbaum Associates.

Paris, D. and Alim, H.S. (eds) (2017) *Culturally Sustaining Pedagogies: Teaching and Learning for Justice in a Changing World*. New York: Teachers College Press.

Porto, M. and Yulita, L. (2018) Language and intercultural citizenship education for a culture of peace: The Malvinas/Falklands project. In M. Byram, I. Golubeva, H. Hui and M. Wagner (eds) *From Principles to Practice in Education for Intercultural Citizenship* (pp. 199–224). Bristol: Multilingual Matters.

Randolph, L.J. and Johnson, S.M. (2017) Social justice in the language classroom: A call to action. *Dimension* 2017, 99–121.

Reagan, T.G. and Osborn, T.A. (2002) *The Foreign Language Educator in Society: Toward a Critical Pedagogy*. New York: Routledge.

Rosa, J. and Flores, N. (2017) Unsettling race and language: Toward a raciolinguistic perspective. *Language in Society* 46 (5), 621–647.

Sims Bishop, R. (1990) Mirrors, windows, and sliding glass doors. *Perspectives* 1 (3), ix–xi.

Teaching Tolerance (2016) Reading diversity: A tool for selecting diverse texts. See https://www.learningforjustice.org/magazine/publications/reading-diversity

Vogel, S. and García, O. (2017) Translanguaging. In G. Noblit and L. Moll (eds) *Oxford Research Encyclopedia of Education* (pp. 32–56). Oxford: Oxford University Press.

Wagner, M., Cardetti, F. and Byram, M. (2019) *Teaching Intercultural Citizenship across the Curriculum: The Role of Language Education*. Alexandria, VA: ACTFL.

Wagner, M. and Tracksdorf, N. (2018) ICC online: Fostering the development of intercultural competence in virtual language classrooms. In M. Wagner, D. Conlon Perugini and M. Byram (eds) *Teaching Intercultural Competence Across the Age Range: From Theory to Practice* (pp. 135–154). Bristol: Multilingual Matters.

Yulita, L. and Porto, M. (2018) Human rights education in language teaching. In M. Byram, I. Golubeva, H. Hui and M. Wagner (eds) *From Principles to Practice in Education for Intercultural Citizenship* (pp. 225–250). Bristol: Multilingual Matters.

4 Building Critical Consciousness through Community-Based Language Learning and Global Health

Joan Clifford

Introduction

As world language educators become more engaged in social justice pedagogy (Caldwell, 2007; Clifford & Reisinger, 2019; Glynn *et al.*, 2018; Osborn, 2006; Randolph & Johnson, 2017; Zapata, 2011), and as undergraduate global health programs embrace more interdisciplinarity (Koplan *et al.*, 2009; Silva & Waggett, 2019; Whitehead, 2019), the intersections between world language and the global health curriculum are expanding. This chapter presents a model that integrates Community-Based Language Learning (CBLL) and global health curricula utilizing principles of critical pedagogy. Working through the lens of global health in the L2 curriculum creates opportunities to study and analyze products, practices and perspectives related to health and wellbeing in innovative ways. The CBLL global health curriculum creates opportunities for decentering constructs of knowledge, understanding positionality and engaging in critical reflection and perspective transformation. Because the COVID-19 pandemic has made more visible the racial, ethnic and class inequities inherent in the US healthcare system, it is even more relevant to find ways to build students' critical consciousness related to health and wellbeing. This chapter explores the pedagogical foundations of this social justice-oriented curriculum and outlines how the CBLL global health curricular model was enacted at Duke University.

Rationale and Framework

Before presenting the critical framework utilized in this curriculum, I first describe two foundational aspects of the model. First, the focus on global health draws on the study of social determinants of health, defined as 'the conditions in which people are born, grow, work, live, and age…, circumstances [that] are shaped by the distribution of money, power and resources at global, national and local levels' (World Health Organization, n.d.). Second, CBLL is a curricular framework for language study designed to include 'interactions that take place between L2 students and heritage/native speakers of the target language residing in the United States' (Clifford & Reisinger, 2019). The interactions vary according to the make-up of local communities and the types of collaborations and levels of co-education possible.

Critical pedagogy in CBLL

The CBLL global health curriculum applies principles of critical pedagogy in various ways. According to Johnson and Randolph (2015), critical pedagogy

> includes any classroom practice that addresses difference, power, or social stratification in the classroom or in the world. Critical classroom practices generally produce one or both of the following: these practices may encourage students to examine social issues and effect social change, or they may emphasize more reflective, critically engaged learning processes within the classroom. (2015: 36)

These critical classroom practices are supported in the CBLL global health curriculum through the study of social determinants of health, learning with community members and opportunities for perspective transformation. Outlined forthwith are the tenets of critical pedagogy that are central to this curriculum: decentering of knowledge, awareness of positionality, critical reflection, and building critical consciousness.

Decentering knowledge

By decentering knowledge, students are prompted to reconsider assumptions, such as their pre-conceived ideas regarding the superiority of Western healthcare systems and biomedicine. Looking at what is and is not at the center of the curriculum is instructive. Where do the readings, films, narratives come from? Whose voices are most represented? In order to create the most opportunity to incorporate underrepresented spaces and unacknowledged, erased and ignored voices and experiences, I curate my own materials (instead of using a textbook), and include counter-storytelling and co-teaching by community partners. This commitment to bring stories from the margins of society into the 'center' of the curriculum secures the inclusion of multiple points of view and diversifies the sources of knowledge in the curriculum.

Awareness of positionality

Awareness of our own positionality related to health and healthcare is also important. Each of us has a different understanding of healthcare, perhaps based on a family member having been hospitalized, a friend newly diagnosed with a disease, our eligibility for health insurance, or personal visits to the doctor. This curriculum supports the exploration of institutionalized medicine, healthcare policy and the conceptualization of wellbeing. Students engage in perspective transformation as they reflect on how they fit into a larger narrative of healthcare and consider issues of access. Expanding our awareness of positionality influences our understanding of the world and provides opportunities to unveil hidden systems of power and privilege.

Critical reflection

Critical reflection is also a fundamental process in supporting the development of critical consciousness since it provides a structured platform through which students offer observations, debrief, reconsider and reimagine their understanding of the world. There are many different models for reflection: the ABC Model (Welch, 1999) is based on Affect, Behavior, Cognition; the DAE framework (Nam, 2012) cycles through Describe, Analyze, Evaluate; the OSEE Tool (Deardorff, 2012) follows the steps of Observe, State, Explore, Evaluate – but I generally utilize the DEAL model (Ash & Clayton, 2009). Through the DEAL model students are led to Describe, Examine and Articulate Learning, thus scaffolding reflection to examine experiences from personal, civic and academic perspectives (Ash & Clayton, 2009). How to engage the student in critical reflection needs to be carefully considered since each student is entering the process at their own stage of development.

Building critical consciousness

Building critical consciousness occurs in this curriculum through an intentional multilayered approach that applies critical pedagogy to a L2 pedagogy. In regards to possible new directions in L2 pedagogy, Trujillo (2009) suggested that the five Cs – communication, cultures, connections, comparisons and communities (ACTFL, 2015) – should be expanded to include an additional 'C' for 'consciousness.' He stated that 'in much the same way that communication takes place in a context defined by cultures, comparisons, connections, and communities, those systems in turn emerge from an environment framed by socially and politically-constructed hierarchies of power and privilege' (Trujillo, 2009: 379). Trujillo defined the proposed sixth standard as: 'Consciousness: Recognize your role in systems of privilege and promote equity' with two subcategories of (1) 'Students recognize the role of language and cultures in systems of privilege and oppression' and (2) 'Students use language and culture to promote equity and social justice' (Trujillo, 2009: 379). This critical approach makes the deep analysis of practices, products and perspectives possible – and ensures that the five Cs do not receive superficial treatment. In addition, this approach encourages the design of problem-posing activities, a key strategy to furthering critical thinking. Shor (1992: 32–33) stated that '[t]he responsibility of the problem-posing teacher is to diversify subject matter and to use the students' thoughts and speech as the base for developing critical understanding of personal experience, unequal conditions in society, and existing knowledge'. L2 educators regularly engage with questions related to student identities (age, origin, etc.) in order to practice certain targeted vocabulary or grammar structures. Critical pedagogy invites L2 educators to consider how to build deeper connections between the students' lived experiences and the curriculum. Shor (1992: 129) indicated that critical consciousness 'refers to the way we see ourselves in relation to knowledge and power in society, to the way we use and study language, and to the way we act in school and daily life to reproduce or to transform our conditions'. Similarly, the CBLL global health curriculum provides ways to make visible the reproduction and/or transformation of our society.

CBLL, critical service-learning and community

The community partnerships developed in CBLL are central to the process of building critical consciousness as well. Service-learning and other forms of experiential learning have become institutionalized in higher education (Bringle & Hatcher, 2000; Furco & Holland, 2009) and the Association of American Colleges and Universities (AAC&U) has identified them as high-impact practices that increase student retention and student engagement in higher education (Kuh, 2008). There are many aspects of community-based learning that can be problematic when power dynamics remain unchecked, but the CBLL global health curriculum follows the principles of ethical engagement defined within critical service-learning. Mitchell (2008: 54) outlined the justice-oriented developmental pathway, stating that:

> Critical service-learning pedagogy fosters a critical consciousness, allowing students to combine action and reflection in the classroom and community to examine both the historical precedents of the social problems addressed in their service placements and the impact of their personal action/inaction in maintaining and transforming those problems.

It is of note that within the general global health curriculum, experiential learning is now an expected and valued complement to coursework since students need 'opportunities to apply their skills and knowledge in a variety of field settings that mirror the broad field of global health to pre-pare them to blend theory and practice' (Whitehead, 2019). The CBLL global health curriculum is an interdisciplinary effort that responds to this interest in exposing students to the real-world context as it supports opportunities for multilingual and multicultural explorations of sociohis-torical systems and social issues related to health and wellbeing.

Thinking about the role of community engagement in higher educa-tion requires a careful consideration of the best practices for sustained community partnerships. Davis *et al.* (2017: 50) identified key character-istics for ethical community partnerships, stating that:

> Mutual sharing of power that produces generative reciprocity enables all stakeholders to … join together synergistically to build capacities and produce outcomes that none could otherwise produce separately. Deliberative civic engagement, mapping intersects of power and reciproc-ity, and attending to capacities for transformative learning are all essen-tial practices in community engaged partnerships.

The concepts of generative reciprocity and transformative learning are present in the CBLL global health curriculum as students work in solidar-ity with communities. When students participate in CBLL, they are chal-lenged to reposition themselves within the campus and community and to examine privilege and power both in personal and societal contexts. In this practice, uncomfortable situations may arise that trigger dissonance for students. It is through the deconstruction of habits of mind that stu-dents have opportunities to transform their own beliefs and practices (Mezirow, 2000). When CBLL germinates critical consciousness, then students begin to challenge assumptions and encounter new ways of thinking about topics. Randolph and Johnson (2017: 17) stated that:

> [p]erspective transformation, the hallmark process underlying transfor-mative learning, is the process of becoming critically aware of how and why our assumptions have come to constrain the way we perceive our world, making possible a more inclusive perspective and allowing the individual to act on new understandings (Mezirow, 1991). The process of perspective transformation is a movement from the conflict, also called the disorienting dilemma, to critical reflection, then to conscious action, and finally to integration, resulting in a new, broader meaning perspective.

As students assess difference and integrate the critiques of systems and policies into their study, they build critical consciousness and engage in perspective transformation that can then lead to conscious action. When these components are integrated into the curriculum it brings into focus how academic themes 'live' in the real world and enact social change. In order for students to connect their individual experiences with larger social systems the curriculum encourages a study of systems of oppres-sion, active listening in the community and the development of critical reflection strategies, among other skills needed to become agents of change. The students are challenged to look at their individual world with new eyes and then apply their new understandings to reconceptualize society at large.

Case Study Context

The extensive resources dedicated to academic advancement in health and wellbeing at Duke University, a private R1 doctoral degree-granting institution, have cultivated an environment in which the creation of different academic pathways connecting language study and global health content is possible. Currently there are four models for language study at the institution: Languages for Specific Purposes (LSP), Health Humanities (HH), Cultures and Languages Across the Curriculum (CLAC), Community-Based Language Learning (CBLL). The flexibility of each language department to integrate these academic pathways differs greatly depending on resources, faculty preparation and the conceptualization of departmental curricula. Many students are motivated to enroll in these courses because they are not interested in traditional language course topics or structures. Other students are ramping up to participate in an immersive study experience or conduct research in the field and want the interdisciplinary experience that exposes them to different professional contexts and collaborations. Duke University is privileged to sustain these diverse models and, because of this, serves as a good site for a case study.

Curriculum models

Each curricular model exposes students to language study and global health themes in valuable ways. Interest in the LSP curriculum stems from the desire to diversify traditional language study that connects to professional content areas, with the most popular focus in business and medical fields (Sánchez López et al., 2017). Examples at Duke University include: 'Business and Culture in the Francophone World,' 'Business and Interculturality in Chinese Society,' 'Business German,' and 'Advanced Spanish Translation.' This interdisciplinary approach has become routine in the commonly taught languages in the US and it has appeared to varying degrees in less commonly taught languages (Hardin, 2015; Hertel & Dings, 2014; Uber Grosse & Voght, 2012).

The emerging field of health humanities (Berry et al., 2017) develops a collaboration between practitioners and scholars in the humanities, arts, and interpretive social sciences, and their counterparts in the health sciences. On my campus these efforts are external to the language departments with an alternative infrastructure for team-based research projects, the 'Health Humanities Lab.' The team includes a vertically integrated 'lab' involving undergraduates, graduate students, postdocs, faculty and community.

The third curricular model is CLAC, a pathway based on the principles that '[s]tudents should have multiple opportunities to apply their knowledge of languages in a variety of curricular contexts, not just within the traditional language classroom' (CLAC Consortium, n.d.). The design of CLAC courses varies greatly; for example, they can be structured as large lecture courses taught in English with breakout sections in a second language or a content course based in a non-language department and taught in a second language (for additional models see the CLAC Consortium website). At Duke University the structure of CLAC is a half-credit course that is pass/fail and offered once a week. Various sections of the course, 'Voices in Global Health,' are offered in Arabic, French, Mandarin and Spanish by native or near-native instructors (graduate students and non-regular rank professors within and outside of world language departments).

Participants and data collection methods

At Duke University the fifth-semester undergraduate Spanish language course 'Health, Culture, and the Latinx Community' exemplifies how global health themes can be merged with the *World-Readiness Standards for Learning Languages* (ACTFL, 2015) to develop a rich educational experience for students. This chapter is a case study of three semesters – Fall 2018 (15 students), Spring 2019 (15 students), Fall 2019 (13 students) – of teaching the course. Designed in a small group seminar format, the course includes undergraduate students from all class levels and a variety of majors. The 12 student voices in this chapter come from a qualitative analysis of the 43 final reflection essays (written in Spanish) submitted by the students at the end of their semester. The course themes, activities and assessments remained constant in each iteration. The service-learning component varied due to the needs of the Durham County Public Health Department and the Sugar Smart Durham campaign, but each semester focused on the research and dissemination of information related to these organizations' efforts to support the wellbeing of the Latinx community in our city. The following is an examination of how critical pedagogy was integrated into the design of the course, as well as how students reflected on their experiences in the course.

Findings

Decentering of knowledge

One topic utilized in the Spanish course with the objective of decentering knowledge is the study of different definitions of wellbeing from various cultures. Discussion of health and wellbeing in the US is dominated by a biomedical perspective, focusing on physical and biological factors of health and treatments of disease. With a biocultural perspective, students are exposed to how cultures approach health, and through that lens, can consider different interpretations and explanations of illness. By introducing an additional way to conceptualize healing and health we create the opportunity to disrupt beliefs and challenge attitudes that assume a superiority of Western medicine. For example, after students interacted with a local Mexican healer in a class visit, they continually referenced the exchange for the remainder of the semester. The inclusion of this community member's voice as a content expert greatly enriched the curriculum and provided additional information about the local community to which students did not have previous access. A student acknowledged a shift in how they thought about health based on their studies of this topic, commenting that: 'the idea of physical, spiritual, mental and environmental wellbeing is new to me. When I think about wellbeing I only think about physical and spiritual health. Before reading these articles and talking in class, when I thought about alternative medicine, I thought about herbs, but now I have more information and I think about it much more' (Student H, translated from Spanish, spring 2019).

By including non-traditional experts in the curriculum, it is possible to delve deeper into the biocultural approach. By creating a broader representation of community voices there is the potential for students to reassess their assumptions based on diversified sources of knowledge (Glynn et al., 2018; Trujillo, 2009).

It is through the study of multidisciplinary health treatments, multicultural beliefs and multilingual sources of information that students understand global health with a global perspective. One student reflected on the sources of information that influenced their biases. They contemplated how most literature identified countries like Sweden and Canada as the best models for healthcare, and so they were very surprised when an article named Costa Rica as the second-best healthcare system in the world. The student stated that 'this opened my eyes to how biases toward Western countries contributed to the use of themselves as examples, when in reality we can learn a lot from Central American countries also' (Student D, translated from Spanish, fall 2018). Another student reported on reconceptualizing their understanding of health on a more individual level, stating that: 'depending on your culture, other people can think about the things that are needed "to be healthy" in a different way than me. Therefore, they could make different decisions related to their health than those that I would make' (Student E, translated from Spanish, spring 2019).

Another source through which to cultivate this process of decentering knowledge is conversations on the students' experiences abroad. Knowing that some students have traveled to different regions of the world – and knowing that students engage particularly well with other students' stories – I invited students to share their experiences of health and wellbeing from their time abroad. Students recounted having confronted challenges in navigating a medical system while living in another country, for example, the different norms for scheduling an appointment, new types of pharmacies, clinics and providers, as well as alternative ways to pay for services. Students abroad discovered that they could buy certain medications over the counter that required a prescription in the US. Most students narrated their experiences naming a superiority of US medical practices or identifying perceived deficiencies of other countries' medical practices. Reflecting on personal experiences was invaluable as an entry point into larger conversations of the biases and assumptions of the superiority of biomedicine and the US healthcare system.

Another example of how a counternarrative can be incorporated into the decentering process is seen in the students' work with the Sugar Smart Durham campaign. A coalition of local non-profit and governmental organizations related to health formed a grassroots effort to design a campaign to reduce the consumption of sugary sweetened drinks in the local African American and Latinx communities. My students assisted the coalition with research on advertisements targeting communities of color and relevant health research studies. The students also helped facilitate story circles, a democratic dialogue tool, after receiving training from a community organizer. As the students practiced this tool in class with the trainer, they immediately understood the strength of this technique to generate knowledge from multiple perspectives. The sessions at a local church with community members included the establishment of group norms and two phases of questions that explored habits related to sugary sweetened beverages. Each story circle had individuals assigned to act in three roles: the facilitator, the notetaker and the timekeeper. All participants (including the facilitators) were invited to share their own stories and observations during a three-minute segment of uninterrupted time. Students and community members shared anecdotes about their habits and beliefs regarding their consumption of sugary sweetened beverages. There were many differences and similarities shared, varying from one community member who always brought a two-liter soda beverage to work since it was a good size, easy to transport and economical, to a student who had never drank soda in his entire life. At the conclusion of phase 1, the facilitators distributed information related to the topic (data on television advertisements and viewing rates among communities of color) and engaged a second time in the reflection process. Finally, the students transcribed important moments of the conversation and wrote a report for the coalition summarizing the knowledge gained in the session. This community-based research project served as a powerful model of a grassroots organized empowerment effort and challenged students to 'center' new models of learning and community-based knowledge.

An additional challenge that we noted in this partnership was how the Sugar Smart Durham coalition created a non-traditional classroom experience and challenged the students' understanding of traditional classroom power dynamics. Since members of the Sugar Smart Durham coalition acted as co-educators in this course, the partnership with these community experts created a unique dynamic when the coalition presented in class and when students prepared assignments to turn in to the coalition. One of our primary partners described the positive outcomes of partnership, stating that the 'class strengthened the capacity of the project by offering their language skills and time to do research, facilitate story circles and do community windshield surveys on marketing of sugary drinks in local grocery stores' (Q. Mallette,[1] personal communication, 19 August 2019). Mallette indicated that overall, the partnership was a success and recognized many of the known benefits and critiques of service-learning partnerships:

> A few pros of having language students involved in health-related projects in the community is that they often have some flexibility in their schedules, such as daytime availability. Students also have different skill sets that can benefit community members, such as researching and writing. Also, rapport may be built with particular community groups and institutions if semester after semester, the same cohort of students are engaged in the same or similar service learning projects with the same community group. Some cons of student involvement are that it is likely limited to a semester term, which does not always allow enough time to fit student projects into community schedules. In the same vein, the turnover tends to be quick (i.e. new students every semester), which helps create challenges in building rapport with community groups and community members. Additionally, students often bring their own biases and limited experience/exposure to the real world and without effective training/orientation there is a risk that their engagement with the community is ultimately unhelpful. Finally, students and community members may face similar transportation challenges, so finding a location where both can meet may also prove difficult. (Q. Mallette, personal communication, 19 August 2019)

Mallette clearly identified the challenges of building authentic relationships and appropriately orienting the students to be with the community – and the community partner voice was essential to navigating these challenges. She stated that the coalition consciously chose the story circle tool since it is 'a way to build rapport with participants because everyone in the space is a co-facilitator' (Q. Mallette, personal communication, 19 August 2019). Co-facilitation was a principle that defined our overall relationship, serving as a cornerstone of the co-education model in the community and the classroom.

The students reacted to this partnership in different ways, which indicated that the co-education model made them reconceptualize their community and their academic experience. For example, one stated that '[o]ur association with Sugar Smart Durham helped me to understand better the seriousness of the problem here in Durham, putting a more personal touch on a social issue' (Student J, translated from Spanish, spring 2019). The following two students commented on how the community partnership shifted how they thought about the academic experience. The first student commented that the information presented during a visit from the leader of the coalition, 'gave a more profound significance to what we were doing this semester' (Student K, translated from Spanish, spring 2019). The second student reflected that their favorite component of the course was the work with the coalition because 'it was the first time that I felt that my course work had a positive impact greater than my own learning ... I learned about some interventions in the Latinx community, social issues, [and] discrimination in marketing' (Student L, translated from Spanish, fall 2018). Creating an environment through which students decenter traditional knowledge constructs, engage with information and understand educational pathways in non-traditional ways was a valuable outcome from the CBLL model.

Awareness of positionality

The CBLL global health course provided opportunities for students to reconsider their identities and how their positions in society impacted their understanding of the world. One student expressed that exploring the concept of cultural competency alerted them to the fact that even the study of cultural competence contained biases. They reflected that:

> this semester I discovered that cultural competency, even though important, is rooted in Western society. It is necessary to recognize our own biases as students who are receiving a Western education ... As the Sugar Smart organizer said, culture has the potential to change systems of power. Therefore, we have to continue emphasizing the need to understand the cultures of others so that we can overcome systemic inequities and better society. (Student I, translated from Spanish, spring 2019)

Building an awareness of biases tied to Western norms was a significant shift in how this student oriented to wider society. Another student reported a similar outcome because they began to 'think more about how our origins influence different health results, including how we interact with the medical system' (Student B, translated from Spanish, fall 2018). Being more aware of how identity impacts access and power dynamics in the healthcare system is one of the ways that language learners reconsidered their positionality.

Various students reflected on how the community-based projects informed their thoughts about their own families' immigration experiences; for example: 'The complexity of the influence of immigration status on health fascinated me, especially because my family and I are immigrants from China. I never thought about the push-pull factors nor the importance, for example of the age of the immigrant or the balance between acculturation and assimilation' (Student C, translated from Spanish, fall 2018). This student ended up incorporating new perspectives about positionality related to immigrants into their own life story.

It is important to consider how the experiences of heritage speakers of the target language of the CBLL course may be considerably different from that of non-heritage language learners. For example, recollecting the conversations about what resources are needed for health education, a heritage Spanish-speaking student revealed their own privileged position, stating: 'Normally when I thought about health, I only thought about the idea of health insurance because in reality that is what is most talked about in the United States. Even though I was born in Mexico and my dad is a doctor, I never thought much about the health problems in the region' (Student G, translated from Spanish, spring 2019). This self-identified Latinx student was exposed to information about Latinx communities in the US that did not reflect their own experiences. The student grew to reposition themselves as they expanded their understanding of positionality through deeper knowledge of realities in healthcare.

Another heritage language learner reflected on how the course impacted their identity in relation to language. The student commented that:

> This class has increased my desire to better my Spanish in order to be able to articulate more complex ideas than the vocabulary that I would use in the locker room with my soccer team. In general, this class was a humiliating experience because I realized that I needed to improve my Spanish – a language that I had listened to my entire life and that I saw as part of my identity. (Student N, translated from Spanish, fall 2018)

Using Spanish in an academic environment and with community members created a challenge to this student's identity and their relationship with Spanish. Through this curriculum, heritage and L2 language learners grew in how they understood their community, but the diversity of personal backgrounds in the classroom created many different lenses that influenced how students approached CBLL.

Critical reflection

In the Fall 2019 course our community partnership was with the local county Department of Public Health. The students were trained by a public health department staff member on their community health assessment protocol. Students then conducted door-to-door surveys in local neighborhoods with a Latinx population of 50% or higher. The students were either paired with another classmate or a community member during their door-to-door survey taking. Engaging in a variety of reflection activities allowed students to explore their experiences in a variety of modes of communication and within different power dynamics. These included written field notes in Spanish after interaction in the community, conversations in Spanish in class with me (the professor), conversations in English in class with a peer facilitator, conversations in English with the organizer from the Department of Public Health, and a final reflection essay in Spanish. Basing the target questions on the DEAL model, we entered into a personal perspective through questions related to how the students felt knocking on people's doors and on how the experience met their expectations. Many reported being uncomfortable or nervous and that it was easier or harder than they expected. Students delved into a civic perspective when we discussed how power differentials between the survey respondent and survey administrator might impact the responses on the survey. They were pleasantly surprised to observe that being a college-aged student seemed to put community members at ease. We discussed at length the different ways the community might have perceived their identities due to town and university relationships, socioeconomic and ethnic differences, and historical and current events. When engaging with the academic perspective, students commented on the social determinants of health they observed in the neighborhoods and through the answers on the survey. The work on the Community Health Assessment provided students with opportunities to reflect on their understanding of the community, their linguistics skills and their own beliefs in new contexts.

Although there are different levels of reflection in which students typically engage (Kember *et al.*, 2008), some students reported significant changes in how they thought about different issues. For example, one student commented in a written reflection:

> In this class, we read a lot about barriers that the Latinx community confronts with respect to health and wellbeing, but also, we had the opportunity to interact directly with members of this community as part of our service-learning project. These two experiences complemented each other, in that I could see how what we learned in class applied in real life. In some way, I have fought to reconcile the two. The members of the community that I met through my service obviously don't live the gloomy lives that many times are shown in the literature about Latinx immigrants who are economically disadvantaged and don't speak English. Rather, they were happy, loving, showed a sense of community and were grateful for what they had. They are human beings whose lives cannot be defined by these big generalizations. (Student A, translated from Spanish, fall 2019)

This student articulated the thought process behind contrasting the reality witnessed and the generalizations provided in materials previously read. The conversations in class around service (in Spanish in class with the professor, in English in class with a peer facilitator, in English with the organizer from the Department of Public Health) supported the student's reflection process in different ways. With me, the students were asked to tackle sociohistorical issues in the community. With the peer facilitator, the students were provided a forum to talk openly about their feelings and observations about the service-learning experience. I worked with the student facilitator prior to the three class sessions to develop appropriate lesson plans, but I did not attend in order to encourage sharing between peers unencumbered by my presence. I received a general summary of the peer facilitation after each session that helped inform the evolution of the collaboration. The final type of reflection conversation was with the representative from the Department of Public Health. Prior to the three visits, I worked with the representative to set target objectives and update her on the status of the project, including student reactions and questions. Students were asked to read assigned materials and prepare questions for the representative's visit. These interactions complemented the other conversations since they provided opportunities to reflect on civic, academic and professional topics.

Although some students responded well to in-class reflection opportunities, other students were not ready to discuss their observations in a public setting, and therefore other less personal entry points to reflection were provided. For example, by looking at national and international newspaper coverage of different policies and initiatives – in English and Spanish – students compared how specific issues were presented to different audiences and what stories were covered in which publication. When students did a systematic review of what and how universal healthcare was presented in print, they compared the views of all stakeholders (including their individual point of view) and amassed information on how individuals or groups of people are treated differently within different healthcare systems around the world. Students had to articulate the different points of view as they debated if healthcare was a human right. This activity, an academic reflection, was not as personalized as other forms of reflection, but it was a useful vehicle to further their exploration of issues related to healthcare.

Due to developmental and linguistic differences in students, the variety of languages and facilitators for the reflection activities was beneficial since it ensured that the students were able to process their thoughts in different ways and through multiple perspectives. The rationale for the design of critical reflection in the course was shared with the students in order to maximize their awareness of the process.

Building critical consciousness

The above-mentioned activities and student reflections demonstrate examples of the students' evolving critical consciousness. The community-based interactions were formative in the exploration of critical consciousness during the three semesters of 'Health, Culture, and the Latinx Community.' One of the Sugar Smart Durham coalition liaisons affirmed the objective of building critical consciousness as part of the motivation to participate in the collaboration. The community partner commented that, '[w]e were motivated by the desire to build critical consciousness for the students to the extent that University students often enter cities with little context for the world outside of their campus. We were aware that this project was intended to raise awareness and understanding of lived experiences of some local residents' (Q. Mallette, personal communication, 19 August 2019).

The collaboration of the partner was key to engaging students in the examination of their individual beliefs around sugary sweetened drinks, researching the health literature and media representations, listening to community stories and considering the wider sociopolitical constructs in play. One student reported that because of the community-based learning, they had developed a new understanding of the individual's experience and larger social issues:

> now I understand better that even though at times behaviors or attitudes related to health appear unalterable, in reality the change involves much more than the individual's choice – at times, it requires change on a much larger scale, on a scale of culture or social and political institutions. In short, by interacting with people in the 'real world,' now I understand the challenge for change, and humanity in general, a little more than before. (Student F, translated from Spanish, fall 2018)

This student was able to reimagine how change could be enacted by moving beyond individual behaviors to consider the issues on a larger social scale. Shor (1992: 127–8) stated that critical consciousness 'allows people to make broad connections between individual experience and social issues, between single problems and the larger social system. The critically conscious individual connects personal and social domains when studying or acting on any problem or subject matter'.

The CBLL global health curriculum was designed to provide students with opportunities to connect personal and social domains and succeeded in promoting new ways of thinking about healthcare and wellbeing. It is unclear how students put their new knowledge into action beyond the classroom experience, but I am confident that this curriculum cultivated strategies for social change and agency by building critical consciousness through the counternarratives that decentered knowledge, brought awareness of positionality and included a process of critical reflection.

Important Considerations

Although the examples provided in this case study showcase one CBLL course in Spanish that deepened skills to view the world using a social justice lens, the incorporation of global health themes is also possible in other language groups and using a variety of curricular pathways.

At Duke University, a colleague teaches 'Global Displacement: Francophone Voices,' an advanced French CBLL course, which includes global health topics. The sustained relationships between the faculty member, a refugee resettlement agency and community members provide meaningful interactions that bridge different groups in the community. A multi-year project includes developing and maintaining written and video resources for DukeHELLO, a website designed to support intercultural and linguistic learning for newcomer communities. Some of the vignettes on the website introduce health topics such as requesting an interpreter at the pharmacy or the differences in where to seek medical attention in the US medical system.

Another advanced CBLL course that developed materials to support a newcomer community in the health arena was the 'Issues in Arabic Language and Literature' course. The Arabic language learners were paired with Arabic-speaking community members with whom they arranged a regular cultural celebration over various semesters. The students developed materials to support the newly arrived Arabic speakers, including a video 'Health Care for Arabs' that used animation to teach about the healthcare system in the US.

A final example based on the CLAC curricular model, 'Voices in Global Health: Mandarin,' supported the development of a series of presentations and brochures on health issues using the target language. The Mandarin language learners introduced the US healthcare system, environmental problems, American lifestyle, stroke prevention and research on sleep problems to Chinese community members at a local senior community center. These presentations were valuable to all participants as they expanded the educational programming at the senior center, introduced more interactions to a linguistically isolated community and provided real-world use of Mandarin to students. The community-based learning was grounded in a comparative study of US and Chinese healthcare and created opportunities for students to critically reflect on their understanding and knowledge of issues related to wellbeing and access to healthcare. The opportunity to demystify US practices for community members required students to critique the systems that perhaps were previously invisible to or unexamined by them.

For many educators, service-learning or community-engaged pedagogy is not viable due to place-based realities, for example, there might be very few native/heritage world language speakers in their community or there are too few resources at their disposal to build a sustained relationship with a community partner. Aspects of the CBLL global health curriculum, however, can be enacted in many different ways in order to create that interdisciplinary language experience. Perhaps a local healer or alternative medicine practitioner lives in your community and could be a guest lecturer in class so that students learn directly from a community member about traditional medicine and holistic healing practices. Alternatively, you might be able to arrange a video chat with a health provider in another country for an in-class conversation. My students used TalkAbroad, a paid online synchronous videoconferencing tool, to converse individually outside of class with native speakers living in other countries about health topics. The students regularly reported that these conversations triggered key moments in perspective transformation. There are also free online tools that could further goals of learning about cultural products, perspectives and practices in other countries. The community's voice is not always heard in the classroom and it is valuable to find ways to expand our inclusion of less visible experts in the field.

Finally, educators should consider that although sometimes it isn't explicitly named as such, we engage with social determinants of health in many different contexts in the L2 curriculum. For example, topics can include health literacy, food security, housing rights, public service announcements, initiatives to improve public areas, police and community relations, post-traumatic stress disorder in marginalized communities, healthcare legislation, linguistic access within the healthcare system, health as a human right, and many more. If we scaffold the themes and the critical reflection effectively, then these modules will also have a significant impact on how the students build critical consciousness by connecting individual experiences with larger social issues.

When designing reflection – a key tool to building critical consciousness – it is useful to keep in mind the distinctive levels of reflection identified by Kember *et al.* (2008). They identified four levels of reflection: habitual action, understanding, reflection, and critical reflection. *Habitual action* can be equated with non-reflective thinking, for example 'when students search for material on a set topic and place it into an essay without thinking about it, trying to understand it, or forming a view' (2008: 373). The level of *understanding* indicates that students are engaged in learning; however, 'the concepts are understood as theory without being related to personal experiences or real-life applications' (2008: 373). In the *reflection* level students are able to apply a concept or theory to personal experiences. *Critical reflection* includes 'evidence of a change in perspective over a fundamental belief' (2008: 375). Students approach reflection from many different entry points due to their level of personal commitment and in combination with their developmental stage. Educators need to recognize that the last level of *critical reflection*, indicative of perspective transformation, is elusive – especially over a short time period (i.e. one or two semesters). Educators are presented with a challenge: to open a dialogue that allows students to process their experiences and to not create a dynamic in which students engage in reflection as a performance in which they are artificially creating narratives of transformation. The most valuable outcome of incorporating reflection practices into the curriculum is that students learn self-reflection strategies that they will then apply in life-long learning.

Conclusion

This interdisciplinary curriculum is a way to stimulate students' exploration of social issues and their agency for change by positioning language as a tool for social change (Caldwell, 2007; Clifford & Reisinger, 2019; Osborn, 2006; Trujillo, 2009; Zapata, 2011). Integrating the study of world languages and global healthcare rises to Shor's (1992) challenge to diversify materials in order to ensure student engagement and opportunities for perspective transformation. Through the application of tenets of critical pedagogy, the CBLL global health curriculum expands the representation of expert voices in academia and decenters and disrupts constructs of knowledge. Critical reflection in both English and the target language supports an exploration of positionality and the corresponding issues of power and privilege at the individual and the societal level. Whether designing this curriculum to be integrated into a world language department or as an interdepartmental project, this interdisciplinary approach creates a platform to connect individual experiences of wellbeing with larger social constructs of health, and in so doing, offers opportunities through which students can build their critical consciousness. By reimagining the content and delivery of our L2 curriculum we ensure deeper engagement between students, colleagues and our communities, and in so doing, we empower language learners to be agents of change and to improve the health and wellbeing of our local and global communities.

Discussion Questions

(1) Reflecting on the themes and activities described, do any of them seem adaptable to your teaching? How could you include more global health themes and topics in the L2 curriculum? Where would you find more resources related to health and wellbeing in the target language? How could you scaffold activities and critical reflections about health and wellbeing to develop skills for social change and agency?

(2) Is it possible to develop a more interdisciplinary curriculum at your institution? How would your department react to this interdisciplinary direction? Who is working in global health at your institution and might be willing to collaborate or be a mentor? How might this interdisciplinary direction impact enrollments? Where might you find professional development opportunities to support this interest?

(3) The models presented emphasize the impact of community-based learning and community voice. Would building a community partnership complement and deepen your current work? What are the barriers to and available resources for establishing a community collaboration? How would you establish a co-educator role with community members or organizations?

Note

(1) Permission was obtained to use Q. Mallette's real name.

References

ACTFL (American Council on the Teaching of Foreign Languages) (2015) *World-Readiness Standards for Learning Languages*. See https://www.actfl.org/resources/world-readiness-standards-learning-languages

Ash, S.L. and Clayton, P.H. (2009) Generating, deepening, and documenting learning: The power of critical reflection for applied learning. *Journal of Applied Learning in Higher Education* 1 (1), 25–48.

Berry, S., Jones, T. and Lamb, E. (2017) Health humanities: The future of pre-health education is here. *Journal of Medical Humanities* 38 (4), 353–360.

Bringle, R.G. and Hatcher, J.A. (2000) Institutionalization of service learning in higher education. *Journal of Higher Education* 71 (3), 273–290.

Caldwell, W. (2007) Taking Spanish outside the box: A model for integrating service learning into foreign language study. *Foreign Language Annals* 40 (3), 463–71.

CLAC Consortium (n.d.) *What is CLAC?* See https://clacconsortium.org/about-2/defining-clac/more-on-clac/

Clifford, J. and Reisinger, D.S. (2019) *Community-based Language Learning: A Framework for Educators*. Washington, DC: Georgetown University Press.

Davis, K.L., Kliewer, B.W. and Nicolaides, A. (2017) Power and reciprocity in partnerships: Deliberative civic engagement and transformative learning in community-engaged scholarship. *Journal of Higher Education Outreach and Engagement* 21 (1), 30–54.

Deardorff, D.K. (2012) Framework: Observe, state, explore, evaluate (OSEE) tool. In K. Berardo and D.K. Deardorff (eds) *Building Cultural Competence: Innovative Activities and Models* (pp. 58–60). Sterling, VA: Stylus.

Furco, A. and Holland, B. (2009) Securing administrative support for service-learning institutionalization. In J. Strait and M. Lima (eds) *The Future of Service Learning: New Solutions for Sustaining and Improving Practice* (pp. 52–64). Sterling, VA: Stylus.

Glynn, C., Wesely, P. and Wassell, B. (2018) *Words and Actions: Teaching Languages through the Lens of Social Justice* (2nd edn). Alexandria, VA: ACTFL.

Hardin, K. (2015) An overview of medical Spanish curricula in the United States. *Hispania* 98 (4), 640–661.

Hertel, T.J. and Dings, A. (2014) The undergraduate Spanish major curriculum: Realities and faculty perceptions. *Foreign Language Annals* 47 (3), 546–568.

Johnson, S.M. and Randolph, L.J. (2015) Critical pedagogy for intercultural communicative competence. *The Language Educator* 10 (3), 36–39.

Kember, D., McKay, J., Sinclair, K. and Kam Yuet Wong, F. (2008) A four-category scheme for coding and assessing the level of reflection in written work. *Assessment and Evaluation in Higher Education* 33 (4), 369–379.

Koplan, J.P., Bond, T.C., Merson, M.H., Reddy, K.S., Rodriguez, M.H., Sewankambo, N.K. and Wasserheit, J.N. (2009) Towards a common definition of global health. *The Lancet* 373, 1993–1995.

Kuh, G.D. (2008) *High-Impact Educational Practices: What They Are, Who Has Access to Them, and Why They Matter*. Washington, DC: Association of American Colleges and Universities.

Mezirow, J. (1991) *Transformative Dimensions of Adult Learning*. San Francisco: Jossey-Bass.

Mezirow, J. (2000) Learning to think like an adult: Transformation theory: Core concepts. In J. Mezirow and Associates (eds) *Learning as Transformation: Critical Perspectives on a Theory in Progress*. San Francisco: Jossey-Bass.

Mitchell, T. (2008) Traditional and critical service-learning: Engaging the literature to differentiate the two models. *Michigan Journal of Community Service Learning* 14 (2), 50–65.

Nam, K. (2012) Building cultural competence: Innovative activities and models. In K. Berardo and D.K. Deardorff (eds) *Building Cultural Competence: Innovative Activities and Models* (pp. 53–57). Sterling, VA: Stylus.

Osborn, T. (2006) *Teaching World Languages for Social Justice: A Sourcebook of Principles and Practices.* Mahwah, NJ: Lawrence Erlbaum Associates.

Randolph, L.J. and Johnson, S.M. (2017) Social justice in the language classroom: A call to action. *Dimension* 2017, 9–31.

Sánchez López, L., Long, M.K. and Lafford, B.A. (2017) New directions in LSP research in US higher education. In M.K. Long (ed.) *Language for Specific Purposes: Trends in Curriculum Development* (pp. 13–36). Washington, DC: Georgetown University Press.

Shor, I. (1992) *Empowering Education: Critical Teaching for Social Change.* Chicago: University of Chicago Press.

Silva, V. and Waggett, C. (2019) Five powerful myths of undergraduate global health education. *Diversity and Democracy* 22 (2–3). See https://www.aacu.org/diversitydemocracy/2019/spring-summer/silva.

Trujillo, J.A. (2009) Con todos: Using learning communities to promote intellectual and social engagement in the Spanish curriculum. In M. Lacorte and J. Leeman (eds) *Español en Estados Unidos y otros contextos de contacto: Sociolingüística, ideología y pedagogía* (pp. 369–393). Iberoamericana.

Uber Grosse, C. and Voght, G.M. (2012) The continuing evolution of Languages for Specific Purposes. *The Modern Language Journal* 96 (1), 190–202.

Welch, M. (1999) The ABCs of reflection: A template for students and instructors to implement written reflection in service-learning. *NSEE Quarterly* 25 (2), 123–25.

Whitehead, D.M. (2019) Curricular coherence and global health. *Diversity & Democracy* 22 (2-3). See https://www.aacu.org/diversitydemocracy/2019/spring-summer/whitehead.

World Health Organization (n.d.) *Social Determinants of Health.* See https://www.who.int/social_determinants/sdh_definition/en/.

Zapata, G. (2011) The effects of community service learning projects on L2 learners' cultural understanding. *Hispania* 94 (1), 86–102.

5 Voces Invisibles: Disrupting the Master Narrative with Afro Latina Counterstories

Krishauna Hines-Gaither, Nina Simone Perez
and Liz Torres Melendez

'Educators must be aware that Afro Latina exists as a category. I
would like to be included, and I would like to feel included.'
— *Bella*

Introduction

Although the terms *Latin American* and *Hispanic* denote a common
heritage and a shared cultural experience, educators must be careful not
to present Latin America as if it were a monolith. In her landmark essay
on intersectionality, critical race scholar Kimberlé Crenshaw (1995: 358)
stated, 'Contemporary feminist and antiracist discourses have failed to
consider intersectional identities such as women of color'. While this content is absent from mainstream scholarship, there is also a gap within
language programs. To this end, content on Afro-descendants has been
strikingly absent from world language textbooks and curricula. The participants of our study on Afro Latina students also revealed a lack of
attention to intersecting identities within their world language programs.
The absence of inclusion is further evidenced by the dearth of publications
that exist on the topic.

Over the past 15 years, multiple scholars have published on race and
racial stratifications within Latin America (Bonilla Silva, 2004; Frank
et al., 2010; Hitlin *et al.*, 2007); however, few US scholars have focused
their work specifically on the experiences of intersecting identities, and
even fewer on Afro Latina women (Armstead, 2007; Hines-Gaither, 2015;
King Miller, 2015; Vega *et al.*, 2012). As world language programs become
increasingly diverse, and as scholarship emerges, our classrooms must
become culturally responsive spaces. All students benefit from inclusive
pedagogy. With the rise of globalization, increased connectivity via the
internet and the browning of the US, exposure to unique perspectives
better prepares students for a 21st-century society.

Randolph and Johnson (2017: 118) affirmed, 'In language education, we need more diverse voices and approaches ... to amplif[y] the voices of the marginalized'. Our study, described in this chapter, addressed this gap in curricula and literature by conducting narrative research with Afro Latina students enrolled in a small liberal arts college in the southern US. The goals of this chapter are:

(1) To provide a platform for Afro Latina students to articulate their lived experiences based on intersecting identities of race, ethnicity, language and gender.
(2) To understand how Afro Latina students experience and navigate their intersecting identities in the context of their world language programs.
(3) To offer strategies, beyond tokenism, for world language educators to incorporate Afro Latina content into their curricula.

Critical race theory and feminist theory serve as the theoretical frameworks for this chapter. This chapter focuses on the personalized narratives of Afro Latina undergraduate students. We incorporate the concept of counterstories in order to disrupt the master narratives that dominate most world language textbooks. This research is a direct response to the scarcity of culturally responsive pedagogy to which many language educators are exposed. Gloria Ladson-Billings (1995: 467), a forerunner in theorizing culturally responsive pedagogy, defines the term as the 'dynamic or synergistic relationship between home/community culture and school culture'. In other words, how do we bring the cultures of our students into the classroom?

According to Lisa Delpit (2006: 229), 'The problem ... is that the cultures of marginalized groups in our society tend to be either ignored, misrepresented, viewed from an outsider perspective, or even denigrated'. We hope that the findings of this chapter may offer strategies to support world language educators in establishing inclusive classrooms that are culturally responsive. Ladson-Billings (1995: 470) acknowledged, '[W]ho I am, what I believe, what experiences I have had all impact what, how, and why I research'. As authors, we believe it is essential to situate our positionality within the framework of this chapter.

Positionality

In her own voice: Krishauna Hines-Gaither, PhD

I am an African American woman who was born and raised in North Carolina. I took Spanish from elementary school through college, and later majored in Spanish and teacher education to become a language educator. I have taught Spanish in higher education for over 20 years.

Although I am African American, many of the counterstories conveyed by the Afro Latina participants were eerily similar to my own lived experiences. This research revealed how my life as a Black woman intersected with the participants' stories of race and gender. However, this study also illuminated our differences of ethnicity, language and cultural heritage. I had to be mindful of these points of convergence, as well as the clear distinctions.

In her own voice: Nina Simone Perez, BA

I identify as Afro Latina. My mother is an African American woman from North Carolina and my father is Puerto Rican. While I grew up in North Carolina, I have been immersed in the two cultures my entire life.

With our research on Afro Latina identity, I could relate to the participants and to their struggles in many ways. I easily engaged with the students that I interviewed, and I appreciated their willingness to be vulnerable with me. I learned so much about myself through the interview process, such as how I have had to navigate and negotiate two ethnicities throughout my life.

In her own voice: Liz Torres Melendez, MA

I am an Afro Latina who was born in Puerto Rico and raised in North Carolina. My identity as an Afro Latina is not because I come from parents of different races or ethnicities. Both of my parents are Puerto Ricans born and raised on the island; however, this was not the case for the majority of our participants.

Because of the way the subject matter impacted me personally, it was important for me to separate my experience from that of the participants. One difficulty for me was to stop myself from turning the interviews into pseudo-therapy sessions. Many of the participants were younger, and therefore, I found myself wanting to comfort them and guide them in their journey to self-acceptance. Knowing how being Afro Latinidad can affect a woman's self-worth and self-love was instrumental for me as I tried to create a welcoming environment where the young women were comfortable being vulnerable and sharing.

Latinidad

The term Latinidad can be a catchphrase for all aspects of what Latin America represents and for what it means to be of Latin American origins. However, many Afro-descendants express a systematic erasure of African descendants from Latin American discourses. Afro-Panamanian scholar and activist Yvette Modestín stated, 'Latinidad leans on whiteness and creates even a white supremacist tone in the use of it. [A]s ... proudly Black identified as I am ... it serves me nothing' (as quoted by Martinez, 2019: para. 9). To the contrary, the term Afro-Latinidad is a reclamation of cultural heritage by Afro-descendants. In addition to race, the term also carries historical, political, economic and social significance.

Theoretical Framework: Critical Race Theory and Feminist Theory

In critical race theory (CRT), the use of stories, often called counter-stories or counternarratives, is essential to opposing the dominant story or the master narrative. Critical race scholar, Richard Delgado (2000: 61) wrote, 'Stories, parables, chronicles, and narratives are powerful means for destroying mindset'. Delgado beseeches researchers to allow participants to tell their own stories. 'Through counter-storytelling, scholars can capture, construct, and reveal marginalized experiences while challenging mainstream narratives that readily may be accepted as objective truths' (Horsford, 2011: 30). In order to expose audiences to genuine images of Black women, we must honor Black women's voices. CRT serves as a tool for reclamation.

Critical race theory as a space for reclaiming voice

Criado and Reyes (2005) spoke poignantly about the double marginalization of women of color.

> Es por ello que las mujeres indígenas, africanas, gitanas, han sufrido una doble marginación y silenciamiento: por ser mujeres y por pertenecer a un grupo racial minoritario. Son como voces aisladas que nunca llegan a encontrarse y que, por desgracia, son pronto olvidadas (Criado & Reyes, 2005: 145).

> [It is for this reason that indigenous, African, and gypsy women have suffered a double marginalization and silencing: for being women and for belonging to a minority racial group. They are isolated voices that never come to find themselves and, unfortunately, are quickly forgotten.]

The silenced voices of marginalized women must be countered. Scholars and educators are in a position to bring these voices from the margin to the center. CRT calls for the valuing of experiential knowledge. This is a tool by which educators can offer space to communities 'that historically have been excluded and marginalized' (Horsford, 2011: 27). The goal of our narrative analysis is to help educators to better understand and incorporate the lives of Afro Latina students. The counterstories of our participants will serve as the foundation for this chapter.

According to Anderson (1995), in an attempt to combat androcentric research that is focused and centered on men, feminist epistemology must begin with women's lives. Adhering to feminist practice whereby women's voices are centered, we will incorporate direct quotes from participants in order to ground their realities.

Methodology

Narrative inquiry

Being aware of our own positionality as researchers enabled us to honor the lives and stories of our participants. In order to better contextualize their narratives, we asked participants to disclose their place of birth and the racial and ethnic identities of their parents. Table 5.1 provides an overview of the participants' demographics.

In narrative research, participants ultimately decide what to share, what to prioritize and how much detail to offer. Although told by an individual, stories are not isolated occurrences (Merriam, 2009). Just as our backgrounds will influence the way that we perceive and describe the world, our participants also construct their narratives within a given social context. 'Narrative analysis uses the stories people tell, analyzing them in various ways, to understand the meaning of the experiences as revealed in the story' (Merriam, 2009: 23).

The key to narrative research 'is the use of stories as data' (Merriam, 2009: 32). Constructing the stories require collaboration and co-construction because 'in narrative inquiry, our field texts are always interpretive' (Clandinin & Connelly, 2004: 85). In order to capture the essence of the participants' stories, in addition to the audio recordings, we took notes during the interviews. We penned their unspoken cues such as pauses, gazes, laughter, smiles, discomfort, and so on. Field texts and transcripts are necessary to fill in gaps created by memory, space and time.

Data collection

We interviewed five Afro Latina undergraduate college students. Interviews were conducted in the summer of 2019 either in person on a college campus or via a virtual platform. Nina Perez and Liz Torres

Table 5.1 Participant demographics

Participants' Pseudonyms	Participants' Birthplaces	Participants' Parental Demographics
Hellen	Born in the United States	• Puerto Rican mother born in Puerto Rico • Black Cuban/Jamaican father born in the United States
Melissa	Born in the United States	• Afro Colombian mother born in Colombia • Colombian father born in Colombia
Jessica	Born in Japan (military base)	• African American mother born in the United States • White Puerto Rican father born in the United States
Bella	Born in the United States	• Black mother born in Guyana • White Puerto Rican father born in Puerto Rico
Felicia	Born in the United States	• African American mother born in the United States • Puerto Rican father born in Brooklyn, NY

Melendez conducted all interviews with participants. Krishauna Hines-Gaither later followed up with participants for member checking. Member checking is a process of ensuring plausibility in which participants are contacted to ask whether data interpretations or findings are accurate (Savin-Baden & Major, 2010: 176). Liz and Nina met with participants once and interviewed them individually. They held interviews both virtually and in-person depending upon the participants' availability and geographical locations. Interviews averaged 45 minutes in length. Upon commencing this study, Liz, Nina and Krishauna had known all participants for approximately two years. The participants and researchers became acquainted at a small liberal arts college. Beyond their two-year relationship, they were previously unacquainted.

We used structured interviews and asked a set of 17 predetermined questions. Participants answered the same questions in roughly the same order. The interview questions related to four main themes: (1) social identity as Afro Latina women, (2) intergroup and intragroup dynamics related to belonging, (3) Afro Latina representation and (4) experiences in world language programs. We worked in collaboration with external transcribers to transcribe the interviews. From the raw data (audio recordings, transcripts and field notes), we analyzed for emerging codes and themes.

Data analysis

'Thematic analysis relies on categorizing accounts or aspects of accounts that are being told' (Lichtman, 2013: 256). In thematic analysis one codes for themes (reoccurring patterns), silences and omissions (omitted stories that are common in other related research narratives or findings), outliers (findings in a transcript that may not be present or common in others) and slippages (when what is said is in conflict with observable reality), to name a few (Casey, 1993). Researchers worked in tandem to analyze the large selection of codes via document analysis of the transcriptions. Krishauna then narrowed the agreed-upon codes into more specific themes and categories (Lichtman, 2013). These codes and themes serve as the foundation for this chapter.

The narrative analysis that follows is based on the research that we conducted with five Afro Latina students. Although not generalizable to the larger population, we hope that educators will embrace the power of these stories and consider how they might bring marginalized voices into plain sight and inform practice in curriculum and instruction.

Key Findings from Afro Latina Student Narratives

Afro Latinidad absent from the curriculum

Participants reported feeling disconnected from their education due to their Afro-Latina identity being underrepresented or altogether omitted.

Although not specific to the world language classroom, we asked participants to reflect on their schooling, overall. When probed if she saw Afro Latina identity represented in her education, Melissa answered unequivocally, 'Absolutely not, no no no, that was not something that I would see.' Felicia also reported that she never recalled seeing Afro Latina identity represented in textbooks.

> I felt disconnected more than connected just because I – I rarely, I never remember seeing anything about biracial people at all. Even in the textbooks, the physical textbooks we had, I've never seen pictures that look like me. I just knew I wouldn't be in that textbook, or even talked about. I think the representation is definitely not there for me.

To this end, Hellen explained, 'I think I always felt kind of disconnected. There wasn't a lot of conversation about anything that happened in the Caribbean. There was a conversation about how a lot of slaves did go there, but there wasn't like much conversation beyond that.'

Although their identity was largely absent from the curriculum, participants shared stories of a few dynamic teachers who incorporated some aspects of Afro Latinidad. These educators were often Black women; however, they were the anomaly. Frustrated by how often Latin America was omitted from her high school history classes, Melissa stated, 'I had one teacher who was Afro Latina, and she was the only one who ever, ever, taught me about any Latin American history.' Since participants did not have the experience of seeing Afro Latina identity represented in their mainstream curriculum, we inquired specifically about their world language classrooms.

Participants shared that they did not experience a greater degree of equity in the world language classroom, either. Bella stated:

> Educators must be aware that Afro Latina exists as a category. I would like to be included, and I would like to feel included. In the Spanish class, I just feel like I am learning Spanish, but I do not feel I am getting any closer to my culture. The language classroom was not specific to my identity. It was never made personable.

However, one redeeming feature of their world language classroom experience was that the participants often had to conduct research and give oral presentations on a particular country. They took advantage of this opportunity to research their Afro Latin American culture and homeland. For them, their research was an act of social justice. They inserted their identities where they had previously been omitted. They also educated their teachers and classmates on their heritage. Hellen remarked:

> For Spanish class, they'd always ask us to do some research projects. So I always jumped to Puerto Rico, and I was like 'I don't give a damn what anybody else says,' I'm going to do something about Puerto Rico. And so … that was the only opportunity I had to learn more about my home, like my family. So I just did it.

Although some participants were determined to bring their heritage into their world language classrooms, they all reported having a negative experience with teachers. Felicia and Liz (co-author, who also shared her story during the interview process) were hurt that their language and culture were not 'good enough' for their language educators. Due to feelings of invalidation, they began to shut down and withdraw. Both subsequently dropped Spanish and pursued other languages instead. Felicia relayed the following account:

> My middle school Spanish teacher was white from the United States, although she studied in Spain. The first day of class, the teacher asked me if I had any knowledge of Spanish. I said yes, and spoke a little to her. She said, 'Who taught you this slang?' I said, 'My *buela* says this to me all the time.' She responded, 'Well that is not correct, your ABUELA (correcting me) does not know what she is talking about.' I cried because that's my grandmother, you can't say that she doesn't know her language. I was so upset that I dropped, and enrolled in French instead. I was so excited to learn Spanish, and really connect as an Afro Latina, but that one experience put fear in my heart as a young girl who was already having a hard time with a dual identity.

Liz had a very similar experience to Felicia. She shared:

> My family moved to North Carolina from Puerto Rico in 2000 when I was four years old. My first experience in a Spanish language classroom (in elementary school) involved the teacher laughing at my accent, and asking me to repeat myself because she could not understand me. From then on, I chose not to pursue Spanish. Instead, I studied Latin in high school and Portuguese for two years in college.

Hellen shared that although she had an unfavorable experience with a white female Spanish teacher, she also had positive experiences with most of her world language educators. She described her issues with the female Spanish teacher: 'I struggled because of her disconnect from the language and the experience of different students with the language. By that I mean, she was very adamant about teaching *Spain Spanish* (*vosotros*), and ignoring that Spanish comes in many different forms.'

Hellen relayed a very positive experience as well:

> My middle school Spanish classes were cool. And then in high school my first teacher for the first two weeks was Puerto Rican so it was like [sound of excitement] 'it's me'! And then they brought in another teacher from Spain. I love love love him, he's my absolute favorite teacher. Every time I go back to my high school, he's the only person I look for. He was just the best teacher I'd ever had in my entire life, and he cares so much about us, but also recognized that I wanted more.

Hellen explained that her teacher from Spain pushed her to go beyond her fears and inhibitions about Spanish. It is of import to note that Hellen appreciated an educator who had higher expectations for her. She explained that he was not solely interested in his discipline, but he also took the time to get to know the students and to build relationships with them. This relationship building increased Hellen's enthusiasm to learn Spanish. As the only fluent Spanish speaker in our study, we wondered if Melissa's experience would be different. Of her classmates, Melissa recalled, 'Then it was always, "I wouldn't expect you to speak Spanish". Then they would say, "well can you say this? Tell me something in Spanish that you really know?" – Excuse me? I don't have to prove myself to you.'

Melissa also incurred a deficit-based approach from her Spanish teachers who often assumed that she did not speak Spanish based on her physical features. Melissa recalled, 'The teacher would always act as if I didn't know Spanish *correctly*.' Melissa emphasized *correctly* to indicate her perception that they saw her variety of Spanish from a deficit perspective. Throughout the study, participants shared that their language teachers and classmates expected them to speak what they considered a bastardized version of the language. According to King Miller (2015: 7), due to years of interacting with teachers who have low expectations of them, Black students have 'to fight against the covert and overt messages conveyed by previous teachers that they do not possess the capabilities to understand such content'. Given the experiences that students shared about their world language teachers, we inquired about their relationships with their peers.

Unpacking belonging

'There's not just one form of being Black' (Hellen)

All participants relayed that they most often engaged socially with African Americans. They felt it was easier to ingratiate themselves into Black spaces due to their similar phenotype and some shared experiences. Of her college experience, Hellen noted, 'Generally, like a lot of the students who I know that identify as Afro Latinx hang out with a lot of the Black kids. So it's like, we're all together.' That said, participants also shared that these were complicated relationships.

Hellen explained that she blended in more with Black people based on her features; however, she also highlighted clear distinctions. 'Like at school I feel like I don't belong in the Black community because they're like "oh you don't do this thing, and you don't do that," but one of the coolest things I've learned about being Black is that there's not just one form of being Black.'

Participants also expressed the concept of belonging within Latin American spaces.

'You want me to prove it because I don't look Hispanic' (Bella)

Having to prove their Latinidad identity in Latin American spaces was a constant for our Afro Latina participants. Since most of them (four out of five) did not speak Spanish fluently, this proved to be a barrier when trying to inculcate themselves within the Latin American community. Jessica narrated her experience with trying to enter the door of Latinidad. She would soon learn that this door was closed to Afro Latinas.

> [After trying to fit into Black spaces], then I tried to go to the Hispanic side or Latina side. The Hispanics and Latinos were not accepting either because they were very close. It was mostly people who had parents that were immigrants … It just seemed like a culture I could never get into because maybe I … didn't speak fluent Spanish, or I didn't have the same cultural background, or whatever the case.

Although Hellen was quite conversant in Spanish, Melissa was the only participant who spoke Spanish fluently. Melissa reported that when she would speak Spanish to her Latin American peers, they would be a little more accepting; however, this acceptance was short-lived given that few light-skinned Latin Americans could relate to an Afro Latina's experience. In those spaces, Melissa felt that she was often dismissed and not embraced as a Latina. Students consistently described siloed environments within their schools. How can educators honor affinity groups, while also creating spaces that promote belonging across differences?

Critical race scholar Tara Yosso (2005: 76) wrote, 'Looking through a CRT lens, the cultures of Students of Color can nurture and empower them'. Just as most educators have not been taught about African descendants in Latin America, students also lack this education. Latin Americans have typically learned very little about their shared heritage with Latin Americans of African origins. It is easier to discount people as the *other* when you are not educated about what connects you. One way to increase awareness, belonging and connectivity is through deliberate representation. Not only did Afro Latina participants report a lack of representation in their schooling, they also reported a lack of representation throughout their lives.

Representation of Afro Latinas in the media

When asked about the representation of Afro Latinas in the media and social media, participants described either a lack of representation or negative portrayals of Afro Latina women. The participants' narratives reveal that invisibility can be as damaging as misrepresentation. Melissa expressed that she was unaware that there were Afro Latin American role models in her younger years. When asked to name a few that she grew up seeing on screen, Melissa struggled. She stated, 'The people who I knew were Afro Latina were Zoe Saldaña (long pause) – I'm trying to think of them. I know there are more, but I can't think of them, not when I was younger. Now, there are definitely more.' Hellen had similar sentiments. She stated, 'Well, I don't like that there aren't any [Afro Latinas] really, like there are very few women who identify as Afro Latina which is kind of lame because I would like for someone to look like me on the TV. Everyone loves JLo, but I don't look like JLo!' Hellen's comment demonstrates that although there is some Latina representation in the media, whiteness is still the rule. The featured Latina is often fair in complexion with highlighted and straightened hair – features not typically associated with Afro Latinas.

Transitioning from physical features to stereotypical portrayals in media, Felicia shared, 'The media likes the hot head, the spicy Latina.' Bella agreed with Felicia's assertion, stating, 'The media wants a Hispanic girl with attitude.' This portrayal is even more damaging for Afro Latinas who are often racialized as Black, and therefore angry Black women. Although there is an obvious paucity of visibility, Felicia reported a shifting trend on social media. 'I follow a lot of Afro Latina YouTubers because I've noticed a recent turnover of people taking pride in both cultures and taking pride in who they are.'

Our classrooms offer a panoramic view of societal norms and practices. Hill Collins (2009: 93) warned, 'Schools, the news media, and government agencies constitute important sites for reproducing these controlling images'. Therefore, just as the media omits Afro Latinas, many language classrooms also neglect to incorporate darker-skinned Latin Americans. For this reason, the classroom becomes a space whereby some identities are omitted and others are privileged. These omissions discourage cultural comparisons and meaningful connections to course content and to target cultures. While Afro Latinas felt underrepresented in the media, they also revealed negative experiences in schools related to their physical attributes.

Dominant beauty standards: Afro Latina hair stories

Critical race theory acknowledges that 'Eurocentric standards of beauty and physical appearance make [problems with body image] especially acute for minority women, many of whom have little chance of meeting them' (Delgado & Stefancic, 2017: 142) due to an unrealistic ideal. The denigration that participants felt based on physical features often manifested in the classroom. Participants relayed a long journey to acceptance. Jessica acknowledged, 'It took me a long time to love my hair, but it is very beautiful.' They struggled to appreciate their natural hair textures in a culture that considered their kinky curls to not fit the dominant standard of beauty nor aligned with the Latina ideal.

Afro Colombian participant, Melissa, was the only Afro Latina among her friendship group. She reflected on her relationship with her predominantly Central American peers.

They would say things like, 'Oh you have Black girls' hair', as if that was like a diss (dismissal) really. The way you're saying it is not a compliment, but also what does Black girl hair mean? Are you trying to say I have ugly hair because I'm Black? And then, am I Black? Because every time I keep saying I'm Latina you guys agree, but then you also say I'm Black. It would really mess with my mind.

Melissa's narrative reveals the psychological toll that rejection based on physical attributes can cause. Her hair was one mechanism by which her Central American schoolmates made it clear that she was not like them. Hellen also commented on the role that her hair played in shaping her early psyche. She stated, 'Not having people that looked like me especially sucked with like my hair. I went to school with people who did not have hair like me my entire life.'

Far beyond just a hair story, participants revealed how African features, such as hair texture, serve as a mechanism by which they are *othered*. By not meeting the white ideal, these stories demonstrate how Afro Latinas are made to feel less attractive, less Latina and less accepted. According to Afro Cuban feminist psychologist, Norma Guillard Limonta (2016: 86):

> What begins as a joke in school can develop into an internalized racism, the hate of one's self for having this type of hair. It causes one to feel rejected and disagreeable with this part of the body and without a doubt it does not facilitate a good development of one's personality and affects one's self-esteem, physical, and mental health.

Acknowledging that these negative experiences often take place in schools and classrooms, the language educator has a prime opportunity to promote inclusion through intentional representation of diverse content and affirming images. The stories that students shared regarding hair politics are branches that stem from a deeper historical root of racism and white supremacy. To understand the narratives related to hair, one must understand colorism and anti-Blackness both within communities of color and beyond.

Colorism and anti-Blackness

Colorism is prejudice and/or discrimination against darker-skinned individuals, usually among members of the same race or ethnicity. Critical race scholars, Delgado and Stefancic (2017: 83) wrote, '[T]hose who most closely conform to the Euro American ideal ... sometimes look down on their darker-skinned brothers and sisters'. To that end, all of our participants commented that they experienced colorism in their Latin American families, Black families and/or within their communities. Both Bella and Jessica noted the prevalence of colorism within Black spaces. Bella reflected that within her mother's family, she 'wasn't Black enough.' Jessica also shared her experience with colorism within the Black community: 'Black girls didn't accept me for reasons that are way beyond my control ... meaning that they could look at me and automatically think "oh she thinks she is better than us because she is light skinned." And it was like, I never had that thought in my life.'

Hellen and Felicia relayed sentiments of colorism and anti-Blackness within their Puerto Rican families. Felicia's great grandmother would say to her darker children, 'You're so dark, you're too dark.' These denigrating comments can lead Afro Latinas to reject the parts of their identities that are associated with pain. These experiences of colorism may lead to resentment and internalized racism for the sacrificed identity.

Hellen shared, 'I feel like my family loves me because I am part of their family, but if I were not, they'd be like "uh, a weird girl." Yeah, my family doesn't really like Black people, which is so sad.' Hellen went on to explain that since her father is Black, she and her brother are the darkest people in her family. Hellen stated that due to her brother's dark skin, her Puerto Rican 'cousins make fun of him for it.'

In an op-ed for *Insider*, Canela Lopez (2020: para 5) explained that anti-Blackness is prevalent amongst Latin Americans. These sentiments are 'connected to the anti-Black statements made by our *abuelas* and *tíos*, of the images we see in telenovelas and Spanish-language news, and of the racial caste system Latin American countries were built on'. The narratives of our participants provide insights into Lopez's assertions. They gave concrete examples of their experiences with schooling, world language programs, belonging, representation, colorism and anti-Blackness. If Latin America is built on the backdrop of racial division, shouldn't this topic be addressed in language programs? Given these findings, we offer recommendations for world language educators.

Implications and Recommendations

The participants' stories provided insights for how educators can create inclusive learning environments. Counterstories can open the doors of understanding by uplifting the voices of those who have been historically omitted. Counterstories can also fill in gaps of knowledge that are beyond an educator's experience or expertise. In his framing of Critical Race Praxis, Roberto García challenged:

> [S]tudents have much to tell and teach us about racism, recent racism. How they see themselves, how they perceive others treating them, and how school treats them. Creating the space, modeling vulnerability and developing racial literacy all have one purpose in mind, to elicit the student-narrated counterstories and make these part of what is learned in the classroom. (García, 2015: 317)

Based on the findings revealed in this study, we offer the following recommendations: (1) Be open to co-construction, (2) give feedback with care, (3) provide diverse linguistic resources, (4) increase visibility of Afro-descendants, (5) think intersectionally, (6) teach about anti-Blackness, and (7) raise your expectations.

Be open to co-construction

Knepp (2012) suggested engaging students in the co-creation of a classroom code, having them talk openly about the kind of classroom environment that would work best for them, especially one that might work best in difficult situations or for controversial topics. Since most language educators have not been trained extensively in diversity, equity and inclusion, we recommend that educators be open to the co-construction of knowledge. Students and their communities can fill gaps where educators and course content may be lacking. Lisa Delpit (2006: 183) wrote, 'I pray for all of us the strength to teach our [students] what they must learn, and the humility and wisdom to learn from them so that we might better teach'.

Give feedback with care

Closely aligned with our recommendation of co-construction is the topic of feedback. 'Inside of a language classroom, giving too much language feedback, especially too much negative feedback, can discourage our students and keep them from wanting to speak up or even to continue learning the target language with us' (Ludwig, n.d.: para. 13). We recognize that feedback is a necessary part of instruction; however, we recommend that educators give feedback in a way that builds students up as opposed to tearing them down. Language educator, Larry Ferlazzo (2017: para 4) wrote, 'Acknowledging, celebrating, and encouraging the use of our students' home languages is just one of the many ways we can look at them through the lens of assets – and not deficits – that they bring to the learning process'. Constructive feedback involves appropriate wait time, attention to frequency of corrections, allowance for self-correction, offering non-hierarchical feedback that does not esteem one target country over another, attention to tone and selection of word choices. Along with consideration of word selection, we recommend that teachers provide students with additional linguistic resources.

Provide diverse linguistic resources

Textbook grammar and vocabulary lists are quite limited in terms of attention to minoritized communities within target cultures. Teachers should examine their textbooks and look for what is missing. For example, diverse descriptions of hair textures, hairstyles, skin tones and mixed identity are most often omitted. For this reason, we recommend that educators supplement their textbooks to include vocabulary, phraseology and grammar that honor the identities of diverse members of the target community, as well as the students that they serve. For example, the poetry of Afro Cuban, Nicolás Guillén, includes both conventional spellings and phonetic spellings associated with Afro Cuban dialects. Educators could incorporate both constructions of his work.

Educators can create assignments where students assist with this expansion of vocabulary. We recommend looking to pop culture, YouTube and other current online sources to find the latest terminology. Having vocabulary that speaks to diverse backgrounds enables students to bring their identities into the classroom. Not providing these resources causes students to speak superficially about their identity or omit certain characteristics altogether.

Increase visibility of Afro-descendants

You cannot value what you do not see. To increase the visibility of African descendants, we recommend that educators take an inventory of their classroom spaces and course content. The incorporation of content on Afro-descendants is most effective when it is evenly interwoven throughout the course, or perhaps into a unit of study to offer a more in-depth examination. Since most textbooks overlook Afro-descendants, educators will likely have to supplement their materials. We recommend hard sources (articles, books, documentaries) as well as soft sources (blogs, YouTube channels, social media). The incorporation of these diversities will draw strong cross-cultural connections and enhance student engagement. Where available, we recommend including racial and ethnic statistics as well as other demographics of the target countries. However, in order that communities are not relegated to numbers, a balance of quantitative and qualitative content should be offered.

Think intersectionally

One way to combat the Black/White binary is to consider how identities intersect. In Crenshaw's (1995: 358) seminal work, she highlighted the 'need to account for multiple grounds of identity when considering how the social world is constructed'. Also of import are the experiences and treatment of diverse populations such as Afro-descendants, indigenous, women, LGBTQ+, varying abilities and other minoritized communities. If we do not account for social identity when teaching culture, we cannot present an authentic representation of target communities. We highlight the need to disaggregate the presentation of culture by breaking down large categories, such as Latin American and Francophone. In doing so, educators can focus on the diverse populations that those categories actually represent, as well as the multiple ways that those identities intersect.

Teach about anti-Blackness

We urge educators to interrogate anti-Blackness within Latin American communities, both abroad and in the US. There is a growing body of research detailing the disparate experiences of racial and ethnic minorities in Latin America (Eduardo Bonilla-Silva, Henry Louis Gates, Krishauna Hines-Gaither, Melva Lowe de Goodin, Kimberly Simmons, Silvio Torres-Saillant, Sonja Watson, etc.). These resources expand the cultural presentations that are found in most language textbooks. Incorporating this content offers world language students and educators a deeper analysis of target cultures and underrepresented communities. If educators examine the multiple ways that anti-Blackness materializes, such as colorism, economic depravity, social (im)mobility, policing, negative stereotypes, and more, students will be better informed and better equipped to make comparisons and connections between the home and target cultures.

Raise your expectations

Participants reported that teachers often had low expectations of their ability to speak and to learn Spanish. Participants felt these negative sentiments were in part based on their African features. In defining stereotype threat, psychologist Claude Steele (1995) noted, 'The existence of such a stereotype means that anything one does or any of one's features that conform to it make the stereotype more plausible' (cited in Steele & Aronson, 1995: 797). Simply put, a student's performance is directly impacted by the educator's perception of them.

Delpit wrote, 'When teachers do not understand the potential of the students they teach, they will under teach them no matter what the methodology' (Delpit, 2006: 175). Therefore, in addition to world language professional development, a serious commitment to diversity, equity and inclusion is key to providing an equitable experience for all students, particularly for students of color and those from marginalized backgrounds. We recommend that educators interrogate their assumptions and implicit biases that may be at play in the classroom, not just for themselves, but also among their students. We recommend that teachers gain more training and education on implicit bias, stereotypes and microaggressions. This education will make teachers more aware of when these deficit-based dynamics are in operation, and in turn, they may be better equipped to combat them.

Conclusion

'The critical race theory family tree has expanded to incorporate the racialized experiences of women, Latinas/os, Native Americans and Asian Americans' (Yosso, 2005: 72). For language educators who are committed to including marginalized identities, CRT can offer the perfect balance between world language theory and inclusive pedagogical practices. A litmus test for its effectiveness hinges on what our Afro Latina participants have described. Succinctly put, they 'want to be included' (Bella). Going beyond the illusion of inclusion to deliberate representation is within our reach. 'Critical race theory draws explicitly on the lived experiences of people of color by including such methods as storytelling, family histories, biographies, scenarios, parables, cuentos, testimonios, chronicles and narratives' (Yosso, 2005: 74). The educators who made the greatest impact on our participants were those who incorporated diverse identities, challenged them to excel, built relationships and included culturally responsive pedagogy. By implementing the recommendations herein, language educators have the power to construct their own counterstories of radical inclusion.

Discussion Questions

(1) Reflecting on your world language programs as a student, to what extent were you exposed to Afro Latin American content?
(2) As an educator, how do/might you incorporate Afro Latin American content into your classroom?
(3) As an educator, how does your course content reflect the demographics of the target culture or the demographics of the students that you teach?
(4) What are the main sources of information that you use in designing your lesson plans?

References

Anderson, E. (1995) Feminist epistemology: An interpretation and a defense. *Hypatia* 10 (3), 50–84.

Armstead, R. (2007) Growing the size of the Black woman: Feminist activism in Havana hip hop. *NWSA Journal* 19 (1), 106–117.

Bonilla-Silva, E. (2004) From bi-racial to tri-racial: Towards a new system of racial stratification in the USA. *Ethnic and Racial Studies* 27 (6), 931–950.

Casey, K. (1993) *I Answer with My Life: Life Histories of Women Teachers Working for Social Change*. New York: Routledge.

Clandinin, D.J. and Connelly, F.M. (2004) *Narrative Inquiry: Experience and Story in Qualitative Research*. San Francisco: John Wiley & Sons.

Crenshaw, K.W. (1995) Mapping the margins: Intersectionality, identity, politics, and violence against women of color. In K. Crenshaw, N. Gotanda, G. Peller and K. Thomas (eds) *Critical Race Theory: The Key Writings that Formed the Movement* (pp. 357–383). New York: The New Press.

Criado, M. and Reyes, J.M. (2005) Raza y etnidad. In M. Criado and J.M. Reyes (eds) *Mujeres de hoy: Textos, voces e imagines* (pp. 143–162). New Jersey: Prentice Hall.

Delgado, R. (2000) Storytelling for oppositionists and others: A plea for narrative. In R. Delgaldo and J. Stefancic (eds) *Critical Race Theory: The Cutting Edge* (pp. 60–70). Philadelphia, PA: Temple University Press.

Delgado, R. and Stefancic, J. (2017) *Critical Race Theory: An Introduction*. New York: The New Press.

Delpit, L. (2006) *Other People's Children: Cultural Conflict in the Classroom*. New York: The New Press.

Ferlazzo, L. (2017) Response: ELL students' home language is an asset, not a 'barrier'. *Education Week Teacher*, 28 January. See https://blogs.edweek.org/teachers/class-room_qa_with_larry_ferlazzo/2017/01/response_aN_ell_students_home_language_is_an_asset_not_a_barrier.html

Frank, R., Akresh, I.R. and Lu, B. (2010) Latino immigrants and the U.S. racial order: How and where do they fit in? *American Sociological Association* 75 (3), 378–401.

Guillard Limonta, N.R. (2016) To be a Black woman, a lesbian, and an Afro-feminist in Cuba today. *Black Diaspora Review* 5 (2), 81–97.

Hill Collins, P. (2009) *Black Feminist Thought: Knowledge, Consciousness, and the Politics of Empowerment*. New York: Routledge.

Hines-Gaither, K. (2015) Negotiations of race, class, and gender among Afro Latina women immigrants to the southern United States. Doctoral dissertation, University of North Carolina at Greensboro. See https://salemcollege.on.worldcat.org/search?queryString=krishauna#/oclc/914234316

Hitlin, S., Brown, J.S. and Elder, G.H. (2007) Measuring Latinos: Racial vs. ethnic clas-sification and self-understandings. *Social Forces* 86 (2), 587–611.

Horsford, S.D. (2011) *Learning in a Burning House: Educational Inequality, Ideology, and (Dis)integration*. New York: Teachers College Press.

King Miller, B.A. (2015) Effective teachers: Culturally relevant teaching from the voices of Afro-Caribbean immigrant females in STEM. *Sage Open*, July–September 2015, 1–14. https://doi.org/10.1177%2F2158244015603427

Knepp, K.A.F. (2012) Understanding student and faculty incivility in higher education. *Journal of Effective Teaching* 12 (1), 32–45.

Ladson-Billings, G. (1995) Toward a theory of culturally relevant pedagogy. *American Educational Research Journal* 32 (3), 465–491.

Lichtman, M. (2013) *Qualitative Research in Education: A User's Guide*. Thousand Oaks, CA: Sage Publications.

Lopez, C. (2020) It's time for non-Black Latinx people to talk about anti-Blackness in our own communities – and the conversation starts at home. *Insider*, 26 June. See https://www.insider.com/anti-blackness-non-black-latinx-spaces-racism-2020-6

Ludwig, J.Z. (n.d.) How to provide positive, meaningful feedback to your foreign lan-guage students. *FluentU*. See https://www.fluentu.com/blog/educator/language-feedback/

Martinez, J. (2019) When it comes to Latinidad, who is included and who isn't? *Remezcla*, 30 July. See https://remezcla.com/features/culture/when-it-comes-to-latinidad-who-is-included-and-who-isnt/

Merriam, S.B. (2009) *Qualitative Research: A Guide to Design and Implementation*. San Franciso: John Wiley & Sons.

Randolph, L.J. and Johnson, S.M. (2017) Social justice in the language classroom: A call to action. *Dimension* 2017, 99–121.

Savin-Baden, M. and Major, C.H. (eds) (2010) *New Approaches to Qualitative Research: Wisdom and Uncertainty*. New York: Routledge.

Steele, C.M. and Aronson, J. (1995) Stereotype threat and the intellectual test perfor-mance of African Americans. *Journal of Personality and Social Psychology* 69 (5), 797–811.

Vega, M.M., Alba, M. and Modestín, Y. (eds) (2012) *Women Warriors of the Afro-Latina Diaspora*. Houston, TX: University of Houston.

Yosso, T.J. (2005) Whose culture has capital? A critical race theory discussion of com-munity cultural wealth. *Race Ethnicity and Education* 8 (1), 69–91.

6 'Sí, yo soy de Puerto Rico': A Teacher's Story of Teaching Spanish through and beyond her Latina Identity

Johanna Ennser-Kananen and Leisa M. Quiñones-Oramas

Introduction

'I felt without a place here.' The sentiment shared by Leisa, a Latina Spanish teacher in the US, is likely one that resonates with many teachers of color (TOC). Educational contexts are not socioculturally innocent and often are places where cultural, linguistic and racial belonging become contested (Yosso, 2005). This chapter tells and theorizes a story of a Latina Spanish teacher who worked at a public high school in an urban context of the northeastern US. Approached through the lenses of critical race theory (e.g. Solórzano, 2019) and Latinx critical theory (LatCrit) (e.g. Yosso, 2006), we offer this narrative as an illustration of the complex identity work that teachers of color do in their classrooms. We present the story as coherently as possible, interrupting it in only a few places in order to offer theorizations and interpretations with the aim of pointing to the larger societal phenomena it illuminates. This process allows us as authors, one of whom is a storyteller, as well as the reader to oscillate between a deep understanding of a teacher's experience and a reflective meta-level, both of which we see as enabling or enhancing critical practice in teaching and teacher education.

In this chapter, we resist the notion that wellbeing and success at school (both for teachers and students) is a result of a neutral and merit-based process (e.g. Condron *et al.*, 2013). We use a Latina teacher's journal entries as our key data point; bring together scholarship from education, applied linguistics and culture studies; and bridge the theory-practice divide in our collaborative analysis and writing and in our addressing of both academic and practitioner audiences. The chapter serves as a contribution to critical practice in teacher education as it highlights the experience of a Latina teacher and the complex interactions of her racial, cultural, socioeconomic and linguistic identity with her teaching, her rapport with her students, and their learning.

Theoretical Framework

CRT and LatCrit

Critical race theory (CRT) originated in the context of legal studies but has since become an interdisciplinary line of work that is situated within and between sociology, women's studies, ethnic studies and education, among others (Matsuda, 1991). Solórzano (1997) proposed five themes that are fundamental to CRT: the centrality of race and racism and its 'intersection with other forms of subordination such as gender and class discrimination' (1997: 6); the rejection of neutral, colorblind, and meritocratic discourses; the 'commitment to social justice' (1997: 7); the importance and legitimacy of people of color (POC)'s 'experiential knowledge' (1997: 7) as captured for instance in stories and other narrative accounts; and the interdisciplinarity of CRT scholarship. He later applied these five themes to teacher education contexts (Solórzano, 2019: 108), reaffirming the centrality and intersectionality of race; the rejection of neutrality- and meritocracy-based practices and policies; and the focus on the 'lived experiences of Students of Color'. He further added an emphasis on transformative practice (theory-practice links) and historical contextualization of educational work to the tenets of CRT. Thanks to Solórzano and many other CRT scholars, critical race studies have gained and continue to gain traction within the field of education (Lynn & Parker, 2006).

Latinx critical theory, or LatCrit, is closely related to CRT as it also centers race in scholarly and activist work, paying special attention to how it intersects with language and accent, nationality, immigration status, surname, and sexuality, for instance (Espinoza & Harris, 1997; Yosso, 2006). Both CRT and LatCrit aim to deconstruct hegemonic ideologies and discourses or, as Yosso (2006) has termed them, 'majoritarian tales,' which are both externally and internally imposed. As Valdes (2005: 148) explains, LatCrit 'is a scholarly movement responding to the long historical presence and enduring invisibility of Latinas/os in the lands now known as the United States', adding that the movement has expanded beyond the US and intertwines scholarly with activist efforts.

Following Yosso (2005), we view schools and education through a CRT framework that 'works toward the liberatory potential of schooling' and 'acknowledges the contradictory nature of education, wherein schools most often oppress and marginalize while they maintain the potential to emancipate and empower' (2005: 74). This is particularly important in the area of world language education, which has, with some notable exceptions such as this volume, been slow to adopt social justice and particularly racial justice approaches to research and teaching.

Literature Review

Counter-storytelling

In line with the theoretical foundations we chose, we contend that storytelling, particularly the telling of counter-stories that are less often heard or that do not align with dominant discourses, is an important tool in the push for increased social justice in language education and all other educational contexts. Solórzano and Yosso (2002: 32) explain:

> [w]e define the counter-story as a method of telling the stories of those people whose experiences are not often told (i.e., those on the margins of society). The counter-story is also a tool for exposing, analyzing, and challenging the majoritarian stories of racial privilege. Counter-stories can shatter complacency, challenge the dominant discourse on race, and further the struggle for racial reform.

Solórzano and Yosso (2002) further point to the long-standing tradition of storytelling in African American and Indigenous communities and differentiate between three forms of stories: personal stories (autobiographical), other people's stories, and composite stories, which draw on a variety of sources, including autobiographical and biographical information. They explain how they bring together storied data, literature, as well as their personal and professional experience, to write counter-stories and name community building; in this way they challenge dominant discourses and beliefs, demonstrate new possibilities, and promote a new reality by bringing together the story with the status quo.

In recognition of these possibilities of counter-storytelling, this chapter aims to challenge dominant discourses and beliefs of school as a colorblind or racially neutral space and hopes to promote new realities by highlighting and analyzing the experience of one Latina Spanish teacher as a basis and call for more racially aware and socially just instruction. In doing so, we are reminded by Chang and Fuller (2000: 1279) that, while storytelling can set free anti-hegemonic powers, it is not in itself a tool of liberation but rather 'a neutral technique that can perhaps be used more easily to maintain the status quo than to attack it'. If used as a transformative practice, they continue, 'the goal of storytelling must go beyond descriptive "accuracy": the "is" must be connected to an explicit or implicit "ought"' (2000: 1280). This 'ought' will be made explicit in the implications of our findings that we address to teachers, teacher educators, and administrators.

Although a growing body of research exists within education and teacher education that uses counter-story frameworks (e.g. Cho, 2017; Maramba, 2013; Milner IV & Howard, 2013; Roy & Roxas, 2011; Settlage, 2011), in world language education (WLE) such studies are difficult to come by. With this contribution, we hope to encourage our WLE colleagues to fill this gap.

TOC narratives as triggers of change and spaces of resistance

With its goal of pushing for change through the centering of a story, our chapter is situated within the narrative approaches that continue to attract attention in educational research. Particularly in teacher education, the value and importance of teacher narratives for renewal of practice as well as theory have been broadly recognized (e.g. Barkhuizen *et al.*, 2013; Clandinin & Connelly, 1985; Johnson, 2001). In addition, teacher narratives, especially TOC narratives, are an important space of resistance, as the following examples illustrate. WLE is in dire need of such spaces of resistance.

In Kambutu *et al.*'s (2009) study, the stories of six racially minoritized teachers 'disrupt orthodox conceptions of teachers of color' and shed light on how 'their experiences with oppression and resistance affect their teaching in rural settings' (2009: 96). Based on the notion that CRT provides an appropriate framework for narratives as tools of decolonization, Kambutu *et al.* (2009) analyzed the oppressive experiences of TOC and how the teachers resisted them. Based on the teachers' narratives, the authors acknowledge the difficult work that teachers of color in rural settings do to develop coping strategies and to resist racial and ethnic prejudice. They conclude that '[n]arratives challenge existing perspectives and provide an alternative worldview' and are thus ways to 'not only learn about the chameleon nature of oppression but also illuminate the efforts by the marginalized to struggle toward a humanizing pedagogy' (Kambutu *et al.*, 2009: 99). In the same vein, we recognize one Latina teacher's stories as evidence of the complexity and difficulty of racial work that is tied to TOCs' professional activities and identities.

Another example of the importance and potentially subversive nature of TOC narratives comes from Kohli's (2009) study. She worked with 12 Asian-American, Black and Latina female pre-service teachers who taught in predominantly non-white school districts in the US. Kohli analyzed these pre-service teachers' experiences of racial injustices from their K-12 education (e.g. racial slurs, teachers' low expectations, curricular erasure), encouraged the teachers to put those stories in connection with their students' 'parallel experiences' (Kohli, 2009: 235), and elicited comments on racial hierarchies within teacher education. From her findings, Kohli concluded that 'we must continue to explore the racialized experiences of Teachers of Color' (2009: 250) and tap them for a pedagogy that promotes social justice within schools and teacher education. In respect to the reflective space (interviews and focus groups) Kohli created for the teachers to share and reflect on their experiences, she underlines the importance of such spaces for fighting racism in schools.

Building spaces of reflection and resistance through TOC narratives was also a central goal of a study conducted by Fránquiz *et al.* (2011). They worked with three bilingual teachers of color from three different teacher education programs, who shared experiences from their learning and teaching trajectories. Their stories represent important counter-narratives to harmful dominant discourses. For instance, they dismantled narratives of Latinx families not caring about or being distant to education or depriving their children of literacy-rich environments. Based on the teachers' lived experiences, the authors recommend using CRT and LatCrit frameworks in teacher education contexts to continue the work of eliciting and sharing counterstories against dominant discourses as well as pushing back against the hegemonic discourses ingrained in teacher education contexts. At the same time, they emphasize the need to support TOC who engage in diversity work: 'We propose a vision for teacher education that situates race, culture, and language at the center and also challenges the assumption that bilingual teachers of color are experts on diversity and do not need additional support and training to teach bilingual learners' (Fránquiz *et al.*, 2011: 280).

In a similar vein, Colomer's (2018) multiple case study of six Latinx teachers at middle schools in the US illustrates their 'racial literacy' and 'experiences with (un)masking' (2018: 194). Colomer understands racial literacy as 'one's ability to resolve racially stressful issues' and unmasking as 'the literal and figurative ways in which one covers or embraces racial markers' (2018: 194–195). She sees storytelling as one of the key strategies of racial literacy. Based on their stories, Colomer documents different ways in which she and her participants did or did not define themselves (e.g. as Hispanic or Latinx) depending on their social environment and the different degrees to which they embraced or resisted social and societal oppression such as monolingual norms or racist comments. Colomer points to the importance of narrative research for creating reflective spaces for identity building. She concludes that storytelling should be included in the preparation of Latinx teachers as one humanizing strategy that helps them and their students become empowered through higher racial literacy.

Encouraged by these examples of TOC resistance through stories and following Kohli's (2008: 180) call to 'encourage these teachers [of color] to reflect on their own educational experiences', we present one Latina teacher's story, particularly insofar as it contains or represents counter-hegemonic beliefs and experiences and can thus be a helpful compass in reorienting traditional (or) colorblind teacher education, which is still common in the area of world languages.

Context

The data we present here is based on Leisa's journal entries. They reflect her experience of teaching at an underfunded high school in a large city on the US American East Coast. According to the 2010 US census, about 52.6% of the city population were white, 25.3% Black or African American, and 9.6% Asian (US Census Bureau, 2010). In 2016, Puerto Ricans constituted the largest Latinx[1] population of the city (40.9%), followed by Dominicans (18.7%) and Central Americans (10.2%). At the time when Leisa worked there, the school, which we call 'Olden' (a pseudonym), served mainly Black students from socioeconomically disadvantaged backgrounds. In the fall of 2016, the total enrollment of the school was 519 students, who attended grades 9 through 12. Of these, 38.5% identified as Black/African American, 26.6% as Latinx, 20.8% as Asian and 12.1% as white. Overall, 59.2% (307) of students were considered 'economically disadvantaged,' 28.5% (148) were coded as students with disabilities, 25.2% (131) were classified as English language learners, and 52.8% reported that their first language was not English. Olden was considered a level 4 school, which is defined as being '[a]mong the lowest achieving and least improving schools'. There was a wide range of experience amongst Olden's 35 teachers. Some had been teaching in the same building for more than 10 years, while others, like Leisa, were new to high school teaching. The majority of them possessed one or more higher education degrees. The class to which Leisa refers in her narrative had approximately 25 students, who were mostly African American and Latinx. Her course was meant to be an introductory Spanish class, and was considered by the district as a graduation requirement. All her students had high proficiency in English; some were heritage Spanish speakers with average to strong oral skills.

Positionality and Process: Who We Are and What We Did

Our academic thinking and writing are heavily influenced by our identities and positionalities, which is why we offer the following positionality statement that we hope explains our intentions, choices and biases. In line with our LatCrit and CRT framework, we recognize that who we are shapes what we do; in other words, our sense-making of Leisa's story and our identities are deeply intertwined.

Johanna: I am a white European woman who works as a researcher and teacher educator at a predominantly white university in Finland. I was born and raised in central Europe, received my PhD in the Midwestern US, and worked at a large private East Coast university thereafter. Seven years of learning, teaching, supervising teacher candidates and doing school-based research in the US had and continues to have a profound impact on how I understand race and racism. As an eternal learner of these issues that permeate all educational spaces, I am (at least partially) aware of the privilege, complicity and responsibility that come with my whiteness. I met Leisa during my time as a teacher educator at the East Coast university. She was a student in some of the courses I taught for pre-service language teachers and the experience and practice-theory connections she contributed to many classes impressed me and stuck with me. We stayed in touch after her graduation, and I remember repeatedly thinking that her stories would be valuable for a larger audience. I consider this chapter as a space to tell a small part of them.

Leisa: I am a queer Spanish teacher, born and raised in Puerto Rico. For the last ten years I have resided in a large city of the Eastern Coast in the US. I can pinpoint my move to this city as the moment when I started questioning my identity and the roles I played as I was increasingly defined by my surroundings as 'Other.' The status that has often been given to me as a 'white-passing' Puerto Rican woman with an 'accent' has in many ways shaped the experiences I have lived in the city. I understand that these experiences, as a 'white-passing' member of the Latinx community, have afforded me privileges that other members of the community haven't had. I moved here to pursue graduate studies in Hispanic Language and Literature at a large private university. After I finished this graduate program, I continued to work in a large public university in the area, as a part-time Spanish lecturer. Nine months after graduating with my first Master's degree, I started a second degree in Education, with an emphasis on Second Language Acquisition. During my third and final year in the program, I started working full time as a high school Spanish teacher at 'Olden,' an under resourced, urban public school. After three years of working there, I was fired, as were all other teachers and staff, when the school was given 'turnaround status.' I decided not to reapply for my position. Currently, I am a middle and high school Spanish teacher at a small, progressive, independent, project-based school. My experiences over the last ten years as a queer Latina, first as a student and then as a teacher; the recurrent and simultaneous feelings of belonging and *otherness*; the different roles that I have had to play within the institutions where I have studied and worked; and the constant evaluation of what and who I am to my classmates, teachers, students and colleagues, have made me interested and aware of *what I do* and *who I am*, and how these two entities shift and shape themselves within parameters of race, racism and identity within and outside education as an institution. Johanna was unequivocally crucial in introducing me to the importance of authenticity within the classroom. I met her the same year I started working at 'Olden.' Her course on Curriculum Development pushed me to rethink what I knew about and did for my own courses. She also pushed and always encouraged me to think about my own story, where it came from and the value it had to guide my journey as a teacher.

***

We started working on this chapter by brainstorming the stories Leisa wanted to share. This mostly happened in the form of email and Skype conversations and jotting down notes in a shared document. The process was driven by Leisa, with Johanna asking mostly clarifying questions and recording the conversations. Shortly after Leisa had decided on some main points to build her stories around, she began to write, sharing her texts with Johanna whenever she felt they were ready enough. This process continued throughout the data analysis and writing stages. After reading the stories, Johanna would sometimes send questions to Leisa, usually asking for clarifications and elaborations. In this way, the stories developed with the main authorship remaining in Leisa's hands and some attention to the questions of a familiar but remote reader. When the main storyline was in place, Johanna made suggestions for the parts that would be included in the chapter and Leisa reviewed these selections. This process was guided by questions of relevance for Leisa and for a wider readership. In other words, we asked: Which parts of the story contain key moments for Leisa? Which parts will readers likely be able to connect with?

Findings and Discussion

Analyzing a story can constitute or feel like an act of violence. However, as most academic genres and discourses demand a theorization of narrative of some kind, we offer an analysis of Leisa's experiences that aims at the same time to preserve the story's integrity. In the following, we present Leisa's story interspersed with interpretations and reflections that intend to highlight its relevance for a larger audience. In particular, we found intersections of race and class as well as accent and skin color to be relevant for how students positioned Leisa.

'You are too white': Feeling without a place

Leisa's story begins with the opening of her first lesson at Olden, a Spanish I class.

> It was 7:45 in the morning, the lesson was about to start. 'Hola, buenos días,' I said as I clicked on my laptop pad and my presentation slide changed to display my words and an image of a sun. 'Me llamo Señorita Quiñones,' another click, another slide, new words. 'Yo soy de Puerto Rico.' At this several things happened all at once. I clicked, new words appeared, and a bunch of images of the island: one of the outlines of its shape, another with a beach in my hometown of Isabela, and another of its flag. Simultaneously, I heard several cries from students. 'From Puerto Rico?' one boy said. 'Nah, nah, you are not from Puerto Rico,' followed another. 'You are too white,' a girl said. Quiet and not so quiet 'yeses' echoed through the room. For a minute I did not know what to do, but

eventually I repeated 'Sí, yo soy de Puerto Rico.' I felt my face turning bright red and tears rushing to my eyes. It must have been 8:00AM, and on my very first day of high school teaching, I was already ready to cry. Several years before, as a Latina newcomer in the city, I had already lived through microaggressions about my heritage. 'Oh, but your English is so good!' 'Really?! You barely have an accent.' 'But you were born here, right?' 'How long have you lived here? Years, no?' were some of the many comments I received and politely answered. Somehow these did not signify much to me then. I deflected them and took them as critiques, or even flattering remarks, about how I talked and sounded. I could not see the relationship between my speech, my physical appearance and my place of origin. It was 8:01AM, I was back in my classroom and surrounded by 15 and 16-year-old students, when a truth about myself materialized before my eyes: 'I was not brown enough to be considered brown by my students, neither was I white enough to be considered "white" in this city.' I felt without a place here.

The moment Leisa described, in this part of the story, is a critical one for several reasons. As she states, 'several things happened all at once.' Maybe most importantly, her identity as Latina was doubted, if not rejected, an experience that has been documented in studies with TOC who teach in high-minority schools (Achinstein & Aguirre, 2008). This called into question her racial and cultural identity and affiliation as a woman from Puerto Rico. Specifically, the students named Leisa's language ('English') skills, accent and skin color as reasons for doubting her identity. Reading this story prompted Johanna to ask Leisa what explanations she had for the students' actions. Leisa offered two explanations, which had to do with how students perceived Puerto Ricans along the lines of race and class.

Two groups of Puerto Ricans

Leisa explains:

After living in Olden for ten years, I have faced an interesting and dual world. On the one hand, this city is filled with Puerto Rican college students and young professionals, who like me, came here to pursue undergraduate and graduate studies, and decided to stay beyond graduation. On the other hand, Olden is an important hub of Puerto Ricans who live in the diaspora. This is noticeable in certain areas of the city. For example, the [part of city], which prior to more recent gentrification used to be a mostly Puerto Rican neighborhood, where low income families live[d]. [...] Even when these two spaces and experiences, that of the young newcomer and the established immigrant, often unite (when the former becomes the latter), it seems that there is a lack of connection between the two. I feel that my students grew up and were often in contact with families that belonged to the second group of Puerto Ricans (established immigrants). I recall a brief conversation with a student who told me he had not met other Puerto Ricans, like myself, who had pursued a higher education degree and were young professionals. To what extent had my students been in contact with young professionals, undergraduate and graduate students from Puerto Rico? I do not know, but I didn't fit the mold.

Leisa's explanations for the students' doubts about her identity also have to do with the conflation of race and class. Urciuoli (2013) lays out the complexity and different meanings of the term 'class,' which is often comprised of a variety of social factors including income, place of residence, occupation, and educational background. Putting the emphasis on individuals rather than on social institutions and systems, such an understanding of class 'becomes morally marked' (Urciouli, 2013: 26):

> In this way, *black* or *Hispanic* or *Puerto Rican* become metonyms for (naturally connected to) the idea of an *underclass*. In this metonymy, class/race difference becomes morally marked. Activities seen as typical of bad citizens (dropping out of school, becoming teenage mothers, taking drugs, committing crimes, going on welfare) are habitually associated with, for example, *Puerto Ricans*, and become 'explanations' for their 'failure'. (Urciouli, 2013: 26)

It may be such discourses that Leisa's students were exposed to and were reproducing, albeit indirectly, through their responses to a teacher who claimed Puerto Rican identity but who did not match these race-class assumptions. In contrast to these discourses, Leisa mentions two existing groups and great diversity among Puerto Ricans in Olden. Through this, she pushes back against (a) a perception of the group as monolithic and (b) the discourse of individual failure, which she redirects towards a description of the city as segregated. Acknowledging her students' limited exposure to a variety of Puerto Ricans as well as the city's socioeconomic segregation (e.g. different groups of Puerto Ricans remain fairly isolated from each other) allows Leisa to address Puerto Rican-ness from a perspective that takes the broader social context, including societal structures and power dynamics, into account.

Skin color and accent

Having outlined the local ways of 'being Puerto Rican' and having explained the intersections of race and socioeconomic status in this context, Leisa continued by addressing race, specifically skin color and accent. She explained the role of 'how you sound' in processes of racialization.

> I wonder if there was also something connected to the color of my skin. My skin is lighter but that is not out of the ordinary in Puerto Rico. Because we are the result of such a rich racial mix, we come in all shades and sizes. I would be lying if I said that there isn't racism in the island, there is, but one is made more aware of it when one leaves and comes to

a place where not only your skin color dictates your origin, but how you sound as well. Did I sound like the Puerto Rican people my students knew or were surrounded by? No, and they told me so several times. To some of them my Spanish sounded too 'polished'.

In her rejection as a Latina from Puerto Rico, several larger social processes are at play that work to oppress members of non-dominant groups. First, a rejection of Leisa's identity can be viewed as part of a larger discourse around racialized identities that do not fit with a Black-and-white paradigm. As Trucios-Haynes (2000: 8) has pointed out, US conversations around race are sometimes literally a 'Black and white' issue: 'Latinas/os are indeterminately raced because racial identity in the United States occurs within a Black-White paradigm, and this paradigm does not incorporate the experiences of Latinas/os and other groups of color'. Being pushed outside the main discourse on race complicates the racial identity work Latinx do because their racial identities are not always recognized. In the case of Puerto Ricans, this may be amplified by the common perception of Puerto Ricans as 'foreign' to the US (Nieto, 2000), which further weakens their position to fully participate in the racial discourses that permeate US society.

In addition, the dynamics of colorism may be at play in Leisa's story. While light skin has been associated with, among others, economic and professional advantages and perceived beauty and intellect, relative to dark skin (Hunter, 2016), it also brings certain disadvantages: 'In societies where resources are divided by race and color, light-skinned people get a disproportionate amount of the benefits. However, light skin may be viewed as a disadvantage with regard to ethnic legitimacy or authenticity. In many ethnic communities, people view darker-skin tones as more ethnically authentic' (Olumide, 2016: 880).

In educational settings, colorism has contributed to a mismatch between how students self-identified and how they were perceived (Fergus, 2009; Hunter, 2016). In addition to Latinx identities falling through the cracks of a Black-and-white discourse and colorism establishing additional hierarchies, the discourse of alignment that is palpable in Leisa's story creates an obstacle for identity recognition. It seems that her students are reproducing a larger societal discourse that expects race, phenotype, nationality/place of origin, language proficiency, and accent, to align in particular ways in order to produce credible Latinx identities. In addition, they might be reacting to a perceived misalignment of class and race: in their view/experience, a light-skinned, university-educated teacher does not fit the stereotypical image of Latinx they are familiar with. Such expectations of alignment not only combine harmful ideologies of racial bias, nationalism and linguistic normativity, they also set impossible standards for Latinx, a phenotypically highly diverse group, whose members can come from a variety of national backgrounds, and whose English proficiency can lie anywhere on a wide spectrum. In combination with discourses that leave little room for nuance between Black and white and promote colorist hierarchies, misalignment of either white or Black features can produce irritation, confusion and rejection for those who are operating within the Black-or-white paradigm.

Leisa's experience of having her identity questioned has its roots way beyond her own classroom. Considering the bigger picture, she worked and lived in a large, predominantly white city in the US, i.e. in a context that is permeated by discourses of white supremacy. As Rosa (2016) has pointed out, the perpetual stigmatization of Latinx in such contexts based on their linguistic practices reaches far beyond a linguistic issue. He explains that 'standardized American English should be conceptualized as a raciolinguistic ideology that aligns normative whiteness, legitimate Americanness, and imagined ideal English' (2016: 165). Such raciolinguistic ideologies act on a societal level to reinscribe structures and processes of white supremacy and on a personal level to create experiences of violence such as othering. Between her students and the larger societal context rejecting her identity as either 'too Latina' or 'not Latina enough,' Leisa experienced a strong sense of non-belonging. Driven by her students' othering as well as the white supremacist context of her professional and personal life, both of which called her identity into question, Leisa decided to integrate her experience of being 'without a place' into her lessons.

Racial identity as race-sensitive pedagogy: Faces of Puerto Rico

Leisa's story continues with her lesson on Puerto Rican identities.

I decided to try something to address their reactions and surprise at my 'Puerto Ricanness.' I compiled images of fellow Puerto Ricans. Famous people (singers, athletes, artists), friends, family members, pictures of unknown people I found on the Internet became the subjects of one slide of my daily PowerPoint. I had planned an activity around origin with the students. They were to communicate where they were from using a very simple structure using the first person present conjugation (*yo soy de...*). Then they were going to learn how to communicate where others were from using the third person present conjugation (*él/ella es de...*). I believe I first had them make guesses about the origins of the people in the pictures, while using the target grammar. I provided a list of possible places for them to use. After they had spent some time sharing with a partner, we opened up the discussion for the whole class and took note of some of their answers on the board. Famous people were easier to identify, of course. However, when I would say that someone wasn't from a particular place, but from Puerto Rico, students' responses varied. Some told me things like 'Nah, nah Ms. you are lying.' In others I could see the disbelief and surprise. Others stayed quiet and seemed not to react.

In this final part of her story, Leisa shares how she addressed her experience of having her identity rejected in her Spanish lessons. With the goal of broadening the students' understanding of being Puerto Rican, she provided pictures and stories of Puerto Ricans from a variety of social and professional backgrounds. In addition, she made connections to the students' backgrounds by involving them into the discussion about origins. Although students continued to express disbelief, this activity opened up two important potential avenues for learning. First, it exposed students to a variety of Puerto Rican identities, thus challenging the monolithic understanding of the group as well as stereotypes and harmful conflations such as that of race with class. In other words, not only did Leisa's lesson center the stories and faces of BIPOC (Black, Indigenous and People of Color) in line with CRT (Solórzano, 2019), it also created a space of resistance to 'majoritarian tales' (Yosso, 2006) of whiteness and Puerto Ricans/Latinx as a monolithic group.

Second, the lesson included the students' selves into the topic, thus creating a space where the (otherwise often racializing and inappropriate) question, 'Where are you from?' could potentially generate debate about the complex relationship of place of birth, living environment, social and racial affiliations, cultural belonging and linguistic practices, etc. By complicating her students' images of Puerto Ricans (and potentially themselves and each other), Leisa went far beyond the identity-as-pedagogy approach she started out with. Rather than limiting her teaching to her own identity, she used her classroom as a platform to a variety of people from a variety of backgrounds, including her students. In other words, rather than using identity, she made space for alterity in her pedagogy, for complex identities and images (e.g. of Puerto Ricans) that resisted the comfort of simplification and stereotyping and opened opportunities for deep learning. Alterity as we use it does not refer to the oppressed 'Other' but rather to ideas that refuse to comply with homogeneity, simplicity and comfort. In this sense, the class functioned as a space of resistance (Kambuto *et al.*, 2009) for Leisa, where she challenged and dismantled both the white norms that surround her and her students' stereotypical views of Puerto Rican/Latinx identities.

Implications: Moving towards Social Justice Education

This chapter has told the counterstory of Leisa, a Latina teacher in a large city on the US East Coast. Although we could only offer a small glimpse into her experience, it is illustrative of the complex work racialized teachers do in such contexts. Drawing on Leisa's experience and our analysis of it, we recommend three concrete steps for implementing social-justice approaches in education and particularly WLE: an alterity-as-pedagogy approach, support for TOC from administrators and colleagues, and the centering of BIPOC's stories in the curriculum.

After Leisa's identity claim was rejected by her students, causing her to feel socioculturally and racially homeless, she was motivated to respond to her students in a way that would promote learning and challenge their biases. In a subsequent lesson, Leisa offered them opportunities to explore their own as well as a variety of Puerto Ricans' origins, acknowledging the differences in (at least) race, socioeconomic status, and professional and educational background. What had started as a self-introduction evolved into a rich lesson that brought together Leisa's background, with the backgrounds of other members of the Puerto Rican community, and those of her students. Leisa thus complicated the question of origin and belonging by showing and inviting a diverse and complex response to 'where are you from?' that challenges a stereotyping or homogenizing approach to racialized identities. We argue that this was a move from identity-as-pedagogy towards alterity-as-pedagogy, a turn from simplification to complication that relies on the recognition of difference to resist homogenization and naïve-celebratory approaches that reduce questions of origin to (seemingly) innocent and often meaningless classroom activities.

This approach enabled Leisa to bring the complexity and richness of the topic of cultural, racial and linguistic identities to the fore. Although an identity-as-pedagogy approach has been shown to be conducive to learning in some contexts (Ennser-Kananen & Wang, 2016; Morgan, 2004), a sole focus on an individual (e.g. a teacher) or on identity as representational, unified and static runs the risk of enabling colorblindness and thus perpetuation of racial and cultural stereotypes and hierarchies. Using the teacher's identity as pedagogy, as suggested by Morgan (2004), further runs the risk of centering the teacher's experiences and denying students the opportunity to share and examine their own experiences while also developing empathy and managing tensions, contradictions and disagreements. Leisa's story can thus be understood as a call on teachers to embrace alterity for pedagogical purposes, for instance to challenge stereotypes and biases. Rather than centering themselves and using their identity as a basis for lesson planning and teaching, we hope our chapter will encourage teachers to look for and address differences in experience, belonging and identities, and guide students in making sense of them rather than minimize, reject or attack them. Additionally, an alterity-driven approach can inspire administrators and policy makers to critically question the assumption of 'cultural match' (Achinstein & Aguirre, 2008) between students and teachers and support their TOC in developing strategies and networks around negotiating their identities, alterities and pedagogies.

Of course, change cannot be brought about by teachers alone, and a call on teachers always implies a call on teacher educators and administrators. As this chapter illustrates, TOC shoulder a large amount of extra work, simply because they bring their identities and experiences to school. Not only are they exposed to racialization and impositions of hegemonic identities and behaviors, they are also often expected or required to do the unpaid emotional, intellectual and social work of educating their students, colleagues and administrators about issues including racism, racial belonging and white supremacy (Dixon *et al.*, 2019). It is up to administrators to build structures that recognize this work, provide TOC with the support they need to do it, if they choose to, and create equitable workloads (especially in regards to socioemotional work) for all teachers. Colleagues of TOC are called to support such efforts by adopting social-justice curricula, educating themselves about the workings of white supremacy, and learning to be agents of antiracist education. A commitment to social justice education would enable WLE teachers to take advantage of the many entry points WLE offers (e.g. via topics of cultural diversity and multilingualism) to antiracist pedagogies.

Leisa's story serves as an opportunity for readers to learn about 'the efforts by the marginalized to struggle toward a humanizing pedagogy' (Kambutu *et al.*, 2009: 99), and be reminded of the damage that color-blind curricula and pedagogies in schools and teacher education can do. The chapter also serves as a reminder that providing spaces for TOC to tell their stories can be an effective tool for dismantling curricula and pedagogies that are colorblind and built on normative whiteness. Leisa's story illustrates how experiences of BIPOC can become the center of the curriculum, rather than merely an afterthought. If world language educators and curriculum developers are serious about antiracist education, we need to build curriculum around BIPOC's experiences rather than sporadically infusing the otherwise white curriculum with token-stories of minoritized and racialized populations. An approach to teaching and teacher education based on CRT and LatCrit that centers race, rejects colorblindness and foregrounds the stories of BIPOC, particularly by focusing on the intersections of race, language and nationality (Espinoza & Harris, 1997), can truly make a difference for TOC. In sum, we echo the call to end colorblind pedagogies in teaching and other educational contexts (e.g. Fránquiz *et al.*, 2011; Kohli, 2009; Solórzano, 2019) and suggest that antiracist pedagogies cannot be a voluntary exercise but need to be at the heart of teacher education programs.

Discussion Questions

(1) For white teachers: What aspects of my racial identity have I used in my teaching? How could I refocus identity-based teaching to invite alterity, for instance by building lessons around images and texts that reflect the diverse experiences of BIPOC without othering or stereotyping them?

(2) For administrators of TOC: What systems can we put in place to support TOC, particularly considering that they are often expected to do a lot of unpaid and unrecognized work for all members of the school community on race and racism? How do we educate school

communities, particularly white students and teachers, not to rely on TOC for these issues?

(3) For teacher educators: What entry points for social justice pedagogies does the world language curriculum offer? What enables my white teacher candidates to delve into sociopolitical and potentially uncomfortable topics such as race and racism together with their students in ways that are conducive to learning and activism? How do I introduce them to this work in ways they will sustain?

Note

(1)   The wording on the official Census website is 'Hispanic or Latino' (www.census.gov).

References

Achinstein, B. and Aguirre, J. (2008) Cultural match or culturally suspect: How new teachers of color negotiate sociocultural challenges in the classroom. *Teachers College Record* 110 (8), 1505–1540.

Barkhuizen, G., Benson, P. and Chik, A. (2013) *Narrative Inquiry in Language Teaching and Learning Research*. New York: Routledge.

Chang, R.S. and Fuller, N. (2000) Introduction: Performing LatCrit. *University of California, Davis Law Review* 33, 1277–1292.

Cho, H. (2017) Racism and linguicism: Engaging language minority pre-service teachers in counter-storytelling. *Race Ethnicity and Education* 20 (5), 666–680.

Clandinin, D.J. and Connelly, F.M. (2000) *Narrative Inquiry: Experience and Story in Qualitative Research*. San Francisco: Jossey-Bass.

Colomer, S.E. (2018) Understanding racial literacy through acts of (un) masking: Latinx teachers in a new Latinx diaspora community. *Race, Ethnicity and Education* 22 (2), 194–210.

Condron, D.J., Tope, D., Steidl, C.R. and Freeman, K.J. (2013) Racial segregation and the Black/White achievement gap, 1992 to 2009. *The Sociological Quarterly* 54 (1), 130–157.

Dixon, D., Griffin, A. and Teoh, M. (2019) If you listen, we will stay: Why teachers of color leave and how to disrupt teacher turnover. *Education Trust*. See https://files.eric.ed.gov/fulltext/ED603193.pdf

Ennser-Kananen, J. and Wang, A.F. (2016) 'I am combined': Chinese teachers' cultural identities and pedagogical learning. *Journal of Language Teaching and Research* 7 (4), 625–634.

Espinoza, L. and Harris, A.P. (1997) Embracing the tar-baby: LatCrit theory and the sticky mess of race. *California Law Review* 85 (5), 1585–1645.

Fergus, E. (2009) Understanding Latino students' schooling experiences: The relevance of skin color among Mexican and Puerto Rican high school students. *Teachers College Record* 111 (2), 339–375.

Fránquiz, M.E., Salazar, M.D.C. and DeNicolo, C.P. (2011) Challenging majoritarian tales: Portraits of bilingual teachers deconstructing deficit views of bilingual learners. *Bilingual Research Journal* 34 (3), 279–300.

Hunter, M. (2016) Colorism in the classroom: How skin tone stratifies African American and Latina/o students. *Theory into Practice* 55 (1), 54–61.

Johnson, G. (2001) Teacher reflection narratives: A poststructural approach. *Journal of Education for Teaching* 27 (2), 199–200.

Kambutu, J., Rios, F. and Castañeda, C. (2009) Stories deep within: Narratives of US teachers of color from Diasporic settings. *Diaspora, Indigenous, and Minority Education* 3 (2), 96–109.

Kohli, R. (2008) Breaking the cycle of racism in the classroom: Critical race reflections from future teachers of color. *Teacher Education Quarterly* 35 (4), 177–188.

Kohli, R. (2009) Critical race reflections: Valuing the experiences of teachers of color in teacher education. *Race Ethnicity and Education* 12 (2), 235–251.

Lynn, M. and Parker, L. (2006) Critical race studies in education: Examining a decade of research on U.S. schools. *The Urban Review* 38 (4), 257–290.

Maramba, D.C. (2013) Family and educational environments: Contexts and counter stories of Filipino Americans. In R. Endo and X.L. Rong (eds) *Educating Asian Americans: Achievement, Schooling, and Identities* (pp. 205–231). Charlotte, NC: IAP.

Matsuda, M.J. (1991) Voices of America: Accent, antidiscrimination law, and a jurisprudence for the last reconstruction. *Yale Law Journal* 100, 1329–1407.

Milner IV, H.R. and Howard, T.C. (2013) Counter-narrative as method: Race, policy and research for teacher education. *Race Ethnicity and Education* 16 (4), 536–561.

Morgan, B. (2004) Teacher identity as pedagogy: Towards a field-internal conceptualisation in bilingual and second language education. *International Journal of Bilingual Education and Bilingualism* 7 (2-3), 172–188.

Olumide. Y.M. (2016) *The Vanishing Black African Woman: A Compendium of the Global Skin-lightening Practice*. Bamenda: Langaa Research and Publishing CIG.

Rosa, J.D. (2016) Standardization, racialization, languagelessness: Raciolinguistic ideologies across communicative contexts. *Journal of Linguistic Anthropology* 26 (2), 162–183.

Roy, L. and Roxas, K. (2011) Whose deficit is this anyhow? Exploring counter-stories of Somali Bantu refugees' experiences in 'doing school.' *Harvard Educational Review* 81 (3), 521–542.

Settlage, J. (2011) Counterstories from White mainstream preservice teachers: Resisting the master narrative of deficit by default. *Cultural Studies of Science Education* 6 (4), 803–836.

Solórzano, D.G. (1997) Images and words that wound: Critical race theory, racial stereotyping, and teacher education. *Teacher Education Quarterly* 24 (3), 5–19.

Solórzano, D.G. (2019) Toward a critical race theory for teacher education. In P.M. Jenlink (ed.) *Teacher Preparation at the Intersection of Race and Poverty in Today's Schools* (pp. 107–112). Lanham, MD: Rowman & Littlefield.

Solórzano, D.G. and Yosso, T.J. (2002) Critical race methodology: Counter-storytelling as an analytical framework for education research. *Qualitative Inquiry* 8 (1), 23–44.

Trucios-Haynes, E. (2000) Why race matters: LatCrit theory and Latina/o racial identity. *Berkeley La Raza Law Journal* 12 (1), 1–42.

Urciuoli, B. (2013) *Exposing Prejudice: Puerto Rican Experiences of Language, Race, and Class*. Long Grove, IL: Waveland Press.

US Census Bureau (2010) See https://www.census.gov/

Valdes, F. (2005) Legal reform and social justice: An introduction to LatCrit theory, praxis and community. *Griffith Law Review* 14 (2), 148–173.

Yosso, T.J. (2005) Whose culture has capital? A critical race theory discussion of community cultural wealth. *Race Ethnicity and Education* 8 (1), 69–91.

Yosso, T.J. (2006) *Critical Race Counterstories along the Chicana/Chicano Educational Pipeline*. New York: Routledge.

Part 2

Resisting and Reworking Traditional World Language Teacher Preparation

7 'The World' Language Education: New Frontiers for Critical Reflection

Terry Osborn

Introduction

In the last decades we have seen growth in how world language instructors at elementary, secondary and tertiary levels are embedding issues related to social justice and critical pedagogy into their curriculum and instruction (see Reagan & Osborn, 2021). Germane to this growth, critical reflection is necessary in a world language classroom oriented toward teaching for social justice and critical pedagogy because it requires teachers and students alike to examine and deconstruct the curriculum, instruction and evaluation in the context in which their work takes place, among other aspects (Osborn, 2005). As we engage in these activities, we are better equipped to challenge those facets that act as impediments to social justice.

The field of world language education is advancing quickly in a variety of ways relative to teaching for social justice and related topics. García *et al.* (2017), for example, have looked at the implications of translanguaging in education and on educational practice. In fact, some have gone so far to suggest that even the constructs of first language (L1) and second language (L2) must be critically questioned which, in turn, provides the impetus for a reconceptualization of world language education. Further, scholars utilizing the approaches of raciolinguistics are examining the interrelationship(s) of language and race (see, for example, Alim *et al.*, 2016). As we see advances in these domains, continuing to evaluate other areas of importance is crucial for the continued development of teacher education in a way that prepares language instructors to teach for social justice, human rights, and to disrupt discrimination. In this chapter, I argue for the inclusion of discussion and debate about colonialism and empire, capitalism and globalization as necessary foci in developing a critical awareness in the preparation of future language educators.

Colonialism

Students and teachers alike typically enter the language classroom with mistaken beliefs related to prescriptive approaches to language study. It tends to be assumed that the language of the teacher and the textbook must be 'correct.' Hence, any alternative language use – whether simply a mistake by a student or the use of a form drawn from a non-dominant variety of the target language – is by definition erroneous and incorrect. Such a view is problematic in two ways. First, when a learner makes an error in the language classroom, this is not necessarily a bad thing. It is by making errors, in fact, that much valuable learning takes place. Errors, properly understood and utilized, can be powerful building blocks for language learning. Further, from the perspective of linguistics, it is generally accepted that the scientific function of the study of a language (and of the use of the language by native speakers) is descriptive rather than prescriptive in nature. In other words, language stands as no more a *pre*scribed phenomenon than a *de*scribed one. In essence, this is a question of authority, that is, who *owns* the language and can determine what is acceptable usage? Do the academics and publishers through their dictionaries and writings make that determination, or do everyday speakers through their use of the language? Language is a constantly evolving phenomenon and, as a result, these multiple forms should be described in a language curriculum in a manner reflecting respect for each. As Donaldo Macedo (2019: 11) observes:

> the inability of most educators to defetish-ize methods and re-historicize the imperialistic desires that give rise to the totalization of the object of knowledge that we call 'language' presents another difficult and ongoing challenge for these language programs – a challenge that results in ideologically making the standard colonial language distinct from its inevitable varieties ... [employing labels] that are socially created by the dominant ruling class with the mere intent to create an ideological distinction so as to devalue, dismiss and dehumanize.

In ancient times, many believed that civilization could only flourish under Greco-Roman rule and that its language learning and literature were superior in nature and, therefore, learning the languages and literatures of these civilizations was a necessary prerequisite to becoming an educated person. When one considers the role of language diversity in terms of contemporary world language education, the same ideology of power can be seen, because such an ideology defines empire (Cannadine, 2001; Howe, 2002a, 2002b; Said, 1979). Any drive for linguistic homogeneity in such a context extends not only intra-linguistically, but inter-linguistically as well. Ratner-Rosenhagen (2019) has argued that in the earliest days of colonizing the Americas, for instance, in order for *translatio imperii*, a giant imperial history to carry forward, the 1000 to 2000 distinct linguistic communities in the settled America would need to be addressed as this diversity was overwhelming to the imperialistic European settlers. As Young (2003: 2) points out, 'Colonial and imperial rule was legitimized by anthropological theories which increasingly portrayed the peoples of the colonized world as inferior, childlike, or feminine, incapable of looking after themselves ... and requiring paternal rule ... for their best interests' (see also Young, 2001). In essence, within the context of language teacher education and language teaching, the ideologies seen in imperialism and colonialism continue to impact the way in which we conceptualize language and language education (see Shin & Kubota, 2008).

In other words, going forward, language teacher education faces the challenge of contextualizing the language(s) being taught within the ideological frameworks related to empire and colonialism. Teacher candidates must understand from the outset that the ascribed value placed on one language form or forms is ideological in nature.

Osborn (2006) argued that a set of primarily positivist assumptions drives language study in ways reflecting a similar ideological system, noting the beliefs that:

(1) Language can be presented as an 'objective' reality.
(2) The language user can be meaningfully separated from the language.
(3) Generalizations and observations regarding language teaching can be presented free from situational and temporal constraints.
(4) Learning to teach a language is or can be a value-free (technicist) process. (Osborn, 2006: para 2)

These assumptions both reinforce, and are reinforced by, ideologies that see one form of language as inherently superior, whether Castilian Spanish, *Hochdeutsch*, Tuscan Italian, and so on, while reinforcing notions of other language varieties as inferior. The ideology that such distinctions are neutral and natural often reflects what has deemed linguistic legitimacy. A critically reflective practice, or praxis, would suggest that such assumptions are clearly antithetical to the goals of a social-justice or democratic orientation in the world language classroom.

We must recognize that language should not be presented as an 'objective' reality, meaning we must intentionally lead reflection, both in ourselves and our students, as to the subjective nature of language knowledge in all language varieties. Since one who uses a language cannot be meaningfully separated from the language itself, our approach to language authority should be descriptive, and even more, we should argue that all rule-governed varieties are held equal in the classroom. This assertion will almost certainly require a change for many language teachers in practice.

In a similar vein, generalizations and observations regarding language teaching should not be presented free from situational and temporal constraints. This suggests that a powerful focus of language educator preparation needs to include a thorough historical perspective of language teaching – not merely a history of language methodology. Rather, what is required as a focus in the preparation of future language teachers is an understanding of the historical contexts in which language teaching has happened, and how historical events shaped language teaching. Future language educators should be familiar with the contexts of our work, which can be achieved by teacher educators centering critical questions such as the following:

(1) When German education was eyed with suspicion in the early decades of the 20th century, which other language professionals presented themselves as a more palatable option?
(2) Why have Japanese, Arabic, Mandarin and Russian historically been added to the high school curriculum? Are these languages viewed differently (by students and by policy makers), and if so, why?
(3) The speakers of which non-English languages have been put into detainment camps in the US and why?
(4) Language discrimination often acts as a surrogate for which other forms of discrimination?

It should be clear to the critically reflective language educator that learning to teach a language is not and cannot be a value-free (technicist) process. Learning a language, at least in a critical manner, requires both teachers and students to critically examine their own mindsets, including attention to greater social, political, historical, economic and ideological contexts. Therefore, in order for language teachers to be equipped to evaluate their work and to be prepared to teach in a way that disrupts discrimination, one important feature of their preparation would be in understanding the processes of colonialism and empire.

Capitalism

A second area demanding further reflection by language teachers is capitalism. One certainly could argue that conceptualizing language curriculum as a vehicle for practicing skills necessary for expanding resource bases and commodity exchange is also reflective of imperial and colonial mindsets, but in this section, I will focus on another aspect of these phenomena. In order to support capitalism, there is an ever-increasing need for exchanges, even if linguistic in nature, to reflect a by-product of consumerism. Smith (2018) explains this with respect to what we find in common world language textbooks: 'Apparently amid the images of happy consumption, no one in the target culture was poor, marginalized, or suffering. The images and words selected for the textbook use implied that normal people, whether at home or abroad, shop a lot, go on foreign vacations, and enjoy horse riding' (2018: 46).

Capitalism should be understood as a multifaceted *-ism* that is not static. It has shifting political, economic, sociocultural, managerial, regulatory and international facets for reflection and consideration. In its American iteration, therefore, it is understandable that there are unique aspects that are not always visible in other capitalist systems. Within the US, for example, capitalism in the form of innovation in financial products tends to predominate and some multinational companies have budgets higher than the gross domestic product of many nation-states (Fulcher, 2015; Steger, 2003).

Yet, capitalism assuredly requires the expansion of markets to continue to grow a wealth of resources. Thorsten Veblen (cited in Ratner-Rosenhagen, 2019: 89–90) asserted that during the Victorian Age in the late 19th century, America permitted a leisure class to exempt themselves from work and to live off the fruits of others (see also Schlereth, 1991). Ratner-Rosenhagen argues that the creep of markets into all facets of life in America prompted the middle class to idealize Victorian culture to protect a democratic culture threatened in part by the rude and decrepit poor. John Hobson argued that imperialism was linked to new fields of investment and Lenin's analysis was that imperialism *was* monopolistic capitalism (see Howe, 2002a: 24), the end of free market competition. Fulcher (2015) ties the expanding markets with an important feature of protecting one's own resources from competitors.

In the context of world language classrooms we are only beginning to unearth the relics of such mindsets. Reflecting on Smith (2018) above, how many instructional activities have been shaped around a world that has in turn been shaped by capitalism, consumerism, competition and the like? In a broader context, how many curricular choices reflect a greater capitalist context? Did we offer Japanese language learning in the 1980s due to expanding competition from Japanese automakers and electronics producers? Are the increases in Mandarin offerings primarily tied to political, economic and national defense interests? Even the simple information gap activity, where one speaking partner attempts to communicate knowledge that a second partner lacks, has echoes of the admittedly exchange-related nature of language.

The importance of exploring such approaches to world language education can be understood from an observation by Spring (2004), who notes:

> Nation-states and global institutions such as the World Bank share an interest in creating an industrial and consumerist paradigm in students' minds for interpreting world events. When, in strong nation-states like Singapore and the United States, government officials refer to attacks on the nation's 'way of life', they are usually referring to attacks on the ability of people to work for the consumption of goods. The industrial and consumerist paradigm results in students' evaluating world events according to their effect on economic growth and the equal opportunity to consume. The hidden curriculum of schools is the imparting to students an industrial and consumerist paradigm. (2004: 165)

It is not difficult to find capitalist echoes in the world language class-rooms of today. Students are engaged in linguistic transactions that only thinly, if at all, veil an ideology reflecting capitalism and capitalist concerns. Students learn to shop and to travel (the hospitality industry itself is a significant economic force, of course). These topics are part of being human, perhaps, but so are love, hate, grief, joy, pain, healing, doubt, fear, courage and outrage. Labor movements and worker/management relations, important features of society as well, are almost universally ignored in our curricula. Indeed, virtually none of these is discussed in the typical day of a world language classroom.

Spring (2004) contrasts the consumerist approach with a human rights and environmental approach in which activist citizens advocate and evaluate world events in light of their effects on human rights or the biosphere, respectively. Obviously, there would need to be a balance struck between proficiency in language skills and a depth of understanding about languages, a balance that is indubitably one of the more important challenges we face today (see Osborn, 2018). In a world language classroom, therefore, it will be important to plan for objectives that are related to language acquisition concomitant with content that empowers activism. One might, for example, discuss homelessness at the same time one teaches vocabulary on houses, rooms, and so on. World language educators who perceive and reflect critically on the influences of capitalism in the world language classroom would be better prepared to deconstruct its influences in curriculum, instruction and evaluation within and beyond the classroom.

Globalization

Globalization is defined by Steger (2003: 13) as: 'a multidimensional set of social processes that create, multiply, stretch, and intensify worldwide social interdependencies and exchanges while at the same time fostering in people a growing awareness of deepening connections between the local and the distant'. When defined in this way, the fundamental concept hardly seems negative – in fact, it could be used as a definition in support for language study. However, if we tweak this definition only slightly after critically reflecting on its components, we might well decide that the following is perhaps a more accurate reading:

> Globalization is an ideologically-proscribed set of inequitable social processes that reinforce worldwide social interdependencies and inequitable exchanges while at the same time fostering in people a growing false consciousness of deepening connections between the local and the distant, connections that ultimately benefit certain parties at a much greater level than others.

When viewed through a critical lens, it is important to note that globalization is neither a neutral nor natural process – it is inherently value-laden and based on relationships of power and is well suited to life in a world dominated by capitalist relations and forms of production.

Globalization takes many forms that are obviously well beyond the purview of this chapter. However, the impacts on language have been well noted by researchers at the University of Hawaii Globalization Research Center. Two of these, in particular, merit our attention here. First, the declining number of languages in the world suggests that globalization has a homogenizing impact on language diversity and, second, that language learning and tourism spreads language beyond national and/or cultural boundaries (Steger, 2003). In the case of both, the phenomena that result from language contact is the purview of experts in contact linguistics.

Related to the impact of globalization in the world language classroom is the concept of foreignness (Osborn, 2005). In the course of the history of the US, this bifurcation between what counts as 'foreign' and what is considered to be 'not-foreign' has played itself out in terms of language, national origin, and religion, among others. The foreignness agenda (see Osborn, 2005) present in world language classrooms includes three features of relevance to our discussion of globalization: geographic fragmentation, English language/American synonymy and paternalistic empowerment.

The logic of geographic fragmentation refers to the idea that there is a natural correspondence between a particular language and one or more particular nation-states. In essence, it asks us to assume that language x is spoken in nation-state y, and furthermore, that learning about y is a necessary part of the knowledge base of learning language x. Often, but not always, this is based on the declaration of language x as the official language of y, meaning that x is used for official political, judicial, educational, commercial and media purposes in nation-state y. Although this conceptualization does have certain uses, it is also very problematic in many settings. The notion of the nation-state, after all, is historically very much a European one. In addition, many former colonial languages continue to have official or semi-official status in their post-independence former colonies, even when the majority of citizens of these countries speak only local languages. There is also the challenge of the native speaker of a language other than x who resides within (and is a native of) nation-state y. Are they part of the 'x-speaking world'? And is such a person considered to be a member of the nation-state in which they reside, irrespective of the language that they speak?

A different, but equally complex, problem is found in the presentation of the place of languages other than English in the US in world language curricula. When speaking of the *mundo hispánico* or the French-speaking world, maps will depict entire nations (usually those with an official language) as speaking a particular language. These images include and are juxtaposed with the US, which is commonly divided into individual states and having specific states highlighted as areas in which the target language is spoken. Louisiana is often shown as (at least to some extent) French-speaking, while states such as Texas, Arizona, Florida and so on, are shown as Spanish-speaking. It is important to note that these depictions do not necessarily reflect any official language status in US states.

Neither Texas nor Louisiana has an official language, while both Arizona and Florida recognize English as their official language. Louisiana is actually a somewhat special case, because although it does not officially recognize French, French has had a special status in the state since 1968 through the Council for the Development of French in Louisiana:

> CODOFIL est le Conseil pour le développement du Français en Louisiane. Comme l'agence francophone de l'état, notre but est de supporter et d'augmenter les communautés françaises de la Louisiane avec des bourses, l'éducation en français, et d'autres programmes.

> [CODOFIL is the Council for the Development of French in Louisiana. As the French-speaking agency of the state, our goal is to support and increase the French communities of Louisiana with scholarships, education in French, and other programs.] (Office of Cultural Development, 2019: para. 1)

Auténtico 1, a widely used introductory-level Spanish textbook, which comes in a special Texas edition, describes a birthday party (*una fiesta de cumpleaños*) in which the 'Country Connections: Explorar el mundo hispano' map shows the following areas highlighted as parts of the Spanish-speaking world: España, República Dominicana, México, California and Texas (Boyles *et al.*, 2018a). Not only is this problematic in its conflation of different Hispanic traditions in particular settings (Mexican-Americans and Guatemalans in Los Angeles may well celebrate birthdays in quite different ways), but it is also flawed since it may lead one to wonder about the person celebrating a birthday in Spanish, for example in Florida, Maine or Nebraska. Does such a person even have a connection to the Spanish-speaking world? Or, are such individuals, as it were, foreigners in their own communities? Such is the ideology of foreignness.

Auténtico 1 presents a similar image with its treatment of housing choices. In this case, the country connections are to España, Venezuela, Chile, Panamá and Arizona (Boyles *et al.*, 2018a). Again, the ideology of foreignness is evident as it is suggested that housing is a relatively united matter elsewhere; only in the US does one find a collection of many smaller entities in which certain behaviors and situations are likely to be found. In *Liaisons: An Introduction to French*, a similar situation presents itself where a map including New England and Louisiana depicts the world as including the highlighted areas of le Maine, le New-Hampshire, le Massachusetts, le Rhode Island, le Connecticut and la Louisiane, in addition to other territories or countries (Wong *et al.*, 2016).

There are, however, signs of progress since my work on this topic (Osborn, 2000) first appeared. For instance, in *Cuadros: Introductory Spanish* (Spaine Long *et al.*, 2012), there is a recognition of the diversity throughout the Americas and beyond as the authors affirm that they 'strive to present the Spanish-speaking world in all its diversity, with particular attention to indigenous and African-Hispanic populations, as well as European and Latin American immigrant populations' (2012: iii). Spanglish is also addressed thoughtfully in the text. It is important to both reflect on and challenge elements of geographic fragmentation in the world language classroom. To fail to do so is to leave students with an understanding of a linguistic identity that is necessarily tied to particular countries in ways that go beyond official business and even law. It positions Others outside those fragmented zones and within a realm of foreignness and as such can ideologically deprive those speakers of their rightful status within their own communities, within and beyond a particular nation-state, or within their state of residence.

A second element of the foreignness agenda is the treatment of the English language and the identity marker 'American' as synonymous (see Osborn, 2005). In this way, there is a normalizing of monolingualism and so-called melting pot mentalities, coupled with a reflection of the pressure placed on those who migrate to the US to do so at the expense of assimilation, giving up their own linguistic, cultural and national identities. Surprisingly, this feature is still regularly found in world language textbooks, as in the following example:

> Social relations are somewhat more formal in Spanish-speaking countries than in the United States. New acquaintances usually greet one another with a handshake. Friends, however, greet each other with a hug or a kiss on the cheek. How does this compare with the way you greet people in the United States? (Quoted in Boyles *et al.*, 2018b)

To be technically accurate, it is likely that social relationships may be more formal in Spanish-speaking cultures than in English-speaking ones, particularly in the US, but it is certainly not the case that the US is not a Spanish-speaking country. Indeed, many texts proclaim the US as one of the largest Spanish-speaking countries in the world. However, a conflation of linguistic and national identities marks the English language/American synonymy and contributes to an overall perception of foreignness. Reflecting on, exposing and challenging this type of logic in the world language classroom is important . Further, positioning a speaker of Spanish, for example, as a 'foreigner' in a US Spanish class is an inevitably troubling blow to any ideal of intercultural competence, democratic education or celebration of diversity that we might claim to support.

Finally, there is the very real risk of a false form of what is actually paternalistic empowerment in which speakers of English are enticed to learn a second language because of the allegedly positive impacts it will have on their use of their own native language (Osborn, 2005). Regrettably, these features are also still prominent in some discourse related to language learning almost to an absurd level. One language learning advocacy website puts it this way:

> It's rewarding to learn Spanish and help someone learn English. Let's face it, English is the language of the business world. In countries like Spain, English is seen as crucial for better work opportunities. You can help! Helping someone makes you feel good. Even if you only have a basic conversational level of Spanish you can find language exchanges and help someone grow their English while they help you grow your Spanish. I don't want to get too deep on you in this article. I was never [planning] on bringing up questions about the meaning of life. But if we aren't here to help others, what are we here for? (Barr, 2015: 5)

Though I am certainly an advocate for learning other languages, and to increasing the time and effort devoted to it, such a position is profoundly insulting on a number of grounds: it is paternalistic, it exhibits linguistic imperialism and, ultimately, it takes the hegemony of English both in the world and in our society as a given and does so uncritically and unreflectively. In essence, it positions the speakers of Spanish as in need of assistance from the speakers of English in ways that are reminiscent of the 'altruism' regarding language and culture of empires of the past.

In the world language classroom, it is important to reflect on the fact that by learning another language, our goal is not to make life better for those supposedly abject speakers of that language by assisting them to learn English. Instead, language learning must become a political act by which one can, alongside others, disrupt the very conditions that seek to privilege speakers of one language above others. Such disruption can only take place as part of changes with respect to how world language teaching is often manifested in classroom practice.

The impacts of globalization on language teaching and learning are indeed much more than making us a smaller 'global community.' Critical reflection by world language educators should provide opportunities to engage in the ideologies of globalization and the ways in which foreignness remains a feature of world language teaching and learning in the US. Through such examinations, world language educators will be able to lead students, likewise, to examine assumptions that they themselves may have.

Progress

As discussed above, colonialism, capitalism and globalization create challenges to world language education that need to be deconstructed relative to practices in the classroom and curriculum. We have already witnessed many strides in taking the insights of critical reflection into account in the activities of the world language classroom, among which are inclusion of issues of social justice, the use of theater and literature, and critical reflection on practice. Glynn (2017) suggests images as one source of inspiration for critical reflection in a world language classroom, invoking topics such as women's rights, Islamophobia, feminism, LGBTQ rights, protectionism, immigration, religion, migrant rights and workers' rights. Such complex discussion topics may already be used by teachers in advanced courses. Glynn argues that we should not wait until the most advanced courses to introduce these issues, because they can be very motivational for students at every level. Insightful connections to world language education comprise products, practices and perspectives. Products include access to tangible and intangible resources. Practices include issues that arise from interactions among people. Perspectives relate to the attitudes and values of those engaged in the interactions (see Glynn *et al.*, 2018).

A variety of other approaches have been suggested to push language teaching in a more critical direction. Glynn *et al.* (2018) outline five categories of activities that would involve critical reflection in a world language classroom such as problem-posing, text analysis, and investigations of rights and policies. Wooten and Cahnmann-Taylor (2014) present a critical and performative approach to exploring race relations through the vehicle of the Brazilian playwright, Augusto Boal's (1979, 1995) Forum Theatre and Rainbow of Desire. In part of this pre-service exercise, participants

> identify those stories of recurring struggle that resonate with the group and then to perform, or spect-act, these stories. Boal's term spect-actor breaks the traditional divide between actors and audience, asking all participants – including audience members – to imagine and perform alternative courses of action for the protagonist. Each spect-actor that volunteers changes the story's end, at which point all spect-actors engage in a 'reality check' to determine how realistic the change in action might be in any future context involving the story's 'protagonist' and 'antagonist.' Each rehearsal aims to expand the protagonist's possibilities for alternative courses of action, thus expanding her/his sense of agency and options for future action, leading to an iterative cycle of action and critical reflection. (Wooten & Cahnmann-Taylor, 2014: 184)

Based on their research, Wooten and Cahnmann-Taylor conclude that a theatrical approach to teacher preparation might deepen critical language awareness for pre-service world language educators and provide examples of a more critical approach.

Kashuba (2017) sees literature as a basis for one approach to teaching for social justice, arguing that:

> Teachers can choose materials from theory to poetry, from revolutionary documents to song, from the Middle Ages to the twenty-first century. This essay proposes pertinent examples and indicates practical applications. The texts show that many problems are global and deeply rooted in human society. They touch upon questions of justice, immigration, and

undocumented immigrants. They offer peaceful solutions to national and international disputes, and emphasize human rights and individual freedom. (Kashuba, 2017: 74)

Cardetti *et al.* (2015) report on a project to integrate intercultural competence and social justice theory into an interdisciplinary unit in mathematics, world languages and social studies. In so doing, they draw among other sources from Kramsch's (2011) work, including the observation that:

> If intercultural competence is the ability to reflect critically or analytically on the symbolic systems we use to make meaning, we are led to reinterpret the learning of foreign languages as not gaining a mode of communication across cultures, but more as acquiring a symbolic mentality that grants as much importance to subjectivity and the historicity of experience as to the social conventions and the cultural expectations of any one stable community of speakers. (2011: 365)

Byram and Wagner (2018: 147–148) draw this connection explicitly:

> There are important parallels between fostering social justice and developing intercultural citizenship. Both concepts promote criticality in that educators enable students to reflect critically on language, discourse, and culture with regard to power and inequality. In both approaches, educators foster students' engagement with important societal issues by applying the skills of intercultural competence, which allow them to make critical judgments based on specific evidence.

Coda (2018) explores ways in which queer theory can be utilized to explore heteronormativity in the world language classroom, in a practice he refers to as queering the world language classroom. Meredith *et al.* (2018) document the use of fairy tales in beginning language classrooms as one avenue of introducing topics requiring critical reflection. Vázquez and Wright (2018) developed an approach for partnering with museums in search for meaningful community dialogues. Caballero-García (2018) offers suggestions on using thematic units to move students from understanding the complexity of our linguistically diverse world to taking action based on their new insights. Finally, Oppewal and Wooten (2018) describe how they critically reflected on units regarding food and housing in the language classroom.

In each of these examples, there are possible approaches to deconstruct the influences of colonialism, capitalism and globalization in world language education. For example, carefully selected literature as reported by Meredith *et al.* (2018) or Kashuba (2017) touch on the themes of colonialism, capitalism or globalization in ways that could be a springboard for discussion in both the 'native' and 'target' languages. Interdisciplinary or thematic units such as those reported by Cardetti *et al.* (2015) and Oppewal and Wooten (2018), or as suggested by Caballero-García (2018), can likewise integrate the themes of colonialism, capitalism or globalization.

Conclusion

In this chapter, I have argued that critical reflection is necessary for teaching world languages for social justice and within a critical pedagogy framework, because we must examine the context in which our work takes place and how the ideological struggles of our context make their way into the classroom as curriculum, instruction and evaluation. I have pointed to the areas of colonialism, capitalism and globalization which create a next frontier for critical reflection. Teachers can advance critical reflection with their own students as they continue the journey for social justice. As teacher practices shift toward deconstruction in these areas, teacher education likewise will benefit from an analysis of these same elements. As we do so, we are better equipped to challenge those facets that act as impediments to social justice.

In echoing this call, and despite all the advances in critical reflection on and in world language education, Randolph and Johnson (2017) appropriately point to continued work needed in the field, including service learning, classroom climate, curriculum development, faculty development and action research. They offer teachers a call to action reflecting the theme of social justice, which of necessity will involve critical reflection:

> Above all, the most important way we can contribute to the current movement of social justice in language education is in our own teaching. In our classrooms, taking one small step at a time, we have the opportunity to share with our students that the world is bigger, more complex, and more beautiful than they know. There are real challenges, but there are also groups of people who choose to work together to address those challenges. There is no better place than a language classroom to explore how to communicate across differences and work together to solve real problems. We leave you now with a call to action: Take small thoughtful steps to promote social justice in your classroom; bring students, community members, and colleagues along as partners in your work; and report back to the community of language teachers. (Randolph & Johnson, 2017: 118)

Indeed, this call sums up the challenge for pre-service and in-service world language educators in embedding issues, understandings or content related to social justice. It points as well to the 'small, thoughtful steps' in a new direction that critical reflection in the field needs to take.

Discussion Questions

(1) How does the author suggest that critical reflection on world language education should examine 'new frontiers'?
(2) What are some additional examples of geographic fragmentation or English language/American synonymy you have encountered in world language education textbooks?

(3) Do you agree with the author's assertion that 'The impacts of global-ization on language teaching and learning are indeed much more than making us a smaller "global community"?' Why or why not?

Acknowledgments

I am grateful to the editors and Timothy Reagan for helpful critiques of this chapter.

References

Alim, H.S., Rickford, J.R. and Ball, A.F. (eds) (2016) *Raciolinguistics: How Language Shapes Our Ideas about Race*. New York: Oxford University Press.

Barr, A. (2015) 25 reasons why English natives should learn Spanish. *Real Fast Spanish*. See https://www.realfastspanish.com/motivation/25-reasons-learn-spanish#more-2096

Boal, A. (1979) *Theatre of the Oppressed*. London: Pluto Press.

Boal, A. (1995) *The Rainbow of Desire: The Boal Method of Theatre and Therapy*. New York: Routledge.

Boyles, P., Met, M., Sayers, R. and Wagrin, C. (2018a). *Auténtico*. London: Saavas Learning Co.

Boyles, P., Met, M., Sayers, R. and Wagrin, C. (2018b). *Auténtico*. London: Saavas Learning Co.

Byram, M. and Wagner, M. (2018) Making a difference: Language teaching for intercul-tural and international dialogue. *Foreign Language Annals* 51 (1), 140–151.

Caballero-García, B. (2018) Promoting social justice through 21st century skills: Thematic units in the language classroom. *Dimension* 2018, 130–145. See https://files.eric.ed.gov/fulltext/EJ1207916.pdf

Cannadine, D. (2001) *Ornamentalism: How the British Saw Their Empire*. Oxford: Oxford University Press.

Cardetti, F., Wagner, M. and Byram, M. (2015) Interdisciplinary collaboration to develop intercultural competence by integrating math, languages, and social studies. *NERA Conference Proceedings 2015* (7). See https://opencommons.uconn.edu/nera-2015/7

Coda, J. (2018) Disrupting standard practice: Queering the world language classroom. *Dimension* 2018, 74–89. See https://eric.ed.gov/?id=EJ1207908

Fulcher, J. (2015) *Capitalism: A Very Short Introduction*. Oxford: Oxford University Press.

García, O., Johnson, S. and Seltzer, K. (2017) *The Translanguaging Classroom: Leveraging Student Bilingualism for Learning*. Philadelphia, PA: Caslon.

Glynn, C. (2017) Social justice in the world languages classroom [video file]. YouTube, 7 December. See https://www.youtube.com/watch?v=2Hc-xAory-I&feature=youtu.be

Glynn, C., Wesely, P. and Wassell, B. (2018) *Words and Actions: Teaching Languages through the Lens of Social Justice* (2nd edn). Alexandria, VA: ACTFL.

Howe, S. (2002a) *Empire: A Very Short Introduction*. Oxford: Oxford University Press.

Howe, S. (2002b) *Ireland and Empire: Colonial Legacies in Irish History and Culture*. Oxford: Oxford University Press.

Kashuba, M.H. (2017) Global citizenship: The literary connection. *NECTFL Review* 79, 73–88.

Kramsch, C. (2011) The symbolic dimensions of the intercultural. *Language Teaching* 44 (3), 354–367. https://doi.org/10.1017/S0261444810000431

Macedo, D. (2019) Rupturing the yoke of colonialism in foreign language education. In D. Macedo (ed.) *Decolonizing Foreign Language Education: The Misteaching of English and Other Colonial Languages* (pp. 1–49). New York: Routledge.

Meredith, B., Geyer, M. and Wagner, M. (2018) Social justice in beginning language instruction: Interpreting fairy tales. *Dimension* 2018, 90–112. See https://eric.ed.gov/?id=EJ1207922

Office of Cultural Development (2019) CODOFIL – Agence Des Affaires Francophones. See https://www.crt.state.la.us/cultural-development/codofil/

Oppewal, A. and Wooten J. (2018) Thematic units and social justice with Anneke Oppewal and Jennifer Wooten [audio podcast]. *We Teach Languages*, 23 March. https://weteachlang.com/2018/03/23/ep-45-with-anneke-oppewal-and-jennifer-wooten/.

Osborn, T.A. (2000) *Critical Reflection and the Foreign Language Classroom*. Santa Barbara, CA: Greenwood Publishing Group.

Osborn, T.A. (2005) *Critical Reflection and the Foreign Language Classroom* (revised edn). Charlotte, NC: Information Age Publishing.

Osborn, T.A. (2006) *Teaching World Languages for Social Justice: A Sourcebook of Principles and Practices*. Mahwah, NJ: Lawrence Erlbaum Associates.

Osborn, T.A. (2018) Foreword. In C. Glynn, P. Wesely and B. Wassell *Words and Actions: Teaching Languages through the Lens of Social Justice* (2nd edn). Alexandria, VA: ACTFL.

Randolph, L.J. and Johnson, S.M. (2017) Social justice in the language classroom: A call to action. *Dimension*, 99–121. See https://eric.ed.gov/?id=EJ1207903

Ratner-Rosenhagen, J. (2019) *The Ideas That Made America: A Brief History*. Oxford: Oxford University Press.

Reagan, T. and Osborn, T.A. (2021) *World Language Education as Critical Pedagogy: The Promise of Social Justice*. New York: Routledge.

Said, E.W. (1979) *Orientalism*. New York: Random House.

Schlereth, T. (1991) *Victorian America: Transformations in Everyday Life, 1876–1915*. New York: Harper Perennial.

Shin, H. and Kubota, R. (2008) Postcolonialism and globalization in language education. In B. Spolsky and F.M. Hult (eds) *The Handbook of Educational Linguistics* (pp. 206–219). Malden, MA: Blackwell.

Smith, D.I. (2018) *On Christian Teaching: Practicing Faith in the Classroom*. Grand Rapids, MI: Eerdmans.

Spaine Long, S., Carreira, M., Madrigal Velasco, S. and Swanson, K. (2012) *Cuadros: Introductory Spanish*. Boston, MA: Cengage Learning.

Spring, J. (2004) *How Educational Ideologies are Shaping Global Society: Intergovernmental Organizations, NGOs, and the Decline of the Nation-state*. Mahwah, NJ: Lawrence Erlbaum Associates.

Steger, M.B. (2003) *Globalization: A Very Short Introduction*. Oxford: Oxford University Press.

Vázquez, K.E. and Wright, M. (2018) Making visible the invisible: Social justice and inclusion through the collaboration of museums and Spanish community-based learning projects. *Dimension* 2018, 113–129. See https://files.eric.ed.gov/fulltext/EJ1207917.pdf

Wong, W., Weber-Fève, S., Ousselin, E. and VanPatten, B. (2016) *Liaisons: An Introduction to French* (2nd edn). Boston, MA: Cengage Learning.

Wooten, J. and Cahnmann-Taylor, M. (2014) Black, white, and rainbow [of desire]: The colour of race-talk of pre-service world language educators in Boalian theater workshops. *Pedagogies: An International Journal* 9 (3), 179–205. https://doi.org/10.1080/1554480X.2014.924005

Young, R.J.C. (2001) *Postcolonialism: An Historical Introduction*. Malden, MA: Blackwell.

Young, R.J.C. (2003) *Postcolonialism: A Very Short Introduction*. Oxford: Oxford University Press.

8 Can Western Armenian Pedagogy be Decolonial? Training Heritage Language Teachers in Social Justice-Based Language Pedagogy

Anke al-Bataineh, Kayane Yoghoutjian and Samuel Chakmakjian

Introduction

In this chapter, we will address the question of teacher education and professional learning with regard to social justice in language education through the lens of an endangered, diasporan language that is taught around the world as a heritage language: Western Armenian. Despite dozens of schools and programs worldwide dedicated to teaching this language, no teacher education program that focuses on *language* pedagogy has been able to survive into recent years. Teachers of Western Armenian have been forced either to study the language from a linguistics or literature standpoint, or study education from a non-language focused standpoint, and then figure out how to optimize their work in teaching the language. Recently, a small group, including some of the authors of this chapter, organized an innovative new program to train teachers, current and future, in Western Armenian (WA) language pedagogy, and set out to embed social justice frameworks into the program. Over the program's first four years, we have encountered a range of barriers and challenges that have made it seem, at times, that social justice pedagogy and heritage language pedagogy might be incompatible. The present authors do not agree that they are, in fact, incompatible, but instead conclude from their experiences and research that for a language teacher training program to embed social justice or, more specifically, decolonial pedagogy, a multi-faceted effort must be made to address deeply-entrenched countervailing forces. The lessons of this experience have direct value for programs which train teachers of other heritage languages. While heritage, minority, indigenous and endangered languages face special challenges and each have their own unique circumstances, the present chapter's findings address more widely applicable challenges in training language teachers in social justice approaches, in such a way that even languages that are not often thought of as 'heritage' languages may experience similar challenges and benefit from similar interventions.

The Context of an Endangered, Diaspora Language

We begin by providing some minimal background on the Western Armenian language, whose context is in ways unique and in ways interconnected with the contexts of all other heritage languages, as well as with so-called 'world' languages, in less direct ways. We put 'world' languages in quotes because languages with fewer speakers are, in our view, just as valuable to their speakers and learners, and often, as in the case of Western Armenian, just as geographically dispersed in their usage, as the official languages of wealthy European, American and Asian states.

Armenian is a distinctive Indo-European language with its own alphabet and highly complex systems of consonant cluster phonemes, vowel diphthongs, seven grammatical cases and considerable diversity in its dialects. Variants of Armenian are classified into two main families, different enough to be considered two languages (Manougian, 2020). While Eastern Armenian is the dominant language in the Republic of Armenia and communities in Iran and Russia, Western Armenian does not benefit from any official state support, but thrives among communities descended from those who inhabited Anatolia until a genocide expelled them in the last days of the Ottoman Empire. Families who survived the mass killings, death marches, starvation and forced religious conversions at the founding of the modern Turkish state mostly took refuge in what later became the states of Lebanon and Syria. While some families fled directly to European or North American countries from Anatolia, many more eventually undertook secondary migrations from the refugee camps of the Levant to Europe, North America, Australia, Latin America and other Arab nations.

Some Western Armenian-medium schools had been established in the Ottoman Empire, but there had also been large numbers of Ottoman Armenians who had adopted the Turkish language and assimilated to local Turkish-dominated culture in other ways. Combatting and reversing these aspects of 'Turkishness' became a matter of collective survival and an essential element of solidarity in a new context. Diasporan schools centered on the teaching of Armenian history and religion and, above all, Western Armenian (WA) language, a campaign known as 're-Armenization.' Within a generation, the Middle Eastern communities were entirely WA-speaking and Turkish was both marginalized and highly stigmatized. Global events soon increased the prevalence of English and French in the Middle East, as well as the number of families who relocated from there to Western countries where those languages dominate, all of which contributed to the decline of WA (al-Bataineh, 2016). In 2010, the language was officially added to UNESCO's list of endangered languages, due to changes in the use of the language among the fourth and fifth generations descended from these founding survivors (Donabédian-Demopoulos & al-Bataineh, 2014; Moseley, 2010).

The US currently has 24 Armenian schools (Karapetian, 2017), which are part of a much larger, global network including many weekend or after-school programs. Traditionally, these schools offer the canonical Euro-American curriculum of mathematics, sciences, literature and history, all focused on Europe and in either French or English, in addition to courses in Armenian language, history, and sometimes religion, from kindergarten through high school graduation. Each school is associated with either a branch of the Armenian Church, or one of the diasporan Armenian political parties.

Since the Armenian diaspora is organized around transnational institutions of either a religious or political nature, cultural activities and materials production are similarly organized (Migliorino, 2008). These organizations are largely based in Beirut, particularly in the Armenian-dominated neighborhood of Bourj Hammoud, and decisions made there about publishing, funding and project development impact communities around the globe. As such, Beirut, and the Lebanese and Syrian communities more generally, are the central, unidirectional vectors of WA learning materials and pedagogy for the global diaspora.[1] Moreover, there is a widespread consensus (Karapetian, 2017) that the teaching of WA is largely failing in its objective to maintain the language's vitality, and teachers in all communities express a sense of despair and isolation when looking at their work in a broader perspective.

An Attempt to Revolutionize WA Language Teacher Training

Context of the program

Several speakers of WA, including a linguist, an applied linguist (al-Bataineh) and a specialist of early childhood education, set out in 2014 to (re)train teachers of an endangered language in order for those teachers to more effectively reverse language shift (the loss of use of a traditional language in favor of a socioeconomically dominant one, cf. Fishman, 2001). This professional development is organized as a certificate program, with courses centered primarily on critical applied linguistics, student-centered pedagogy and communicative language teaching (cf. al-Bataineh, 2019a), all with the aim of creating more engaging and effective Armenian language classrooms in diaspora communities. This graduate-level professional certificate program is still in its early years, and is being actively improved and reworked after each cohort of teacher trainees, in an effort to increase its impact. al-Bataineh is a central organizer of the program and teaches three of its courses, while Yoghoutjian and Chakmakjian have both completed the program as students, and have subsequently taught in its practical setting: an immersion summer camp for WA learners from around the world. This chapter relays a combination of our lived experiences as two lifelong members of the diaspora community and one experienced teacher educator, as well as a wide variety of our research and that of our diasporan colleagues.

The summer camp setting was intentionally imagined and developed in order to counteract the assumptions of power and identity that are endemic to WA language classrooms: there are no textbooks, there are no desks, no one is referred to as a 'teacher', and in fact one of the co-founders talks to trainees about being 'non-teachers' in the learning environment: in WA, *'ch'ousoutsitchner'* (not-teachers) rather than *'ousoutsitchner'* (teachers). Those who come for training are explicitly forbidden from leading camp activities so that they can instead watch and learn from teenagers and non-teachers, and can see for themselves how effective language acquisition is when it happens in a natural, democratic, creative and empowering environment. Teacher trainees observe camp activities and make structured notes, and discuss them with program organizers to help make meaning of what they see. Another especially innovative part of the program is the 'Unknown Language Course,' in which teacher trainees are given a fully immersive course in a language with which they are completely unfamiliar. This was designed because many are native speakers of WA, and they have a hard time appreciating how inscrutable the language is for learners whose first languages are English, French, Arabic, Greek, Turkish, etc. The program's design assumes that empathy building and embodied, lived experiences are as important, or more, than theory courses (cf. Borg, 2011; Donato, 2016; Ferguson & Donno, 2003), and this has been borne out consistently by participant feedback on the program (al-Bataineh, 2019b). The following theoretical framework has informed both the content of the formal courses, as well as the informal structure of the program, which is residential and intensive and therefore involves heavy interaction between instructors and participants outside of classes as well as inside, throughout its four years of operation.

Theoretical framework of the program

Gounari (2014) proposes that rethinking heritage language education through the lens of critical pedagogy necessitates a recognition that assimilation, acculturation and language loss were indeed conscious goals of the national curriculum in the first place; that language loss is neither natural nor inevitable, but intended by the powerful. In short, critical pedagogy for Western Armenian, and for other heritage languages, would fundamentally reject the premise of the capitalist nation-state, whereby anyone choosing or forced to live within an arbitrary territory is economically, if not legally, excluded if they do not submit to the culture and language repertoire prescribed by the most wealthy and powerful residents.

Paris and Alim (2014) describe practical attributes of resistance pedagogy in calling for teachers to move beyond asset pedagogy that focuses on subaltern students gaining access to dominant norms of interaction, and toward pedagogy that questions power imbalances and aims for 'explicitly pluralist outcomes.' Youth cultural and linguistic practices, which often challenge normative paradigms by creating novel and hybrid language patterns, have value in their own right, according to these authors, and in fact have instrumental value in a world in which multilingualism and multiliteracies are rapidly becoming more common than monolingual or monocultural practices. They propose a democratic project of schooling that explicitly endorses cultural pluralism and rejects the dominance of white, middle-class norms, but also overly deterministic representations of race, language, literacy, cultural practice, and their connections. Paris and Alim (2014) amplify Pennycook's (2005) call for pedagogies that 'go with the flow,' scrapping prescriptive legitimacy for the valorization of global linguistic flows (Alim, 2007) and 'ill-literacies' (Alim, 2011). The authors anticipate resistance both from dominant groups and from within subaltern communities, as their model replaces simplistic glorifications of static 'traditions' with critical, student-centered engagement at all levels. We discuss below some ways in which precisely this resistance manifests among WA teachers.

McClaren (2014) proposes a postmodern approach to multilingualism and multiculturalism as part of a 'pedagogy of resistance and transformation.' A postmodern approach recognizes the realities of hybridity, transgressions of boundaries, combinations and influences in lieu of rigid boundaries around concepts and identities. This framework naturally incorporates translanguaging pedagogy (García et al., 2017) and multiliteracies pedagogy (Cope & Kalantzis, 2000). This has been the point of most direct resistance and questioning of legitimacy from participating teachers in the novel program. The 'multiple monolingual' framework is deeply internalized by language leaders in the Armenian diaspora (al-Bataineh, 2015), and hybridity is seen as antithetical to legitimacy. A first shock occurs when a non-native speaker, imperfectly fluent in a highly stigmatized dialect, is introduced as the instructor of the program's core course. While most participants respond politely to this change, older and higher-status participants predictably reject the ideas of hybridity and multilingual practices.

McCarty *et al.* (2009), writing with a focus on US indigenous languages, propose a pedagogy that recognizes youth themselves as language policy makers, and their knowledge of their heritage language, however limited, as a valuable, relevant resource in their lives, and not only as a symbol. Their scholarship specifically addresses the core issue for endangered languages that is almost entirely overlooked in heritage language scholarship and which focuses so narrowly on Spanish in the US and French in Canada: what if transmission has greatly declined or ceased, such that the 'heritage' language and the 'home' language are not synonymous? This is the case for well over half of learners in WA schools. This has a double implication for teachers: they cannot simply elevate the value given to 'home language practices' in their classroom, nor can they rely on creating community-based language learning experiences as a method and motivation for their students. There may be small elements of these principles that can be integrated into their approach, but endangered language teachers have no choice but to work against the tide of certain community language practices. Positioning youth who are learning their language as the policymakers is then a primary available strategy for empowerment of endangered language learners. This is part of McCarty and Lee's (2014) reconceptualization of Paris and Alim's (2014) Culturally Sustaining Pedagogy framework, which the former term 'Critical Culturally Sustaining Pedagogy.'

Based on this reality of declining or irregular intergenerational transmission, Cushing-Leubner *et al.* (2019) perceive a need to prepare heritage language teachers to reimagine 'developmental stages' according to their students' realities, to reverse the pathologizing of their students' multilingualism, to design assessments that measure meaningful skills and not only conformity to prescribed norms. Heritage language teachers must teach heterogeneous learners without excessive friction from imposed curricula, and hold language acquisition to standards that transcend neocolonial objectives. A first step toward this is preparing teachers to question their own identities with regard to prevailing power structures and white supremacy. This immediately raises the questions, for WA teachers, of who should provide this training, and how. Concretely, what right do Western academics like al-Bataineh have to (re)train language teachers in ways that contradict their existing self-perceptions and perceptions of their role? From where can in-group reformers like Chakmakjian and Yoghoutjian draw legitimacy, if not from Western academic sources? These remain open questions and sites of struggle for the present authors.

We offer here our original summary of the preceding theoretical frameworks as together articulating a vision of social justice pedagogy in heritage language contexts. We see an effective, decolonial and social justice teacher education program as having the following minimal attributes:

(1) Recognition of language loss as a result of oppression, and of language maintenance or revitalization as an act of resistance to power.
(2) Democratic systems in which students are empowered throughout their language learning journey, and of which the explicit goal is a pluralist vision of society.
(3) An approach to language norms and practices that is more descriptive than prescriptive and situates the language's users, and especially its young users, as experts in its use.
(4) Embracing transgression of boundaries and hybridity as steps toward pluralism, including hybrid language practices such as translanguaging and multiliteracies.
(5) An approach to proficiency assessment that centers skills in use rather than conformity to prescribed norms.
(6) A fundamental questioning of white supremacy and social dominance of certain cultural and linguistic groups.

Sites of Resistance to Social Justice Pedagogy in the Western Armenian Teacher Community

We will share here some brief summaries of our findings about Western Armenian language pedagogy, drawn from published research by the present authors and our colleagues working in language maintenance in the Armenian diaspora, our personal experiences, informal and formal participant observations, more than 150 interviews about language pedagogy (al-Bataineh, 2015; Donabédian-Demopolous & al-Bataineh, 2014) and dozens of personal communications with other members of the Armenian diaspora community.

Challenges to a decolonial pedagogy

In order to fully understand the challenges of adopting a decolonial pedagogy to train WA teachers, it is important to address the first point of our framework and its underlying premise: that speakers of heritage languages are oppressed by white supremacy and its related power structures in society, and the sixth point, that language acquisition and use are challenges to social dominance and assimilation pressures.

In the US context, Armenians have a long, though contested, history of asserting and benefiting from social Whiteness. The first waves of Armenian immigration to the US were in response to the Hamidian Massacres in 1894–1896, and American Protestant missionaries played a key role in facilitating the Christian Armenians' entry to the US, despite a context of mounting nativism, xenophobia and exclusionary policies, such as the Chinese Exclusion Act. Each subsequent generation of Armenians born in or immigrating to the US has had to confront a central question of identity: how do Armenians fit into the racial paradigm of the US?

> [M]any Armenians in the United States have managed to 'pass' as best they can in the dominant culture, and still remain centrally involved with the Armenian community. On the whole, Armenians in the United States have not suffered intensive economic oppression. To survive, we have shifted our value systems to accommodate capitalist, industrial society by becoming literate in the language of the oppressor. (Boudakian, 1994: 34)

Armenians have largely benefited from their position at the fringe of what American society and institutions recognize as 'Whiteness,' yet the fact that each generation revisits this question is a testament to the community's perpetual racial insecurity. Armenians fought in American courts in 1909 to be considered 'free white persons,' then in 1923, leveraged their Christianity to again claim legal Whiteness in *US v. Cartozian*, but individuals have often contested this communal self-identification, based partly on their own experiences of racism. Boudakian (1994) wrote about feeling more comfortable among women of color than among white women; Okoomian (2002) complicates the Whiteness of Armenians from an emic perspective; and in 2013, two (Western) Armenian UC Berkeley students successfully campaigned to establish the SWANA (Southwest Asian/North African) racial category as distinct from 'white' in the UC system's demographic data. Armenians' categorization as white in the American system is incongruous with the community's collective memory of oppression, but the tenuousness of the community's relationship with Whiteness results in very few conversations about racial awareness, racial justice or racism. 'Although neither Armenia nor Turkey was colonized in the conventional sense, both nations were among the West's many Others. Both were subjected to the Orientalist desire to comprehend, and to secure Western authority over, the differences manifest in their cultures. Both also were profoundly affected by Western Imperialism' (Okoomian, 2002: 216).

Ironically and poignantly for our discussion, one significant way in which Western imperialism affected Armenians was by (re)creating and defining their modern pedagogy. The pedagogy used in the post-genocide refugee communities to re-Armenize survivors and combat cultural disappearance was largely imported from schools founded in the Ottoman Empire by Francophone and Anglophone Christian missionaries. Because the missionaries delivered the curriculum largely in WA, it was seen as belonging to the community, but there has been no study to establish how close or far it was from the pedagogies used by Armenians dating back to the creation of the Armenian alphabet in the fifth century, or earlier. It stands to reason that the missionaries imported their British, American and French curricula and translated them, as they did most places in the world for the purposes of proselytization.

> [T]he Christians who had been living and worshipping as Christians for hundreds of years posed a challenge [to American missionaries] of bringing Christianity to the natives. Since they were already Christian, the darkness that the missionaries had imagined as the prime justification for a mission in Syria (and elsewhere) was contingent on the claim that they were the true disciples of Christ and that Oriental Christianity was not only corrupt but selfish, bigoted and out of touch with the common man. (Makdisi, 1997: 691)

The complicated relationship between Armenian language and structures of oppression reaches back even further. Even in the earliest days of Armenian literacy, the language was a tool for fortifying the dominance of Christian philosophy and suppressing polytheist heritages or monotheist competitors. For centuries, the clergy were the only people who had access to education. Classical Armenian, the language seen as acceptable for speaking to God, was distant from the vernacular dialects, making even comprehension difficult. Since only clergy were trained in writing this inaccessible standard, history books were also authored by them, often focusing on Christianity as the main identity of the Armenian nation (Karakashian, 2016).

The Western Armenian language itself was born of a standardization movement that was Eurocentric in nature. At the beginning of the 19th century, young WA-speaking intellectuals were increasingly traveling to France, Belgium and Germany for education. Upon returning to the Ottoman Empire, this new *intelligentsia* wanted a cultural revolution, and felt that a standardized language in the image of French, German, Italian, etc. was indispensable. Classical Armenian had long fallen out of vernacular use, so dialects were highly diverse and bore a great many contact influences. A concerted effort was made to remove markedly rural features from the standardized variant and to replace loanwords with either neologisms or lexemes from Classical Armenian, which created grammatical irregularities that continue to baffle learners. At the heart of this effort was the Mekhitarist congregation in Venice and Vienna, which embarked on a massive translation of foreign literature to WA and, subsequently, created the first history, language, science and math textbooks in WA. There is thus no clear line between the Western European or Christian imperialist worldview and pedagogical tradition, the purview of those who saw the Armenians, who had been universally Christian for 13 centuries, as 'heathens' and 'pagans' in need of civilizing (Ümit, 2014), and what might be called an indigenous Armenian approach. We see here a paradox that challenges teacher training efforts: a decolonial approach is needed for language maintenance and revitalization to occur, whereby learners and speakers understand the costs of transitioning to English or French as home languages and resist the pressure to do so, but the very idea that there is anything to be decolonized is not readily apparent to many of the language's speakers and teachers.

A curriculum at odds with social justice education and decolonial pedagogy

Practical challenges also exist. Much of teacher training in Lebanese and Armenian universities, and in former, now-defunct institutions dedicated to language teacher training, has focused on preparing teachers to use textbooks, thereby excluding and discouraging teacher-centered or student-centered rethinking of these values or redesign of courses and materials. The content and theoretical framework of textbooks thus has enormous influence over the experiences of WA learners in classrooms around the world. Karapetian (2017) has astutely noted that Armenian language pedagogy is neither aligned to any standards nor organized around objectives. There are, however, strong and consistent themes in textbooks and syllabi used across the diaspora, which Yoghoutjian (2018) has quantified for grade 4–6 textbooks (see Table 8.1).

The textbooks analyzed contained 160 readings (the main modality through which language is taught) and demonstrate what Gulludjian (2014) has dubbed the 'shrine mentality,' wherein nationalist (*azkayin* [≃ ethnic]) ideology is embedded in language instruction without giving opportunities for critical engagement. Gulludjian (2014) points out that this curriculum has the unintended function of relegating Armenian language to the domains of Norms, Symbols, Contemplation, Commemoration, Icons and Hierarchy, while distancing it from everyday, secular and contemporary

Table 8.1 Most prominent themes in Armenian textbooks

Table of percentage of the most repeated themes throughout the 3 volume of the series

Themes	%
Glorification of Ethnic Identity	18.3%
Value/Moral	18.3%
Nature/Animal	11.1%
Culture	10.1%
Friendship	8.3%
Tale	7.8%
Patriarchal Hierarchy	6.7%
Family	6.1%
History	5.0%
Teacher	4.4%
Religious Themes	3.9%

Source: Yoghoutjian, 2018

life. We see that much of this pedagogical paradigm is incompatible with social justice themes of social responsiveness, pluralism, decentralization of power and the embracing of novel and creative uses of language.

Common teacher discourses and practices that are passed down across generations of WA learners and teachers also embody resistance to social justice frameworks. We will summarize these conflicts by contrasting the remaining four tenets of our social justice framework with staple phrases heard in WA classrooms around the world.

Tenet #1: Democratic systems in which students are empowered throughout their language learning journey, and of which the explicit goal is a pluralist vision of society

'*Char es*' [you are bad/naughty]. Armenian pedagogy contains strong moral themes, and teachers generally see themselves playing moral roles in the upbringing of children. As such, one frequently hears teachers refer to children as '*char*' (bad/naughty) and their behaviors (fidgeting, speaking out of turn, writing outside the lines) described in this way. In a decolonial model, students would have ownership over their space and their learning, and would work collaboratively to reach their learning goals. Small behaviors like fidgeting would not be perceived as transgressions, and behaviors that genuinely harm the community or learning environment would be addressed through collaboration and communication and would themselves be opportunities for learning and connection-building.

'*Mart bidi ch'ullas*' [you'll never be anyone]. Similarly, teachers often make comments about children's relative value and potential, and define these within narrow hierarchies of talents, personality traits and language practices. This is a pillar of authoritarianism in which appealing to teacher approval is defined as success, even when that approval is unrelated to academic learning. Yoghoutjian experienced this commonplace comment, translated as 'you'll never be anyone,' from her own teacher, related to her interest in modern dance and wearing of clothing that transgressed local gender norms. A decolonial approach values and uses students' interests and talents, whatever they may be, to drive their engagement with language and their acquisition of additional registers and domains. A student's love of modern dance would be an opportunity for a project wherein comparisons are drawn or connections are built with speakers through various discussions, debates, presentations or studies of topics within modern dance.

Tenet #2: An approach to language norms and practices that is more descriptive than prescriptive and situates the language's users, and especially its young users, as experts in its use

'*Hayeren che*' [it's not Armenian]. The prevailing perception of multilingual cognition in the Armenian community has been dubbed the 'multiple monolingual' model (cf. Rothman & Treffers-Daller, 2014). Speakers are expected to speak as though they knew no other language, avoiding all loanwords and contact influences. Although all speakers habitually use loanwords such as *telefon* [telephone], *oto* [car] and *zaytoun* [olive], teachers create such a strong norm of scolding these usages that children adopt the habit, reminding one another and even, in Yoghoutjian's experience, their teachers, that only the respective terms *heratsayn* [telephone], *inknasharj* [automobile] and *tsitabdough* [olive] should be used, as the others are 'not Armenian.' This thinking even extends to erroneously (Donabédian-Demopoulos, 2006) stigmatized grammatical features, especially the use of the present progressive tense, which is absent from the academic register but is heavily used in daily life. For example, in a group of teenagers in Boston, one youth, who had minimal Armenian schooling, was asked a question in Armenian using the universally used, but academically stigmatized, present progressive particle *gor*. (cf. Donabédian-Demopoulos, 2012). The youth responded, 'I don't know what that means, but I know that *gor* isn't Armenian.' The youth's memory of this prescriptive rule, taught and enforced by his former teacher, outlived his ability to understand or use the structure itself.

Because teachers of Armenian language are thought of, first and foremost, as model speakers, there is a strong preference among school principals globally to hire women who grew up in either Lebanon or Syria, where vitality is highest. Although these communities are, in fact, highly multilingual and linguistically diverse, their speakers are seen as more legitimate (closer to imagined WA monolinguals) than those raised in other communities, whose prosody or phonemic realizations often reveal their proficiency in the dominant local language. Although numbers require it, hiring teachers who speak with non-Middle Eastern accents is often staunchly opposed by parents and institutional authorities (Donabédian-Demopoulos, 2001). A decolonial pedagogy would reverse this thinking, embracing and celebrating multilingualism and multilingual practices. It would push beyond the elite multilingualism (De Costa, 2019) paradigm of seeing English and French as harmless or prestigious, but Arabic and Turkish as threats, to an embrace of local hybridities and innovations as inherently valuable and positively associated with students' identities.

'*Arants khosilou!*' [Without talking!] Classroom discourse is a foundational component of power relations in the classroom (Kumaravadivelu, 1999) and verbal interaction in the language classroom is a key component of developing communicative competence. The norm in Armenian classrooms, however, is that the teacher controls talk time (frequently shouting '[do this] without talking!'), requiring students to ask permission to speak most of the time (al-Bataineh, 2015). Most permitted student talk is of the teacher-directed, elicited response type, and teachers often complete the expected answer once a student begins giving it; so frequently, in fact, that students often anticipatorily trail off. A decolonial pedagogy questions and disassembles this power structure, giving over much of the learning time to student-led communication and a relatively free exchange of ideas.

Questioning would be critical and beneficial to the student, not only constructed for the teacher's benefit. Students would communicate directly with each other during most of the class activities, with the teacher serving in a supportive, facilitator role, and would have agency in both individual and group activities.

'*Skhal krele*' [incorrect writing]. Armenian youth both within and outside of Armenian schools consistently express high anxiety about writing in the Armenian alphabet, as they anticipate corrections for confusing letters that are phonemically similar. It is so common among the adult and youth generations to write Armenian words in Latin letters, using either English or French spelling conventions, that writers often transfer those spelling conventions to Armenian alphabet compositions, a highly criticized tendency. Professionals often hesitate to write emails or official documents in Armenian for fear that the reader will find errors and criticize their status as speakers, a fact that has accelerated the loss of the official and professional domains to WA language use. A decolonial approach to literacy instruction would embrace translanguaging and other multilingual practices as valuable and shared, and would explicitly support students in developing multiliteracies. Not only do all speakers of WA read multiple alphabets, but they also read in multiple media, analog and digital, and in multiple domains, formal, informal, informational, conversational, ritual, etc. Literacy in a context where Latin letters are used to send WhatsApp messages is as vital to building connections and belonging to the speaker community as is reading published poetry, and arguably more so.

Tenet #3: Embracing transgression of boundaries and hybridity as steps toward pluralism, including hybrid language practices such as translanguaging and multiliteracies

'*Amot e*' [it's shameful]. An Armenian professor was once asked, while opening a professional development session on critical thinking in the classroom, how Armenian teachers could possibly promote critical thinking, when their job was to make sure that Armenian children believe that Mount Ararat (in the Caucuses, an ethnic symbol) is the most beautiful mountain in the world. Many teachers in attendance agreed with the anxiety expressed: they saw critical thinking as inherently antithetical to the transmission of values with which they believed themselves to be charged. Students are also aware of this paradigm. When Yoghoutjian assigned a historical essay to students in which they were asked to question an Armenian king's decision, a top student concluded her essay by commenting that such an assignment 'is shameful' and inappropriate in an Armenian school. Ethnic nationalist rhetoric is the expected norm. A decolonial approach, particularly one grounded in Paris and Alim's (2014) Culturally Sustaining Pedagogy framework, supports pride in identity and positive self-image without being uncritical or prescriptivist in its representations of culture and history. Such a framework requires a shift both in published curricula and in teachers' understanding of their role in children's education.

Tenet #4: An approach to proficiency assessment that centers skills in use rather than conformity to prescribed norms

'*Sahoon gartale*' [fluent reading]. The teaching of literacy currently revolves around the practice of 'fluent reading.' This is a decoding-focused practice that gauges progress by having students read aloud in front of the class, the teacher announcing any errors, while taking no inventory of their comprehension of the text's meaning. A decolonial pedagogy would focus on functional literacy that engages authentic uses of written language and builds students' interpretive, expressive and communicative capabilities.

'*Ardasanele*' [recitation]. Another central tenet of literacy teaching is 'recitation', wherein students are assigned a piece of literature to memorize and publicly recite. Once again, comprehension is not considered, and students are not permitted to engage with the material creatively or editorially. A decolonial approach would indeed teach the presentational mode of speaking, but through meaningful activities in which students explore topics of identity, community, connections and critical thinking. Students would be supported in expressing their own points of view, and peers would respond as critical interlocutors.

Community Institutions as Seats of Power

While we have shared testimony of teacher-led practices that occur at the classroom level, we in no way mean to imply that teachers themselves are ill-intentioned or unwilling to change. Rather, they lack professional development resources and, in the rare cases that those resources become available, such as when they attend the program discussed above, they receive little support and often great resistance from their institutional leaders, whether those be principals, boards of directors or parent committees. Armenian institutions are, like most institutions, somewhat resistant to change, both by their very design, as well as by their ideology (Karapetian, 2017).

To bring social justice pedagogy to schools, teachers need a supportive principal or administrator who is willing to accept new methods and create new structures that support those methods. Principals, however, usually answer to both boards of directors and parents in ways that make them feel very limited in their ability to innovate. Any effort to reform instruction must then engage parents and community leaders, so that they might support and accept an experimental phase and a type of instruction that does not look like what they remember from their own days in Armenian school. In fact, Karapetian (2017) suggests that they may need to go several steps further. In order for teachers to engage in the kind of sustained, profound, reflective practice and risk-taking that is involved in transforming one's teaching, they need sufficient motivation. The experience of the training program we describe is evidence that teachers believing in the project is not, on its own, sufficient to transform classrooms. She suggests that teachers need material and symbolic rewards for their participation, such that their salaries, promotions, awards, titles, etc. reflect the extra efforts they have made. This would require large-scale institutional buy-in.

Finally, there are interpersonal and intrapersonal factors that cannot be overlooked. The work of being a teacher is done out of passion, and teachers are subjected to intense judgments and criticisms. Teachers of WA are generally an aging population, generally underpaid (diminishing both the attractiveness of joining the profession and the ability of teachers to seek out professional development opportunities), and usually offered little to no training focused on pedagogy, much less on the pedagogy of language. Teachers joining the present program are often unfamiliar with concepts such as lesson-planning, alignment to standards, Vygotsky's (1978) Zone of Proximal Development (McLeod, 2019) or formative assessments. Each of these factors primes teachers to feel insecure or disempowered in various aspects of the training program. The program often involves great shows of emotion and teachers reflecting, after the fact, that it has been transformative for them on both personal and professional levels.

There is a perception in most Armenian communities that those who become language teachers do so because they were unsuccessful in more prestigious academic endeavors. Most language teachers are married women, whose husbands are the primary breadwinners, while subjects such as math and history are often taught by Armenian men. Textbooks, however, are often written by male language experts, referred to somewhat idiomatically as 'linguists.' Paradoxically, since teachers are imagined to be paragons of authoritative language and guardians of acceptable language practices, their perceived 'mistakes' are severely scrutinized and they tend to exhibit high levels of anxiety around the legitimacy and 'perfection' of their language (Donabédian-Demopoulos, 2017). Younger teachers are often criticized, mocked and have even been publicly rejected by parents and community leaders who perceive their language practices to be illegitimate.

Significant support is thus needed for teachers to take risks, invest additional labor and question their own upbringing and habits. For those young teachers, raised in Western contexts, whose linguistic practices and philosophy of teaching often challenge inherited paradigms, the present training program offers a sort of liberatory space, wherein their sentiments about student-centeredness, respect for youth and youth culture and their embracing of hybridity receive unprecedented validation. It is the translation of this validation into innovative methods that presents both practical and philosophical challenges for the trainees. For this, they need structures within which they can support one another in informal, personal ways throughout the professional transition, as well as coaching that allows them to reflect on their personal practice in non-judgmental, productive ways. We have attempted to offer this through monthly mentoring sessions over Zoom, but have not yet succeeded in sustaining the engagement needed from teachers to maintain the momentum they have at the end of the intensive program. We mentioned above that sustaining such programs has historically been financially infeasible, and indeed our own program involves hundreds of hours of unpaid labor from professors who have to combine this program with full-time, paid work to make it a reality. These realities point to further unanswered questions of practicality in social justice training for language teachers.

Intersections with Training Needs of 'World' Language Teachers

While heritage languages are special in many ways and have unique needs and challenges, world languages are also often heritage languages, so the dichotomy is somewhat false. Also, the term 'world languages' implies that heritage languages, by contrast, are important on something less than a global scale, which is often false, especially in a case like that of Western Armenian, which is spoken on six continents, and this assertion is also largely irrelevant to questions of pedagogy. While 'world language' teachers may have access to a far greater number, and therefore variety, of written materials for instruction, they are no less obligated to examine the discursive frameworks of those materials for their relationship to empowering and justice-minded pedagogy. While most learners of a heritage language will encounter complex emotions relating to identity and community acceptance that may complicate their learning journey (Karapetian, 2017), learners of 'world' languages should also be introduced to critical thought about identity, privilege and acceptance, and will also sometimes relate to their target language through complicated family heritage. Moreover, if WA teachers face institutional, interpersonal and intrapersonal barriers to implementing a decolonial or critical language pedagogy framework, many of those barriers also exist within schools that have not taken language maintenance or transmission as central to their mission. We therefore conclude that the lessons of this teacher education program and its participants will serve as useful guides for all teacher training programs wherein a decolonial or social justice framework is sought.

Conclusion

There are both theoretical and practical challenges for the adoption of social justice or decolonial pedagogy in the Western Armenian context. On a theoretical level, there are gaps in at least two areas. First, heritage language frameworks have yet to sufficiently account for the paradoxical language practices and resources that face teachers of languages with limited vitality. WA teachers in the US are understandably anxious about allowing youth to act as language policymakers, given the poverty of exposure they have to traditional linguistic forms and the overwhelming dominance of English in the home and other domains. Second, theories of belongingness and acculturation offer rich explanations for both the successful and unsuccessful experiences of US heritage learners of WA, but less on the establishment of supportive environments for community-based language learning in cases where white supremacy, Eurocentrism and capitalist values are deeply ingrained in both individuals and communal discourses.

In terms of practical teacher training, the beginnings of a decolonial approach may be discernible in the present teacher training program, which centers on the application of communicative language teaching and project-based language learning, but the program lasts only four weeks in residence, and most teachers fail to take full advantage of the year-round coaching offered because they feel insufficiently supported in the material, institutional, interpersonal and intrapersonal domains (al-Bataineh, 2019b). While most of the participating teachers demonstrate great motivation and openness, we see how the paradigms proposed by the program and those widely adopted in the schools are diametrically opposed. Furthermore, we see that the program is only marginally or temporarily impactful for most teachers, which is in line with research about teacher reform through training more generally (Borg, 2011; Donato, 2016; Ferguson & Donno, 2003). Even a longer, more comprehensive program should expect significant inefficiencies without coordinated support in the other domains.

Generally, we conclude that a move away from authoritarian hierarchies and toward student-centeredness, away from purist prescriptivism and toward authentic multilingual instruction, away from static representations of culture and toward relevant, responsive and dynamic cultural pedagogy does not only require a shift in the external conditions such as available teaching tools, class sizes and formats, assessment protocols and classroom discourses. We find that it also requires profound internal changes in individuals' self-concepts, in institutional structures, and in visions for what successful language pedagogy would achieve. No one limb of the pedagogical body can achieve this in isolation, and it will be near impossible to justify the needed efforts in financial terms alone. WA community institutions are already threatened by limited funds, political instability, demographic shifts and declining participation. WA language teachers already have to endure a loss of usage domains for the WA language, a lack of training and resources, unrealistic community expectations and students who lack buy-in to their mission. While a decolonial pedagogical model appears to address most areas of the map of threats to WA language survival, and to represent many realities of community members' lived experiences, many different actors will have to embrace counter-intuitive principles and take radical actions within their respective spheres of influence in order to give this model the momentum it needs to stem the tide of decline and disengagement from the language, particularly in the US. Who has the right to define this new path and where the pedagogical center of the diaspora should lie, if there should be one at all, are unavoidable questions, though not easy to answer. 'World' languages may not face such dire circumstances, but are certainly always contested in terms of funding, value and institutionally-adopted objectives. The same questions must be reckoned with before social justice approaches can become central to program design and teacher work: who is centered in the charting of the course of the language program, and who has the right to drive the teacher training agenda?

Discussion Questions

(1) How does the target language you teach relate to the concept of decolonization? Is it a language of colonizers, of the colonized, or both?
(2) In what ways would successful acquisition of your target language empower students within the socioeconomic power structure? In what ways would it disempower them?
(3) In what ways is your curriculum teacher-centered or authoritarian? In what ways could it be handed over to the students and centered on their interests and needs?
(4) What barriers are you or your teacher trainees likely to face if you or they commit to decentering the teacher and decolonizing the ideology of the language program?

Note

(1) This chapter was written before the explosion in Beirut, Lebanon on 4 August 2020, which has been compared in magnitude to the bombing of Hiroshima. One of the authors was displaced as a result of this and related events. Our hearts are broken by the devastation of this beautiful and diverse country, and we feel a great weight for the cultural and linguistic consequences of the devastation of the Armenian Lebanese community. We are, frankly, at a loss for further words about this pain and grief.

References

al-Bataineh, A. (2015) Cent ans après: Politiques scolaires et la vitalité des langues en danger le cas de l'arménien occidental. Unpublished doctoral thesis, Institut National des Langues et Civilisations Orientales.
al-Bataineh, A. (2016) Is Western Armenian an endangered language in Lebanon? Comparative qualitative perspectives on an unanswered question. In A. Donabédian, L. Choueiri and L. Dimachki (eds) Proceedings of the Multilingualism across Disciplines Conference, American University of Beirut, April 7–9, 2014. Washington, DC: Georgetown University Press.
al-Bataineh, A. (2019a) Communicative competence: A necessary approach for Western Armenian language vitality. Proceedings of Challenges in Teaching Western

Armenian in the 21st Century Conference. Paris: Études arméniennes contemporaines.

al-Bataineh, A. (2019b) *Training Endangered Language Teachers to be at the Forefront of Project-based Learning*. [Presentation]. Future of Education Conference, Florence, 19 June.

Alim, H.S. (2007) Critical hip-hop language pedagogies: Combat, consciousness, and the cultural politics of communication. *Journal of Language, Identity, and Education* 6 (2), 161–176.

Alim, H.S. (2011) Global ill-literacies: Hip hop cultures, youth identities, and the politics of literacy. *Review of Research in Education* 35 (1), 120–146.

Borg, S. (2011) The impact of in-service teacher education on language teachers' beliefs. *System* 39 (3), 370–380.

Boudakian, M. (1994) Crossing over to the other side. In J. Kadi (ed.) *Food for Our Grandmothers: Writings by Arab-American and Arab-Canadian Feminists* (pp. 32–38). Boston, MA: South End Press.

Cope, B. and Kalantzis, M. (eds) (2000) *Multiliteracies: Literacy Learning and the Design of Social Futures*. London: Routledge for New London Group.

Cushing-Leubner, J., Eik, J., Vang-Moua, B., Yang, P., Schornack, M. and Her, K. (2019) *Antiracism, Anticolonialism, and Culturally Sustaining Approaches to Language Teacher Education*. [Presentation]. Society, Identity, and Transformation in Language Teacher Education: 11th International Language Teacher Education Conference, Minneapolis.

De Costa, P. (2019) Elite multilingualism, affect and neoliberalism. *Journal of Multilingual and Multicultural Development* 40 (5), 453–460.

Donabedian-Demopoulos, A. (2001) Langues et diasporas: enjeux linguistiques et enjeux identitaires. Réflexion à partir du cas de l'arménien occidental. In Ecole Française d'Athènes (ed.) *Arméniens et Grecs en diaspora: approches comparatives* (pp. 523–538). Athens: Ecole Française d'Athènes.

Donabédian-Demopoulos, A. (2006) Les 'turcismes' dans le lexique de l'arménien occidental parlé : approche typologique et fonctionnelle. In S. Bosnali and M. Bozdemir (eds) *Contact des langues II, les mots voyageurs et l'Orient (actes du colloque les mots voyageurs en Orient, Istanbul)* (pp. 239–256). Istanbul: Presses universitaires de Bogazigi.

Donabédian Demopoulos, A. (2012) Evidentiel et progressif: quel statut grammatical pour la saillance prédicative? *Faits de langues*, 39(1), 65–82.

Donabédian-Demopoulos, A. (2017) Cent ans après, l'arménien occidental au Liban: Vernaculaire et littératie au carrefour des enjeux identitaires. In C. Babikian Assaf, C. Eddé, L. Nordiguian and V. Tachjian (eds) *Cent ans après, l'arménien occidental au Liban: Vernaculaire et littératie au carrefour des enjeux identitaires* (pp. 253–260). Beirut: Editions de l'Université Saint-Joseph.

Donabédian-Demopoulos, A. and al-Bataineh, A. (2014) *L'arménien occidental en France: dynamiques actuelles*. Délégation Générale de la Langue Française et des Langues de France. See https://hal.archives-ouvertes.fr/hal-01103172v1

Donato, R. (2016) Becoming a language teaching professional: What's identity got to do with it? In G. Barkhuizen (ed.) *Reflections on Language Teacher Identity Research* (pp. 32–38). New York: Routledge.

Ferguson, G. and Donno, S. (2003) One-month teacher training courses: Time for a change? *ELT Journal* 57 (1), 26–33.

Fishman, J.A. (ed.) (2001) *Can Threatened Languages Be Saved?* Clevedon: Multilingual Matters.

García, O., Johnson, S.I., Seltzer, K. and Valdés, G. (2017) *The Translanguaging Classroom: Leveraging Student Bilingualism for Learning*. Philadelphia, PA: Caslon.

Gounari, P. (2014) Rethinking heritage language education in a critical pedagogy framework. In P. Trifonas and T. Aravossitas (eds) *Rethinking Heritage Language Education* (pp. 254–267). Cambridge: Cambridge University Press.

Gulludjian, H. (2014) *Linguistic Compartmentalization in Heritage Language Speakers: Observations in the Armenian Diaspora* [Conference session]. The 2nd International Conference on Heritage/Community Languages, Los Angeles, March.

Karakashian, M. (2016) Հայերի Դասթարակությունը՝ 21-րդ Դարու Սկիզբ-ՃամՑգոյ ու Նոր Մարտահրաւէրներ. *Aravot. See http://www.aravot.am/2016/03/29/672277/*

Karapetian, S. (2017) Opportunities and challenges of institutionalizing a pluricentric diasporic language: The case of Armenian in Los Angeles. In O. Kagan, M. Carreira and C. Hitchens Chik (eds) *The Routledge Handbook of Heritage Language Education* (pp. 145–160). New York: Routledge.

Kumaravadivelu, B. (1999) Critical classroom discourse analysis. *TESOL Quarterly* 33 (3), 453–484.

Makdisi, U. (1997) Reclaiming the land of the Bible: Missionaries, secularism, and evangelical modernity. *American Historical Review* 102 (3), 680–713. https://doi.org/10.1086/ahr/102.3.680

Manougian, H. (2020) International recognition for the Western Armenian language. *EVN Report*, 9 January. See https://www.evnreport.com/raw-unfiltered/international-recognition-for-the-western-armenian-language?fbclid=IwAR02qCQ3jlzT0UU21_TCnmeJ5RhvmmE6GfaTKCHufplSn-xJlxPVXgSgkVQ

McCarty, T. and Lee, T. (2014) Critical culturally sustaining/revitalizing pedagogy and Indigenous education sovereignty. *Harvard Educational Review* 84 (1), 101–124.

McCarty, T.L., Romero-Little, M.E., Warhol, L. and Zepeda, O. (2009) Indigenous youth as language policy makers. *Journal of Language, Identity, and Education* 8 (5), 291–306.

McClaren, P. (2014) Multiculturalism and the postmodern critique: Toward a pedagogy of resistance and transformation. In H.A. Giroux and P. McLaren (eds) *Between Borders: Pedagogy and the Politics of Cultural Studies* (pp. 192–224). New York: Routledge.

McLeod, S. (2019) The zone of proximal development and scaffolding. *Simply Psychology.* See https://www.simplypsychology.org/Zone-of-Proximal-Development.html#:~:text=Vygotsky's%20Definition%20of%20ZPD,-The%20concept%2C%20zone&text=%22the%20distance%20between%20the%20actual, 86).

Migliorino, N. (2008) *(Re)constructing Armenia in Lebanon and Syria: Ethno-cultural Diversity and the State in the Aftermath of a Refugee Crisis.* New York: Berghahn Books.

Moseley, C. (2010) *Atlas of the World's Language in Danger* (3rd edn). Paris: UNESCO.

Okoomian, J. (2002) Becoming white: Contested history, Armenian American women, and racialized bodies. *Journal of the Society for the Study of the Multi-Ethnic Literature of the United States (MELUS)* 27 (1), 213–237. https://doi.org/10.2307/3250644

Paris, D. and Alim, H.S. (2014) What are we seeking to sustain through culturally sustaining pedagogy? A loving critique forward. *Harvard Educational Review* 84 (1), 85–100.

Pennycook, A. (2005) Teaching with the flow: Fixity and fluidity in education. *Asia Pacific Journal of Education* 25 (1), 29–43.

Rothman, J. and Treffers-Daller, J. (2014) A prolegomenon to the construct of the native speaker: Heritage speaker bilinguals are natives too! *Applied Linguistics* 35 (1), 93–98. https://doi.org/10.1093/applin/amt049

Ümit, D. (2014) The American protestant missionary network in Ottoman Turkey, 1876–1914. *International Journal of Humanities and Social Science* 4 (6), 16–51.

Yoghoutjian, K. (2018) Do Western Armenian language textbooks used in Armenian schools in Lebanon serve as a compartmentalization tool for the language? [Unpublished paper]. Haigazian University, Lebanon.

9 Learning *from, with* and *in* the Community: Community-Engaged World Language Teacher Education at Rutgers Graduate School of Education Urban Social Justice Program

Mary Curran

Introduction

As we prepare future world language teachers at Rutgers Graduate School of Education, our faculty believe that to teach and advocate for social justice, teacher candidates must have the disposition and skills to build strong relationships with students, families and communities in order to better understand themselves, their students and the complex and dynamic roles of language, culture and power. Often these kinds of opportunities happen in ad hoc ways in teacher education programs, or do not happen at all. We believe that language-focused, community-engaged experiences and deep reflection upon those experiences need to be intentional, institutionalized and offered to all pre-service teachers. When teachers are grounded in a deep understanding and respect for their students' linguistic and cultural repertoires, they are able to enact pedagogy which sustains and cultivates the diverse linguistic and cultural resources that will support full participation in many communities of practice over the students' lifetime.

Community-engaged pedagogy for social justice is key in the field of language education, as we know that 'linguicism has taken over from racism as a more subtle way of hierarchizing social groups' (Phillipson, 1992, as cited in Celebi, 2019: 247). It is urgent that we create pedagogical spaces based on critical pedagogy (Freire, 2000; Giroux, 1983; hooks, 1994; Macedo & Bartolomé, 1999; Paris & Alim, 2017; Flores & Rosa, 2015) where the status quo is questioned, the voices and languages of the marginalized and oppressed members of our communities are at the center, and educational efforts and resources are mobilized for the emancipation of *all* students (Austin *et al.*, forthcoming). We urgently need world language teachers who are prepared to do this important work as they affirm, sustain and nourish their students' linguistic and cultural repertoires. As such, these elements must be directly addressed in teacher education programs grounded in social justice education.

After a careful examination of pre-service teachers' experiences at Rutgers Graduate School of Education (GSE), we recently reformed our two-year graduate-level teacher education programs to put social justice at the core. Now pre-service teachers of all disciplines enter a program in which they are prepared and immersed in the strengths and challenges present in urban settings; the rich linguistic and cultural diversity and resources of our communities; culturally responsive and sustaining pedagogies (Ladson-Billings, 1995; Paris & Alim, 2017); and community-engaged education (Zeichner *et al.*, 2016; Zygmunt & Clark, 2016). Believing that university-school partnerships have the potential to provide mutually beneficial, transformative spaces for candidates, students and teachers (Austin *et al.*, forthcoming; Burroughs *et al.*, 2019), we developed the GSE Community School Partnership Network, in which our teacher candidates engage in sustained clinical work in schools and required community-engaged placements in urban partner districts. This chapter describes the Urban Social Justice Teacher Education Program experience for world language teachers in terms of program-wide requirements; example language education coursework and course assignments; clinical and community-engaged opportunities; and capstone requirements. In our program, we have moved beyond a traditional approach that includes only classroom-based experiences, to engage our students in classrooms and the community over their two years in the program. The chapter concludes with some of the impacts, challenges and future plans for our program development.

Rutgers GSE Urban Social Justice Teacher Education Program

At Rutgers Graduate School of Education, we offer two pathways to certification: five-year and post-baccalaureate programs. These programs are for two years, and students graduate with a master's degree and a recommendation to the New Jersey Department of Education for a teaching license. Our program redesign puts social justice at the core of the teacher candidates' curricular and clinical experiences.[1]

According to the website:

> The Graduate School of Education's (GSE) Teacher Education Program is designed to develop teachers to be engaged in and committed to excellence, equity, and social justice in their teaching practice. New Jersey is a uniquely diverse and urban state as defined by the following: large numbers of students from historically marginalized linguistic, economic, and cultural backgrounds; high-poverty districts or schools; and population density combined with educational inequality. The GSE Teacher Education Programs aim to develop a diverse generation of teachers prepared according to the *New Jersey Professional Standards for Teachers* with the skills and dispositions to both teach and advocate for all students, as well as to learn from students and their communities. Teachers prepared at the GSE will learn to critically analyze the social politics of urban, rural, and suburban schools and use that analysis to advocate for each other, their students, and the families that they serve as they engage in the most effective instructional practices built upon deep knowledge of their students. (Urban Social Justice Focus, 2020)

Note that we struggled as we named our program, as we understand that the phrase 'urban education' may not completely nor accurately represent our program focus. We are well aware that rural and suburban districts face similar challenges. For our purposes, the *urban social justice* focus is on preparing teacher candidates to work in schools with large numbers of students from historically marginalized linguistic, economic and cultural backgrounds; high poverty; and population density combined with education inequality.

Through these clinical and course-driven experiences, we prepare candidates to:

- develop meaningful understandings of diverse students and their experiences and communities, and the social, economic, historical and political dimensions of urban settings and schools;
- effectively teach diverse students, including those from historically marginalized linguistic, cultural and economic backgrounds;
- identify and disrupt instances and patterns of discrimination and marginalization, and develop their students' critical and active citizenship capacities;
- balance constructivist, student-centered approaches with explicit instruction and scaffolding;
- deeply understand their disciplines, research-based current/best practices in their disciplines, and student learning in their disciplines; and
- be caring, competent, rigorous and reflective practitioners. (Urban Social Justice Focus, 2020)

At the core of this new program is our Community School Partnership Network, a partnership between the GSE and local school districts. To support these collaborations, the GSE has created a new faculty position and hired Partnership Leaders, clinical faculty members whose work is to build relationships with school administrators and teachers, facilitate district placements, teach in the GSE teacher education program, and supervise GSE student teachers.

While at the GSE, all teacher candidates complete four semesters of coursework and clinical practice, which lead to both a master's degree in education and a New Jersey teaching license. Each semester includes clinical experiences, and all pre-service teachers are required to take the following courses: Urban Education I and Urban Education II, and Teaching Emerging Bilinguals I and Teaching Emerging Bilinguals II. These courses, along with Principles of Language Learning, Foundations of Language, and Methods for Teaching and Assessing World Language Learners, are offered during the candidates' first year in the program. Over the summer, they take Classroom Organization in Inclusive and Special Classrooms. In the second year, they spend the first semester engaged in a full-time clinical experience in a partnership, and then in their fourth semester, they take Language in Society, Language and Culture; Inclusive Teaching in Education; and the community-engaged course, Students, Communities and Social Justice.

Importantly, we employ a critical, funds of knowledge framework (Moll *et al.*, 1992), which centers learning *from*, *with* and *in* communities. An important new program addition is the Students, Communities and Social Justice course that provides a vehicle to bridge the university and community so teacher educators and candidates collaborate with district leaders, community organizations and parents to provide community services – for example, developing a reading center at a local community organization or offering after-school tutoring. This learning is shared with the local and global educational community at our annual conference, Teaching the World/Urban Teaching Matters, in which teacher candidates, teachers, administrators and community members present innovative pedagogical activities informed by a social justice perspective. Keynote speakers present on relevant, important topics, such as the school-to-prison pipeline, white privilege and issues of equity in an urban context.

Each semester of the program, candidates are guided to acknowledge, affirm and build on community strengths, while confronting their own deficit orientations, reflecting upon their and others' educational experiences, and considering their roles, responsibilities and possible actions when teaching for social justice.

Rutgers GSE Language Education with WL Certification Program

What does this program look like for a world language (WL) teacher candidate? Upon acceptance, pre-service WL teachers attend a summer orientation workshop that provides a welcome and overview to the program and its social justice orientation and program requirements. They meet with faculty who share their enthusiasm and excitement about entering the teaching profession and the unique role of language teachers in the US education context (Curtis, 2021). In our program, we prepare future bilingual, ESL and WL teachers. Educating these language education pre-service teachers together in one program offers our WL teachers a broader context to understand the responsibilities of language teachers (indeed, *all* teachers) to be leaders and models who affirm multilingualism, acknowledge the rich linguistic and cultural contributions and assets of our students and communities, educate their colleagues about the experiences of emerging bilinguals, and advocate for emerging multilingual communities. To meet these aims, we engage our WL candidates in community-engaged programming, which is a growing trend for language education (Palpacuer Lee *et al.*, 2018b).

To provide an overview of the program, Table 9.1 outlines the required world language courses, clinical placements and community-engaged activities.

In the first year of the program, the WL pre-service teachers enroll in Introduction to Teaching Emerging Bilinguals (TEB) I and II and Urban Education (UEd) I and II. These courses provide foundational orientations to social justice and equity and our linguistic and culturally diverse communities, and the students join members of their own disciplinary cohorts for these courses (we have sections for pre-service teachers in language education, science/math, elementary, social studies, etc.). Interestingly, to indicate the value of both courses and not privilege one over the other by offering it only in the first or second semester, we decided to offer each section for a seven-week half semester for 1.5 credits. For example, a student will take TEB I for seven weeks, followed by UEd I for seven weeks (or perhaps in reverse order). In their second semester, students take the two courses: TEB II and UEd II. To fulfill a three-credit teaching load, instructors teach two sections of one of the courses back-to-back (first seven weeks and then second seven weeks) per semester to different cohorts, or they may teach a section of TEB and UEd to the same cohort.

Teaching Emerging Bilinguals I and II

This two-part course supports students as they develop an understanding of the strengths and needs of emerging bilinguals and their families, and a foundation upon which they can build a set of general and content-specific pedagogical practices. In TEB I, the focus is on dispositions, and fostering perspectives toward emerging bilinguals that includes an understanding of the relationship between language and power and the social-political context of learning English and other languages in the US public school context. We consider the impact of deficit labeling and thinking (García *et al.*, 2008; Moll *et al.*, 1992), and we begin by

Table 9.1 Rutgers Graduate School of Education world language courses and clinical and community-engaged programming

Phase 1 Senior Fall	Clinical Experience Phase I
	Urban Education I
	Teaching Emerging Bilinguals in PK-12 Classrooms I
	Principles of Language Learning: Second and World Language Acquisition [*includes community-engaged programming*]
	Foundations of Language
Phase 2 Senior Spring	Clinical Practice Phase II
	Urban Education II
	Teaching Emerging Bilinguals in PK-12 Classrooms II
	Methods for Teaching and Assessing World Language Learners
Phase 3 Fifth Year Summer	Classroom Organization for Inclusive and Special Classrooms
	Elective
Phase 3 Fifth Year Fall	Clinical Practice Phase III (Student Teaching)
	Clinical Practice Phase III Seminar
Phase 4 Fifth Year Spring	Students, Communities and Social Justice [*includes community-engaged programming*]
	Inclusive Teaching in Education
	Language and Culture [*includes community-engaged programming*]
	Language in Society
	Capstone: Poster Session

reflecting on our use of *emerging bilinguals*, referencing Ofelia García's (2009) use of this term to put our asset-based approach in action. The term highlights our students' bilingualism as a positive characteristic, one that is an advantage and builds on the strengths of their first language as a resource. Moreover, this label can be applied to all of us as we develop our potential as multilinguals. Course content includes language rights as protected in education policy, key court cases defending language rights, and the New Jersey state code regarding languages and education. In TEB I, example key assignments include, for example, an immersion simulation experience (Curran, 2003), watching the video 'Immersion' (Media That Matters, 2009); writing guided reflections; and conducting a linguistic landscape ethnographic inquiry (Curran, 2018) in a partnership district. The linguistic landscape assignment is one we return to over the course of the program. For this assignment, candidates observe the language in signage in the community where they are conducting their clinical placement. Candidates research community demographics and analyze their findings (for example, in terms of 'bottom up' (handwritten) versus 'top down' (official) signs, order and font size of the languages, etc.) to reveal the symbolic messages about power, language and community membership in the linguistic landscapes where they are teaching.

In TEB II, we add a focus on building a toolkit of strategies and practices that support language development and heritage language preservation while practicing culturally sustaining pedagogies (Paris & Alim, 2017). In the second session, key assignments included lesson plan development and making theory-practice connections in reflections on clinical experiences. Some of the key questions from the syllabus are:

- Why is this course called Teaching Emerging Bilinguals?
- Who are emerging bilinguals?
- What do emerging bilinguals need from and bring to schools and educators?
- What is academic English?
- How can educators design culturally responsive instruction?
- How is our public space symbolically constructed? What role does language play?

Introduction to Urban Education I and II

In the two-part UEd courses, pre-service teachers examine urban education from multiple perspectives in order to develop their understanding of the social, political, historical and structural foundations of inequality in US society and their implications for educational settings. The goal is for students to be able to articulate and implement a capacity-based approach to teaching in urban communities. According to the course syllabus, students engage in the following key questions:

- What defines urban? What constitutes an urban community?
- How do urban contexts shape schools and schooling?
- What are the historical, political, social and economic contexts in which urban schools are situated? How might understanding urban schooling within these larger frameworks help educators?
- What is the role of schooling in urban settings? How might schools reproduce or reduce economic inequality?
- How do youth develop as learners in urban settings? What practices push this development in a positive direction?

Course assignments in the UEd courses include a mapping project of an urban community and its schools; an autoethnography; and educator and community member inquiry projects.

Both the TEB and UEd courses are grounded in sociocultural, social justice frameworks and are linked to guided reflection upon the clinical experiences in PK-12 classrooms and activities in surrounding communities. Seminar discussions aim to foster a critical perspective on policy and pedagogy in which students consider their roles and responsibilities in settings with urban challenges, which serve emerging bilinguals. Importantly, instructors guide reflection on the self and others, pushing our pre-service teachers to dig deeply into understanding how their own backgrounds influence what they believe about teaching and learning, reconsidering how they want to act to support all of their students, and inquiring deeply about the lives of their students, families and communities.

Clinical placements

Beginning in their first semester, pre-service teachers are placed in schools in the GSE Community School Partnership Network. These districts have been chosen based on their demographics (those with schools with large numbers of students from historically marginalized linguistic, economic and cultural backgrounds; high poverty schools; and population density combined with education inequality), administrative interest and willingness to collaborate. To manage these placements, the GSE hired several faculty members in the role of Partnership Leaders. To be hired as a Partner Leader, candidates needed strong PK-12 teaching and leadership experience, a clear vision for social justice education, and content and teacher education pedagogical knowledge. The Partnership Leaders hold the important and challenging role of communicating and sustaining the GSE mission of social justice in practice. The Partnership Leaders serve as liaisons, linking theory to practice and supporting communication between the university and districts. They provide the key element for the GSE to implement its Urban Social Justice program.

Students, communities and social justice

In the second year in the program after their full-time clinical placement in the fall, candidates return to the GSE and participate in a required, three-credit, community-engaged course, Students, Communities and Social Justice (SCSJ) during their spring semester. The SCSJ course focuses on learning in outside-of-school settings (like libraries and health clinics) and from students, families, community members and community organizations. We offer several course sections, designed by instructors who focus on different issues and make unique community connections. For example, one section was designed around collaborations with several community organizations in which teacher candidates and community members created health and safety videos, a reading corner in a local clinic, and a community fair at the public library. In the course, students engaged with local community activists, community organizers and parents as they deepened their understanding of the community's history, strengths, challenges, hopes and dreams, and experienced the power of connecting with, learning from and taking action together with community members.

We have created several sections of this course that address issues of language and power, including a section focused on Community-Based Language Learning. In this course, pre-service teachers are prepared to serve as Conversation Facilitators at English Conversation Cafés in local community organizations for adults who are looking for opportunities to practice the English language in informal, comfortable settings. More information about the Conversation Café program and its objectives and outcomes will be provided below when describing world language specific courses.

The SCSJ course also has a local-global option in partnership with the Universidad Autónoma de Yucatán's (UADY) School of Education and meets in Yucatán, Mexico. This section requires an additional fee and takes place in Mexico during the winter session and continues in the local New Brunswick, New Jersey community in the spring semester. While all attempts are made to keep program costs down, only small groups of students (averaging about 10 per group) join the program. This Community-Engaged Education in Yucatán program offers pre-service teachers an exposure to formal and informal education contexts in Mexico and the US. The course structure allows students to build relationships with Mexican K-12 and pre-service English teachers as they learn about Mexican history, cultures and languages.

Community members share their experiences with community-engaged education – for example, a primary teacher shares information about an after-school Mayan language and culture preservation program; women from a cooperative community organization introduce the group to their library and tutoring program, a health clinic, and an artisan workshop in a small pueblo; and students and teachers from the Unidad Académica Bachillerato con Interacción Comunitaria (UABIC), a high school with a community-engaged curriculum, provide a tour of their school grounds (including a tilapia pond and eco-friendly vertical gardens) and explain how their curriculum incorporates community engagement.

The program focuses on issues of language and power. While visiting a Spanish/Mayan bilingual primary school, the pre-service teachers participate in a Mayan immersion experience, which prompts reflection upon the experiences of emerging bilinguals in US classrooms. The pre-service teachers facilitate Conversation Cafés in English for UABIC high school and UADY university students, using strategies of making language comprehensible, meaningful and engaging that they can utilize in their future classrooms. Course excursions to Mayan archeological sites, renovated haciendas and eco-preserves expose the candidates to pre-Colombian, colonial and contemporary influences that inform Mexican history, cultures, languages and identities, which prepare the candidates to embark on a life-long inquiry into a deeper understanding of the different family backgrounds and experiences of the Latinx students that they will have the honor to teach in their future classrooms.

Students who do not register for the section of Students, Communities and Social Justice course that takes place in Yucatán have the option of registering for one of the many other sections which take place in the local community. For example, one section of this course, taught by Dr Kisha Porcher, focused on pairing teacher candidates with members of local community organizations in which they partnered on several projects (for example, fundraising for and building a library of children's books at a local health clinic, or creating informative videos on safety and housing). At the end of this course, the teacher candidates collaborated with the local public library to offer a fair which highlighted the partnership projects and disseminated information about the community organizations. In the coming semester, another section of the course will focus on partnering with a local labor rights organization to offer a remote, community-engaged English class. There are usually around seven to eight sections of the Students, Communities and Social Justice course offered each spring semester; the specific focus or community-engaged components may vary.

World language coursework

In addition to core classes required of teacher candidates of all disciplines, world language teachers are required to take courses in language acquisition, sociolinguistics, language pedagogy and applied linguistics. In this section, we focus on two classes, Principles of Language Learning and Language and Culture, to provide a window into the way that we have embedded community-engaged, social justice perspectives into the program.

Principles of Language Learning: Second and world language acquisition

Pre-service world language teachers take the Principles of Language Learning (PLL) course during their first semester. The course offers an introduction to the field and history of language education, focusing on how we learn first and second languages from a social-cultural framework (Lantolf & Thorne, 2006), while highlighting the importance of participation and membership (Lave & Wenger, 1991). Our social justice perspective requires that we illustrate how power dynamics influence this process, for example, the ways that society privileges which language learning experiences are supported and valued, who has access to language learning experiences, and the way formal and informal instruction can impact validating and sustaining linguistic and cultural identities (Paris & Alim, 2017). We focus on scholarship in the field which acknowledges and builds upon the strengths and resources of all students (Moll *et al.*, 1992), for example, the body of work on translanguaging (García *et al.*, 2008). A translanguaging practice truly puts a student-centered pedagogy in practice, as we shift the traditional world language educator's focus on solely the target language and culture to the centering of the linguistic and cultural repertoires of the students. With students' identities at the center, educators can draw upon all of their strengths, and students bring their whole selves and identities to the learning process as they participate in target language and culture instruction. Using a trans-languaging approach, students are encouraged to learn about, affirm and draw upon their own linguistic and cultural strengths and histories, while making connections to the target language.

The PLL course takes place in the evening and is offered on-site at an elementary school in one of our partner districts. As part of the course, pre-service teachers and their instructor embed an English Conversation Café (ECC), offered to immigrant parents in the district who are looking for opportunities to practice English. The GSE pre-service teachers are prepared as Conversation Facilitators, and the district invites and registers parents who attend an eight-week program which occurs within the class time. The goal is to offer programming that benefits the district and the community, while supporting the development of pre-service teachers' asset-based disposition and technical skills.

This community-engaged programming offers the WL pre-service teachers the experience of interacting with parents and reflecting upon those interactions with their instructors, using PLL course content as an analytical lens. The activity provides a forum in which the pre-service teachers learn from the first-hand experiences of parents; experiment with strategies to make participants feel a sense of membership and belonging; and practice techniques for making language comprehensible and meaningful. Many language learning concepts (like employing 'wait time,' and which corrective feedback is most helpful, i.e. 'recasts' or 'elici-tation,' and the way power and status influence lived experiences with language) are observed and reflected upon in these sessions. Pre-service WL teachers are guided to unpack important questions and concepts that influence language learning – for example: Are schools and communities welcoming to immigrants in the US? What resources in the community are available to people who are new to English? How does it feel to move to a new country and learn the language? What helps and hinders this process?

We offer childcare at these ECCs, and pre-service teachers also have the opportunity to observe and engage in guided reflection upon the ways English and home languages are used among family members or across generations. We have engaged in qualitative research on this program in order to document its impact on pre-service teachers (Curtis, 2018, 2021; Palpacuer Lee & Curtis, 2017; Palpacuer Lee *et al.*, 2018a). For these studies we engaged in a discourse analysis of student course contributions (for example, written reflections and final papers), interactions with community members, classroom discussions and focus group discussions. The analysis of the findings reveals an impact on candidates' identities, instructional practices and dispositions (discussed in the impact section below), and as always, urges us to continue to engage in future research.

Language and Culture

In the last semester of their program, pre-service WL teachers take Language and Culture, a course designed to expose them to 'languaculture' (Agar, 1994) and our responsibilities as language educators to prepare students to navigate linguistic and cultural dimensions of our social world. We focus on the multiple definitions of culture; how we can use 'rich points,' moments of surprise when there are differences in cultural expectations which then become teachable moments (Agar, 1994) in our language teaching; how we can teach languages for global competence; and how we can create authentic, meaningful thematic instruction grounded in global issues that are meaningful to students.

For the past two years, a key element in this course has been the opportunity for virtual and face-to-face exchanges with pre-service English teacher candidates and their instructor at the Universidad Juárez del Estado (UJED) de México. The groups have engaged in a local-global community art focused project designed to spark inquiry into these questions: What does it mean to be from New Jersey? What does it mean to be from Durango? To begin this inquiry, the two groups investigated murals in their communities. Both groups engaged in community-walks and created presentations on their findings, which were shared virtually. Through their self-introductions and presentations on the murals, several 'rich points' of investigation were identified, for example, (1) identities: how the two groups identified themselves culturally; and (2) differences in murals: where murals are displayed, how they are funded and implemented, and what symbolism is used in the two communities. This required that the groups delve into their own 'emic' understanding of their identities and mural art, and find a cultural frame to explain this understanding to their partners. At the second virtual meeting, the groups reacted and responded to these 'rich points.' A third session was held at the annual Teaching the World Conference at Rutgers, when the two groups joined (the Rutgers students in-person, and the UJED students via Zoom) to share the impact of this experience in a professional conference setting.

One 'rich point' came in response to the Rutgers pre-service teachers' introductions. They introduced themselves as 'Chinese American' or 'Colombian American.' When their Mexican peers responded with surprise at these labels (saying that they had 'broken identities'), the Rutgers students chose to examine their reasons for how they identify themselves and the complexity and validation of hybrid identities (Nieto & Bode, 2018: 139) in the US context. They spoke with passion about pride in their identities, how one can be patriotic while acknowledging one's multiple identities and allegiances and that this should not lead to a fear of difference or calls for nationalism.

Another 'rich point' came when the Rutgers students reacted with surprise at the many images of indigenous people and symbols in the Mexican mural imagery. The Rutgers students expressed sadness that few symbols or evidence of indigenous people exist in New Jersey, and they shared an admiration for the ways that indigenous populations are valued and recognized in Mexico. This reaction sparked an investigation on behalf of the UJED students. They carefully analyzed the indigenous images in the murals and noticed that most images were of Aztec communities; however, there had not been an Aztec influence in their region. They expressed surprise and regret that images of local indigenous groups – like the Tepehuán, Hoichol, Náhuatl and Tarahumara – were not depicted. This sparked a discussion of the contrast between the frequency and visibility of indigenous images in the mostly government-funded murals with the actual conditions of indigenous populations and their inclusion in society. The students also noticed that most Mexican murals were officially commissioned works, coming from 'top down' sources; the US murals often grew from more local, grassroot, 'bottom up' initiatives. Both groups of students discussed the impact of the project on their understanding of their own and their peers' identities and cultures and what their new understanding means for their future teaching of 'languaculture.' The Mexican group went a step further to take action and requested (and received) permission from the Escuela de Lenguas to paint a 'bottom up' mural on one of the building walls.

Language education poster session

In their final semester, the bilingual, ESL and WL teacher candidates participate in a poster session in which they choose three artifacts they have produced over the course of their program (for example, a unit or lesson plan; reflections from a Conversation Café; a research paper; feedback on student work; an annotated bibliography). Using those artifacts as an anchor, they engage in an analysis in which they reflect upon their experiences in the GSE Urban Social Justice Language Education program and how they have linked theory to practice, developed a teaching philosophy grounded in social justice, and how they imagine their experiences will influence their future teaching. The poster session is a celebration of their efforts and learning in the program and a moment to reinforce our commitments as life-long learners. First-year students are invited to the event and have the opportunity to learn from their peers.

Impact and Challenges

Our Urban Social Justice World Language Teacher Education program is new. Our second cohort graduated in 2020, and we are collecting data and evidence to document program outcomes and challenges so that we can use this information for accreditation and future planning. At this point, we have gathered some initial reflections on the new program and its multiple forms of impact and challenges.

Impact: Research

In research investigating the impact of the language-focused community-engaged programs at Rutgers GSE (Curtis, 2021), analysis reveals that the students' opportunity to engage with multilingual community members impacted their understandings of identities, instructional strategies, and dispositions. For example, data revealed the following kinds of change: (1) language awareness (of self and others); (2) connections to future teaching (practices and beliefs); (3) an ability to recognize funds of knowledge in community resources and the need for reciprocity; and (4) awareness of how power and language operate in conversations and in our social world. Here is one example of how participation may have prompted change:

> At the [Conversation Café] event where community members were painting posters and signs for an upcoming rally, I ran into one of my former student-teaching kids ... The night of the poster painting, I learned about an essential element of my student's life as a member of the community. Looking back, I cannot help but wonder what kinds of conversations she and I could have had if I had known this when I was her teacher. (Curtis, 2021: 208)

This candidate reveals how important it is to get to know our students and see their strength within their community. Another student writes, '[i]n most cases, I expect the listener to always understand what I am saying ... [A community member] made me cognizant of both the words I was using and the burden that I place on those that listen' (Curtis, 2021: 208). This student's experience will help her as she designs lessons and works to create comprehensible input (taking on this burden herself, instead of placing it on the learner). Comments such as these from journals and class discussions demonstrate how interactions with community members have the potential to change beliefs and impact future practice.

More research on the impact of the program and community-engaged model is necessary. We need to follow our graduates into practice to document their successes and challenges and use the findings as we continuously make adaptations and, hopefully, improvements to the program. We are also getting feedback from our district partners, and ideally, we want to collect evidence from our graduates' future students on the impact of their instruction.

Impact: Hiring

Given the world language teacher shortage we are facing in New Jersey, our graduates are getting hired quickly, and we even have district administrators asking to meet with our students prior to graduation, hoping to enlist them into their ranks as soon as possible. One of the positive impacts of the program is that the partnership districts, where the candidates have done student teaching, regularly hire our WL teachers. This pipeline works well as the districts and teacher candidates become familiar with each other over the two years of clinical experiences, making it easier for them to learn about each other and if they will make a good match. We hope these new graduates, with a firm grounding in social justice, will one day become future hosts for a new generation of student teachers.

Impact: Teacher advocates

We hear, anecdotally, that some of our graduates are putting their social justice education into action by creating community-engaged programming and taking action to support students of color in the districts where they are working. For example, one graduate created an English Conversation program for parents in the school where she's teaching, modeled on the GSE community-engaged program in which she participated. In this way, another program outcome appears to be that some of our graduates are, very early in their careers, taking leadership and advocacy roles around issues of social justice.

Impact: Community programming

Another positive impact is the programming we are able to offer because of our community-engaged model. For example, we offer English Conversation Cafés (to date we have facilitated more than 10,000 hours of interactions between Rutgers students and community members) in local libraries, community organizations and schools. As a result of our virtual global exchange, we will be hosting two UJED pre-service English teachers and their instructor at our annual conference. In this small way, we appreciate the possibility of changing the often uni-directional opportunities for study abroad (in which US students travel to other countries) and instead receive this small delegation from Mexico. This opportunity allows us to focus on the important skills of *hosting and welcoming*, and its requisite time, attention, altruism and kindness, skills we also want to develop in our teacher candidates.

Challenges: Host teachers

At the same time, we also notice new challenges. One difficulty is finding enough practicing teachers who share our social justice perspective who are willing to host student teachers (it is difficult to find teachers to host in general, and even *more difficult* to find ones who align with our perspective). Ideally, we want to find instructors who have experience teaching in K-12 settings from a critical, culturally sustaining pedagogy grounded in principles of translanguaging – a tough order to fill. Another issue is that our candidates expect to encounter teachers and leadership committed to social justice in the field, and they are disappointed and angered when this is not always the case and they witness acts of oppression or disrespect in the classrooms in which they are placed. We change placements (removing candidates from challenging placements) when necessary; however, this is never easy and always a sensitive situation. We are also aware that we need to take responsibility to prepare our candidates for the difficult, courageous conversations and actions (Singleton & Linton, 2005) that they will inevitably face.

Challenges: Hiring

As we are a large research university, in addition to full-time faculty, part-time lecturers teach many of our courses. It is challenging to find enough people with content area experience, a social justice framework, and time. Time is also a factor when hiring and preparing these part-time faculty members as we need to expose them to our program mission and vision and prepare them to put culturally sustaining teacher education pedagogies into practice. In language education, we are now responsible for up to eight sections of the two Teaching Emerging Bilinguals courses each semester. While we are pleased to have this required course on the books, it adds to faculty workload as we now need to recruit, hire, prepare, communicate with and evaluate many more part-time instructors.

Since reforming our teacher education program, when hiring full-time faculty, in additional to experience with research, external funding, and PK-12 and higher education teaching experience, we ask candidates to demonstrate 'evidence of demonstrated commitment to addressing diversity, equity, and social justice issues in pre-K-12 education' (Job posting, Assistant/Associate Professor of Language Education, 13 February 2020). In terms of teaching evaluations, we are now asking questions like these: What guidelines and criteria should we be using to evaluate someone's orientation to social justice? And what evidence should we look for that reveals this perspective in practice?

Challenges: Workload and race

Our Partnership Leaders, clinical faculty members who have the role of communicating and acting at the intersection between the GSE and our district partners, face challenges as well. As clinical faculty, they have heavy workloads that include teaching, large numbers of student teaching observations, and service. While not part of their formal work responsibilities, most of them continue to engage in research as well. They have expressed feeling the brunt of the responsibilities of this new program, and given that they are women of color, this raises stark issues of equity among our faculty. The Partnership Leaders have expressed concern regarding the way the (mostly white) GSE pre-service teachers at times respond to them with resistance and the ways this may impact their course evaluations and opportunities for advancement. As a faculty, we are grappling with what our social justice focus means for us as a diverse group of faculty members who are white and people of color, and what responsibilities should fall to each group so one group is not at the receiving end of resistance or carrying more than their share of the burden of this social justice work, which reinforces inequities within our own faculty and program implementation (Macchia & Porcher, 2019). We are ourselves engaging in many difficult conversations, working to acknowledge our own implicit biases, and acting to make urgent changes in order to move toward full participation in communities of practice for faculty, pre-service teachers and their students.

Challenges: Candidate diversity

Like the majority of programs across the country, our pre-service teacher population is made up of predominantly white women. This is another challenge as we work to find ways to increase our enrollment of bilingual students of color; however, this also leads to new challenges as we realize we may not have adequate support structures for this population. One of our Partnership Leaders, Lisa Knox-Brown, has formed a network for our pre-service teachers of color and is conducting research on the retention and enrollment of Black pre-service teachers at predominantly white teacher education programs (Knox-Brown, 2020).

Challenges: edTPA

Another challenge comes from our context in New Jersey as one of the states requiring passing edTPA scores for teacher licensure. We find that we must devote many class sessions to preparing for this assessment, which takes time away from other possible conversations and activities. In spite of this, even while preparing for the edTPA, we apply a social justice lens; however, we find that may lead to a critique of the edTPA requirement itself (Gitomer et al., 2019).

We also face challenges when conducting research on the program. It is difficult to maintain contact and access to our graduates, making program impact data difficult to collect. We are also aware of the difficulties in analyzing and generalizing from this data given the myriad factors that influence their future teaching and learning contexts and effectiveness in addition to their pre-service teacher preparation.

The Future

We are at an exciting moment at Rutgers GSE as we have staked our claim and made a commitment to prepare WL (and all teachers) for social justice. As we institutionalize this decision, we see opportunities and challenges, and there are few models to follow. We are creating our path as we walk it, as the much-cited quote from Antonio Machado advises: '*caminante no hay camino, se hace el camino el andar* (walker, there is no path, we make the path by walking)'. It a difficult path, especially in the US within our current divisive and nationalistic context, but this only makes the commitment more imperative. As Alison Phipps (2019: 7) writes in *Decolonising Multilingualism*, '[i]f we are going to do this then let's improvise and devise. This is how we might learn the arts of decolonizing'. She acknowledges that 'we aren't going to get it right the first time,' but gestures to possible pathways, including changing who we are publishing and reading; thinking deeply about our relationships and who we are partnering with; listening carefully to multiple and perhaps silenced voices, including those of artists and poets; linking to both local and global contexts; and centering multilingualism.

Similarly, at the GSE we are entering a new way of learning and teaching with and through difference, which may not lead us to landing on a definitive 'one way' or 'best practices' approach to teaching WLs. According to Bartolomé (1994), 'teachers can begin the reflective process, which allows them to recreate and reinvent teaching methods and materials by always taking into consideration the sociocultural realities that can either limit or expand the possibilities to humanize [WL] education' (1994: 178). This changes our understanding of our standards, and especially how we conceptualize *communities* as communities who are now positioned as the leader, as the linguistic and cultural knowledge bearers *who will teach us*. Our new program promises to prepare future teachers who are life-long learners committed to the difficult journey of continually developing one's disposition grounded in social justice and the complex and dynamic skill sets to sustain and cultivate linguistic and cultural repertoires, based upon teaching and learning *from*, *with* and *in* our local and global communities.

Discussion Questions

(1) In what ways does your world language teacher preparation program offer candidates the opportunity to learn beyond the school setting?
(2) At which points in your world language teacher preparation program could you develop and implement community-engaged education?

(3) What do you see as the potential impact and challenges for including community-engaged activities in your world language teacher preparation program?
(4) What kind of learning or professional development would your team need to engage in community-engaged education?
(5) If you have not developed strong relationships with community organizations, how can you begin to identity and develop respectful, mutually beneficial, and sustainable relationships?
(6) Given the high costs for students to engage in a study abroad program, what creative ways can we use to support program funding? What ways can we offer experiences in the local community with similar outcomes?

Acknowledgments

Developing the GSE Urban Social Justice World Language Teacher Education programs is a team effort and is a work in process. Faculty, staff and students have all contributed to this effort, especially Tasha Austin, Jessie Curtis, Marina Feldman, Nydia Flores, Jessica Hunsdon, Nora Hyland, Ariana Mangual Figueroa, Julie Ochoa, Kisha Porcher, Christelle Palpacuer Lee and Anel Suriel. Soliciting and listening to the feedback of our students, community partners, including the New Brunswick Free Public Library, New Labor, the Puerto Rican Action Board, Youth Empowerment Service and our district partners has been integral to guiding our community-engaged teacher education collaborative efforts as well.

Note

(1) A video describing the program reform can be found at the Rutgers GSE YouTube site: https://www.youtube.com/watch?v=3HMySIDMcEg.

References

Agar, M.H. (1994) *Language Shock: Understanding the Culture of Conversation.* New York: William Morrow.
Austin, T., Porcher, K., Curran, M., DePaola, J., Pelaez, J. and Raffaelli, L. (forthcoming) We still have work to do: Community-engaged experiences and impact in an urban social justice program. In P. Clark, E. Zymunt, S. Tancock and K. Cipollone (eds) *Community-engaged Teacher Education: Voices and Visions of Hope and Healing* (proposed title).
Bartolomé, L.I. (1994) Beyond the methods fetish: Toward a humanizing pedagogy. *Harvard Educational Review* 64 (2), 173–194.
Celebi, H. (2019) Mapping the Web of Foreign Language Teaching and Teacher Education. In D. Macedo (ed.) *Decolonizing Foreign Language Education: The Misteaching of English and Other Colonial Languages* (pp. 241–263). New York: Routledge.
Burroughs, G., Battey, D., Lewis, A., Curran, M., Hyland, N.E. and Ryan, S. (2019) From mediated fieldwork to co-constructed partnerships: A framework for assessing K12

school-university partnerships. *Journal of Teacher Education* 71 (1), 122–134. https://doi.org/10.1177/0022487119858992

Curran, M.E. (2003) Linguistic diversity and classroom management. *Theory into Practice* 42 (4), 334–341.

Curran, M. (2018) *Our Linguistic Landscape: Preparing Students to See, Hear and Affirm the Community* [Paper presentation]. AERA Annual Meeting, New York.

Curtis, J.H. (2018) Negotiating identity in a language-focused service-learning project. Unpublished dissertation, The State University of New Jersey, New Brunswick.

Curtis, J.H. (2021) Multilingualism and teacher education in the United States. In M. Wernicke, S. Hammer, A. Hansen and T. Schroedler (eds) *Preparing Teachers to Work with Multilingual Learners* (pp. 191–215). Bristol: Multilingual Matters.

Flores, N. and Rosa, J. (2015) Undoing appropriateness: Raciolinguistic ideologies and language diversity in education. *Harvard Educational Review* 85 (2), 149–171.

Freire, P. (2000) *Pedagogy of the Oppressed*. New York: Continuum International.

García, O. (2009) Emergent bilinguals and TESOL: What's in a name? *TESOL Quarterly* 43 (2), 322–326.

García, O., Kleifgen, J. and Falchi, L. (2008) From English language learners to emergent bilinguals. *Equity Matters: Research Review No. 1*. New York: Teachers College, Columbia University.

Giroux, H.A. (1983) *Theory and Resistance: A Pedagogy for the Opposition*. South Hadley, MA: J.F. Bergin Press.

Gitomer, D., Martinez, Battey, D. and Hyland, N. (2019) Assessing the assessment: Evidence and reliability in the edTPA. *American Educational Research Journal* 58 (1), 3–31. https://doi.org/10.3102/0002831219890608

hooks, b. (1994) *Teaching to Transgress*. New York: Routledge.

Knox-Brown, L. (2020) Through their eyes: The impact of intersectionality on enroll-ment/retention in a predominantly white institution (PWI). Unpublished doctoral dissertation, The State University of New Jersey, New Brunswick.

Ladson-Billings, G. (1995) Toward a theory of culturally relevant pedagogy. *American Educational Research Journal* 32 (3), 465–491.

Lantolf, J. and Thorne, S. (2006) *Sociocultural Theory and the Genesis of Language Development*. Oxford: Oxford University Press.

Lave, J. and Wenger, E. (1991) *Situated Learning: Legitimate Peripheral Participation*. Cambridge: Cambridge University Press.

Macchia, M. and Porcher, K. (2019) Rough waters of resistance: Black instructional coaches affected by implicit bias. In D.A. Thomas, A.J. Mayo and L.M. Roberts (eds) *Race, Work and Leadership: New Perspectives on the Black Experience* (pp. 223–228). Cambridge, MA: Harvard Business Review Press.

Macedo, D. and Bartolomé, L.I. (1999) *Dancing with Bigotry: Beyond the Politics of Tolerance*. New York: Palgrave.

Media That Matters (2009) *Immersion* [video file]. See https://www.youtube.com/watch?v=I6Y0HAjLKYI.

Moll, L.C., Amanti, C., Neff, D. and González, N. (1992) Funds of knowledge for teach-ing: Using a qualitative approach to connect homes and classrooms. *Theory into Practice* 31 (2), 132–141.

Nieto, S. and Bode, P. (2018) *Affirming Diversity: The Socio-political Context of Multicultural Education* (7th edn). New York: Pearson.

Palpacuer Lee, C. and Curtis, J.H. (2017) 'Into the realm of the politically incorrect': Intercultural encounters in a service-learning program. *International Journal of Multicultural Education* 19 (2), 163–181.

Palpacuer Lee, C., Curtis, J.H. and Curran, M. (2018a) Stories of engagement: Pre-service language teachers negotiate intercultural citizenship in a community-based English language program. *Language Teaching Research* 22 (5), 590–607. https://doi.org/10.1177/1362168817718578

Palpacuer Lee, C., Curtis, J.H. and Curran, M. (2018b) Shaping the vision for service-learning in language education. *Foreign Language Annals* 51 (1), 169–184.

Paris, D. and Alim, S. (2017) *Culturally Sustaining Pedagogy: Teaching and Learning for Justice in a Changing World*. New York: Teachers College Press.

Phillipson, R. (1992) *Linguistic Imperialism*. Oxford: Oxford University Press.

Phipps, A. (2019) *Decolonising Multilingualism: Struggles to Decreate*. Bristol: Multilingual Matters.

Singleton, G. and Linton, C. (2005) *Courageous Conversations about Race: A Field Guide for Achieving Equity in Schools*. Thousand Oaks, CA: Corwin.

Urban Social Justice Focus (2020) See https://gse.rutgers.edu/academic-programs/five-year-teacher-education-programs.

Zeichner, K., Bowman, M., Guillen, L. and Napolitan, K. (2016) Engaging and working in solidarity with local communities in preparing the teachers of their children. *Journal of Teacher Education* 67 (4), 277–290.

Zygmunt, E. and Clark, P. (2016) *Transforming Teacher Education for Social Justice*. New York: Teachers College Press.

10 Enacting Social Justice in Teacher Education: Modeling, Reflection and Critical Engagement in the Methods Course

Jennifer Wooten, L.J. Randolph Jr. and
Stacey Margarita Johnson

Introduction

'This is the first time that I've had a conversation about race with some-one of a different race.'

(High school Spanish II student)

Tasha, a Black teacher candidate, is surprised to see the student reflec-tion quoted above and learn that the first time the student had engaged critically in a conversation about race in a diverse setting was during Tasha's high school Spanish II class.

'You're just a white girl who ain't even from here. You don't know any-thing about me.'

(Middle school student)

Jessica, a white teacher candidate, reflects on what a Black middle school student told her during one of her field experience interactions. Helpless, and genuinely interested in building a relationship with the stu-dent, Jessica responds, 'You're right. Teach me about who you are.'

'Why didn't I know?', 'Is it right?', and 'What can we do?'

(James, graduate teacher candidate)

James, a Black teacher candidate, asks why he never learned about the African diaspora in Spanish-speaking countries or even saw representations of Black people in his K-16 Spanish classes. Realizing the injustice of having never seen himself in the curriculum, he pledges to focus on diversity as he prepares his high school Spanish classes.

Enacting social justice in and through world language education depends on teachers who are willing to do the hard work of intentionally and continually developing new skills and habits of mind, including grappling with critical moments like the ones in the quotations above. The core language pedagogy course required in teacher education programs, often called the 'methods' course, presents opportunities for teacher educators to emphasize the foundational importance of social justice in language education. The three authors of this chapter are methods instructors as well as language teachers, and we see our focus on social justice in our respective methods courses as direct action to promote social justice. We believe that our work can inform how our methods students think about their role as world language educators, their students and their communities, which can in turn influence how they interact with their students, how they construct their curriculum and how they challenge their students to act to improve the world.

In this chapter, we will explore how certain practices not only help our methods students develop expertise in social justice-focused language teaching, but also promote deep, meaningful learning by aligning with what we know about how adults learn. Our goal is to share how we do this work in our methods classes via modeling, reflection and critical engagement. We show how our teacher candidates comprehend what teaching for social justice means, how they learn skills to include social justice themes in the curriculum and how they can reflect on their own values to decide how they will incorporate social justice instruction in their classrooms.

Students in our methods courses include pre-service and in-service K-12 teachers, graduate students serving as instructors in a university language program, as well as teachers preparing to teach in diverse contexts such as fully online tutoring, adult education and various contexts abroad. Because the students we teach in our methods classes are so diverse, calling them all 'teacher candidates' is not always appropriate. In Crane's (2015) discussion, she chose the term 'learning teacher' (adopted from Wright, 2010) over the term 'apprenticing teacher' in order to draw attention to the developmental nature of learning how to teach. However, to simplify the terminology in this chapter, whether our methods students are graduate or undergraduate, pre-service or in-service, K-12 or post-secondary, we will refer to all of the students who take our methods courses as teacher candidates (TCs).

The Role of the Teacher in a Social Justice Context

As described in the previous section, our methods courses need to provide TCs with the tools to teach language, culture and critical engagement as well as develop the intellectual tools to continue growing and developing for the rest of their careers. Kumaravadivelu (2003) identified three roles that teachers perform in their classrooms: the passive technician, the reflective practitioner, and the transformative intellectual.

The passive technician (Kumaravadivelu, 2003) understands and uncritically accepts the theory, research and strategies that lead to good results. Such technicians rely on professional experts as the source of professional expertise and work to become effective replicators of that knowledge in their own classrooms. We would argue that, typically, methods courses are seen as spaces where passive technicians are developed to their full potential and made ready for the classroom. Comparable to Pennycook's (2001: 127) 'language learning machines', the traditional methods course aims to mass produce *language teaching machines* rather than assisting TCs in developing as people and as critically engaged teachers. Freire's concept of *banking education* (Freire, 1970/2000) alludes to the passive technician aims of the methods class where TCs uncritically receive knowledge from the instructor and other experts in the field about effective practice.

All of this standardized knowledge does not allow for personalizing, challenging or taking ownership of the material, however, and that is where Kumaravadivelu's (2003) second teacher role comes in. A reflective practitioner is one who arrives at knowledge by combining expert accounts with results from actual practice in context. Before, during and after teaching, reflective practitioners question the goals, values and outcomes that guide their teaching. Analyzing and evaluating language pedagogy as a reflective practitioner can also form part of a typical methods course, although according to Wright (2010), this is a development that represents a stark departure from the second language teacher education approaches of 30 years ago.

Yet, being a reflective practitioner within the confines of the classroom does not necessarily mean that teachers will make the leap to connecting classroom experiences and expert knowledge with the social and historical realities outside of the classroom. The final teacher role identified by Kumaravadivelu (2003) is the transformative intellectual, a teacher who is not limited to expert accounts like a passive technician and their own personal and classroom experiences like a reflective practitioner. Rather, a transformative intellectual is able to make sense of how wider social hierarchies, world events and power relationships interact with their language teaching practices and the social context of the classroom. A transformative intellectual works to effect change in the world through their work in the classroom.

In our discussion, we describe any teacher who embodies all three of Kumaravadivelu's (2003) teacher roles as a critically engaged teacher. Such a teacher is technically proficient, is reflective, knows what is happening in the world and in the community, and is able to bring that proficiency and knowledge into the classroom to challenge the status quo. hooks (1994) described the politics and the practices of challenging the status quo in the classroom as 'teaching to transgress,' a pedagogy to 'open our minds and hearts so that we can go beyond the boundaries of what is acceptable, so that we can think and rethink, so that we can create new visions ... a movement against and beyond boundaries' (hooks, 1994: 12). hooks' use of 'we' here is purposeful; she emphasizes that every student must be acknowledged, encouraged and valued both as an individual and as an active member of the learning community. Osborn (2006: 28) declared that '[t]eaching world languages for social justice begins with a teacher who is concerned about social justice and holds a belief in the students' humanity'. The critically engaged teacher, then, recognizes that starting from students' lived experiences to create purpose and content in the language classroom, merging the private and the public, is impactful pedagogy.

With social justice as the goal of the courses we teach, critical pedagogy is the framework of critical classroom practices and topics we enact as teachers, practices that address 'difference, power, or social stratification in the classroom or in the world' (Johnson & Randolph, 2015: 36). These critical practices and topics 'may encourage students to examine social issues and effect social change, or they may emphasize more reflective, critically engaged learning processes within the classroom' (2015: 36). Ensser-Kananen (2016: 560) advocates for a 'pedagogy of pain,' which she describes as 'a deliberate and systematic engagement with themes that are uncomfortable, taboo, or suppressed, for the benefit of thinking and acting towards social justice'.

Recent research literature shows that world language educators are doing this work; they explore sexual identities (Coda, 2018), race (Hines-Gaither *et al.*, this volume; Schwartz, 2014; Wooten & Cahnmann-Taylor, 2014), gender roles (Meredith *et al.*, 2018), ecospirituality (Goulah, 2011), interculturality (Conlon Perugini & Wagner, this volume) and community and place-based study (Clifford, this volume; Curran, this volume; Vázquez & Wright, 2018) in language classrooms and teacher education programs.

It is clear that a social justice-oriented methods course must push TCs to embrace all three of Kumaravadivelu's (2003) teacher roles, critical pedagogies, as well as the skills, knowledge and mindsets that inform social justice-oriented teaching as described in the research literature.

The State of the Methods Course in Language Teacher Education

In the previous section we described what critical pedagogy is in a language classroom context. Researchers working in language teacher education programs reach similar conclusions about what practices fall under the critical pedagogy umbrella. Hawkins and Norton (2009) describe three categories of critical pedagogy in language teacher education. The first is critical self-reflection including one's identity, perspective and context. The second is critical pedagogical relationships between teacher and learners (Hawkins & Norton, 2009), referred to by Ekiaka-Oblazamengo (2018) as demystifying practical and pedagogical power structures. Finally, Hawkins and Norton (2009) propose critical aware-ness through consciousness raising. Ekiaka-Oblazamengo (2018: 59) would also add a fourth category of critical practices to this list: asking 'tough questions' to encourage critical thinking.

Evidence from research suggests that the knowledge, skills and mind-sets necessary for critically engaged language teaching are not always present in language teacher education. In Grosse's (1993) study of lan-guage teaching methods courses, no topics related to diversity, inclusion, critical pedagogy or social justice were found in the 157 course syllabi studied. Wilbur's (2007) more recent survey of 31 world language meth-ods courses revealed no evidence of critical topics, and only a cursory inclusion of culture in 22 of the courses. 'While some of the microteaches and class presentations were required to be on a cultural topic, for the most part, practice teaching was performed on language topics (i.e., how to teach a particular grammatical feature, how to teach listening)' (2007: 90). As Shaull (1970/2000) stated in the foreword to Paulo Freire's *Pedagogy of the Oppressed*, 'There is no such thing as a *neutral* education process' (Shaull, 1970/2000: 34, emphasis in original). The lack of a criti-cal engagement described by Wilbur is of grave importance because that supposed neutrality reinforces the status quo of imperialism and oppres-sion, including the racism, sexism, xenophobia and linguicism that are often deeply rooted and embedded in the study of languages.

Recent scholarly work in the subfield of world language education has echoed the sentiments described above and has called for more critical, social justice-oriented and politically conscious approaches (e.g. Glynn *et al.*, 2018; Osborn, 2006; Randolph & Johnson, 2017). Researchers have also focused on teacher education programs as spaces in which TCs can engage in social justice pedagogy (Chubbuck & Zembylas, 2016; Lee, 2011; Mills & Ballantyne, 2016). For example, Chubbuck and Zembylas (2016: 490) called for 'holistic teacher education programmes, where knowledge, skills, and dispositions related to socially just teaching are coherently embedded'. One challenge of embedding such themes in the methods course is that the goals of such courses are often broad and far-reaching. In addition to teaching methods, such courses might include theory and practice in second language acquisition, strategies and mechan-ics for unit and lesson planning, and even test preparation for licensure exams. In theory, it may seem that these courses have the potential to incorporate a variety of diverse, practical content; however, in practice, as noted by Wilbur (2007), the methods course can reflect a superficial, information-focused curriculum that tends to produce more passive tech-nicians (Kumaravadivelu, 2003) than not.

One way to reform methods courses is to engage TCs in constant criti-cal reflection, questioning and deconstruction of the 'methods' being studied. However, this process cannot be teacher-driven. Olson and Craig (2012) argued that effective teaching for social justice in teacher preparation courses happens 'not through overt telling (indoctrination) but through participatory showing in which students arrive at their own conclusions by interrogating their own lives and experiences, propelled by [the instructor's] ongoing questioning' (2012: 444). Below, we discuss how adult learning theory can inform the reflective processes necessary for social justice pedagogy in the methods course.

Meeting the Needs of Our Adult Learners

While methods instructors typically are experts in how people acquire language, in order to inspire the deep, transformative learning that will lead TCs to incorporate social justice pedagogies into their future work, methods instructors must also become experts in the processes and pedagogies that lead to personal and ideological change. Adult learning theory and research have much to teach us about how to help TCs grow personally and professionally and how to maximize their experience.

If a TC comes into our methods course having only experienced one kind of teaching, for example a grammar-focused language classroom that reinforces dominant cultural perspectives and standardized language varieties, how can we help them evolve beyond that limited perspective? How can TCs begin to see their profession and their passions through a new lens? In addition, how can we help TCs experience the discomfort of the learning experience without disengaging or rejecting the learning? In order to answer these questions, we draw on the adult education framework of *andragogy* to understand the needs of our teacher candidates.

Used as early as 1833 (according to Rachal, 2002), the term *andragogy*, formed from the Greek meaning 'the teaching of adults,' was not formalized as a theoretical framework until Malcolm Knowles (1968; Knowles *et al.*, 2005) used it as an alternative to *pedagogy*, which refers to the teaching of children. As a theory of adult development, andragogy has been applied widely in the last 50 years and has been improved and expanded through connections with other adult learning research (Merriam, 2002), as a result of critiques from feminist perspectives (Tisdell, 1998), womanist critiques (Sheared, 1994) and Africentric models of knowledge (Sheared, 1996), among many others. As it stands, andragogy is based on several underlying assumptions about how adults learn, of which the three most salient are discussed in more detail below.

Adult learners draw on experience

Adult learners draw on their reservoir of experiences for learning. This tenet of andragogy is echoed in the literature on language teacher education (Wilbur, 2007) and presents a hurdle for methods instructors to overcome when TCs have been students in language courses that lack a critical or social justice focus. How can our teacher candidates teach in a way they have never experienced as a learner? How can they replicate what they have only heard described but never lived? When a TC has been a successful language learner, it is natural for that TC to begin to believe that the conditions that led to their own success are, in fact, universally beneficial for all students. Wilbur's (2007) research on methods courses supports the assertion that teachers draw on their own experiences of acquisition and other recent observations to construct their own beliefs about second language acquisition and methods. Velez-Rendon's (2002) review of the literature revealed that experiences as a learner can be even more important in determining future teaching practice than teacher education coursework.

As an example, a look at the data related to racial disparities in education indicates that upper-level language courses consist primarily of white students (Glynn & Wassell, 2018) and public school teachers at all levels are overwhelmingly white (82+%; US Department of Education, 2016). The data for who succeeds as a language teacher or language student indicate racial disparities in access. Yet, even when a TC understands that these disparities exist and that they themselves will need to learn new ways of teaching in order to have a more inclusive, representative classroom, that same TC only has their own reservoir of language learning experiences on which to draw, experiences that privilege the white teachers and students involved in those courses. Here the second pillar of andragogy guides our methods course design. If adults learn by making connections to their own experiences, then we as methods instructors must provide TCs with a substantial number and variety of social justice-oriented language learning experiences on which to draw through modeling and examples.

Adults use knowledge to solve problems

Adults want to solve problems and apply new knowledge immediately. This implies that a social justice-oriented methods course would center practical classroom problems, simulations, a practicum, microteaching or other open-ended situations that would give TCs an immediate opportunity to see how their learning is useful and relevant. However it is done, social justice-oriented methods courses must focus on what is practical, actionable and applicable for TCs in order to meet their needs as adult learners.

In our methods classes, we observed for years that TCs would participate enthusiastically in conversations about the theory and research of teaching for social justice, but that there was little uptake. In other words, there were few examples of TCs creating activities, lessons or units that had social justice principles and practices at their core. When we asked our own methods classes about this disconnect, the reason cited by nearly all TCs was that they did not know how to put teaching world languages for social justice into practice. It was good in theory since it helped them think more critically about the field and their own experiences as learners, but it was not relevant or meaningful to them as educators if they could not go into the classroom in the near future and put it into practice. Hawkins (2011) observed the same phenomenon in a social justice-focused ESL methods class:

> Teachers were focused, as might be expected, on the daily work of teaching in their classrooms and schools, and responded with greater enthusiasm to topics and issues that they perceived could lead directly to ideas for implementation and improvement in ways recognizable to them and to the institutions in which they worked, and to which they were accountable. (Hawkins, 2011: 110)

The *new* – that is, new ways of thinking about language teaching and learning vis-à-vis social justice – does not have the currency of the *now* when TCs are faced with the daily demands of planning and instruction.

As methods instructors, we must emphasize that teaching world languages for social justice means taking action, not talking about taking action – that is, imagining, formulating and enacting plans, rather than remaining in the theoretical space. Beyond providing TCs with real samples from the classroom, we must guide them in learning how to adapt samples for their own contexts and in creating a framework in which they can create new social justice activities, lessons and units efficiently.

Adults are internally motivated

Adults are motivated by internal forces to a greater degree than by external pressures. In a methods course, this implies that adults not only bring their own set of motivations and preferences to the table, but also that those internal forces must be respected, surfaced, discussed and included in the learning practice. Reflective activities that allow TCs to connect their internal motivations to the course content will result in more effective learning.

Despite the clear theoretical foundation for including extensive reflective activities that help TCs tap into and evaluate their own assumptions and perceptions at various points in the course, in Wilbur's (2007) survey of 31 methods courses, only one of those courses had a structured reflective activity while six in total required TCs to reflect on their beliefs. Thirteen courses out of the 31 had reflective activities that required TCs to connect classroom observations with theory from the readings, but that sort of reflection focused on the external elements of learning is less likely to invoke deep personal connection or result in transformative learning.

Methods instructors must first understand that our adult TCs will buy into our carefully crafted learning experiences when they are building on their own base of expertise and experiences, applying their learning to solve problems and can connect with their own internal motivations. Then, as we plan day-to-day learning experiences, the previous discussion can guide that preparation in order to maximize not only learning but also TCs' receptiveness to that learning.

Modeling Social Justice Pedagogy in Methods

Because TCs may not have experienced a social justice-focused language classroom, methods instructors should not be surprised if TCs cannot immediately process the methods course content and therefore ignore or reject it. If methods instructors do not provide compelling, recent examples of critical pedagogical practice, they are dooming TCs to superficial learning and to being passive technicians (Kumaravadivelu, 2003) of prescribed practice rather than moving on to be reflective practitioners and transformative intellectuals. Furthermore, giving TCs time, space and guidance on how to tune in to their internal learning processes can help make conflict and stress productive rather than negative experiences in the classroom. Reflective practice also allows TCs to tap into their internal motivations for learning, make sense of how their learning can be applied in different parts of their lives, and how their new roles are being shaped by their current learning experiences (Crane, 2018), all elements that promote a more meaningful learning experience in the andragogy framework (Knowles *et al.*, 2005).

In the section that follows we will describe the specific ways we ensure that TCs in our methods courses are exposed to high-quality examples of critical pedagogy and social justice as well as concrete strategies for promoting reflection and recognizing growth. We each use examples from our methods courses to expand upon connections to adult learning and Kumaravadivelu's concept of the transformative intellectual. Specifically, we focus on four categories of practice: autobiographical narratives, inductive analysis of sample lessons, responding to methods course goals, and reflecting on the role of personal diversity development.

To provide some context for the examples we present, it is important to note that the three of us teach in different contexts, and yet many of our practices overlap. L.J. teaches a combined undergraduate and graduate level K-12 methods course for world language TCs at a regional public research university. Jennifer's methods course is for graduate teaching assistants who teach a variety of world languages to undergraduates at a large flagship university. Stacey's methods courses at a private research university are aimed at two groups. One course is for PhD students in different departments who teach language courses as instructors of record. The other is a master's-level course for people who intend to teach languages, in particular English, outside of the US at any level Pre-K through adults.

Setting the stage with autobiographical narrative

Returning to the example of Jessica from the chapter opening, in that situation she was confronted by a student who challenged Jessica's investment in the student's life, highlighting Jessica's race as one of the contributing factors. Although Jessica responded in what she believed to be a humble manner ('Teach me'), she gave herself a passive role in the reconciliation of the relationship, thereby absolving herself of the responsibility of critically examining her own biases and reflecting on how those biases and associated behaviors may have led the student to make such an observation in the first place. To be fair, there are certain situations and interactions that cannot be planned for in advance. Nonetheless, teacher educators should consider how critical skills can be embedded into teacher education rather than relying on on-the-job training.

In L.J.'s methods course, the stage for a social justice pedagogy is set from the first day as students engage in 'drawing on their own experiences' (Knowles *et al.*, 2005) to make connections among their experiences and motivations as adult learners. In doing so, TCs critically examine their own identities and reflect on intersections among those identities. These collaborative reflective practices establish community and guide TCs to identify, critique and deconstruct power, privilege and bias at the individual, institutional and societal levels. As recommended by hooks (1994), teachers must engage in the same level of critical self-reflection as their students: 'When education is the practice of freedom, students are not the only ones who are asked to share, to confess ... Professors who expect students to share confessional narratives but who are themselves unwilling to share are exercising power in a manner that could be coercive' (hooks, 1994: 21). Thus, L.J. also completes these assignments along with the TCs in his courses. For example, one of the first readings in the course is chapter 2 ('Preparing to Teach for Social Justice') of *Words and Actions: Teaching Languages through the Lens of Social Justice* (Glynn *et al.*, 2018). Early in the chapter, TCs complete an activity titled 'Circles of My Multicultural Self.' The activity asks TCs to list several descriptors of themselves. TCs then critically examine those descriptors through lenses of intersectionality, power, stereotypes and discrimination, among others. For example, how might a TC who identifies as a white, gender nonconforming, second language learner of Spanish have a different critical lens from a TC who is a cisgender Latina heritage speaker of Spanish? And how might their lived experiences with Spanish (educational and otherwise) afford them different assets and challenges in the instructional contexts where they will complete their student teaching internships and eventually be employed as certified teachers?

Another activity that TCs complete during the first days of the class is an autobiographical narrative. Using the medium of their choice (text, images, multimedia, etc.), they respond to the following questions about the language they will teach: (1) How/Why did you learn the language? (2) Why do you want to become a language teacher? (3) How have your experiences shaped your views on the teaching and learning of the language? (4) What biases about the teaching and learning of the language will you bring to the classroom? and (5) What are some of your goals as a future educator?

In Jessica's case, perhaps her interaction with the student would have been more fruitful if she had the tools to critically engage with that student. In fact, it was during those preliminary activities at the beginning of the course when Jessica shared that story and reflected on how her biases and experiences impacted her response (or lack thereof) during the conversation with the student. That is, the onus should not lie on the student to be a cultural ambassador; rather, the student and the TC should 'co-construct the classroom space' together (Emdin, 2016: 27). This type of self-reflection and exposure/critique of bias is a first step in L.J.'s methods course, because it is a first step in social justice-oriented teaching that embraces cultural responsiveness. As Emdin (2016: 43) stated, '[w]ithout teachers recognizing the biases they hold and how these biases impact the ways they see and teach students, there is no starting point'.

An inductive approach to teaching social justice pedagogy

From top-down to bottom-up

Jennifer's methods courses evolved in three stages over a decade: from using traditional methods textbooks and making passing comments about social justice in her own language classes, to including readings on teaching world languages critically after focusing on the Cultures standard (Freire, 1970/2000; Kubota, 2003; Osborn, 2006; Glynn et al., 2018) à la 'social justice week,' to infusing social justice readings throughout the course. TC buy-in seemed to increase with each change, but no more than a handful of TCs incorporated social justice principles and practices in their own teaching.

Feedback from TCs suggested that Jennifer was encouraging them to teach in a way that they had not been taught – that is, teaching removed from their experiences – and that did not seem immediately actionable. In other words, she had not acknowledged two key assumptions about working with adult learners, that they draw on their own experiences and that they want to immediately apply what they have learned (Knowles et al., 2005). The focus on social justice in her methods course changed radically as a result. Rather than starting from scholarly texts, as a first step, Jennifer now shares classroom examples from several sources, including her own practice as a university Spanish professor, from university instructors who have contributed sample materials for public use in her department and from K-12 colleagues dedicated to social justice work. What follows is a walk-through of how Jennifer shares lesson plans focused on social justice themes with TCs more than once and for multiple purposes. One lesson plan from her own classroom practice as a Spanish instructor is shared briefly to illustrate this process.

When TCs first review a class activity, a lesson plan or unit plans, they analyze them for features related to the pedagogical standard or practice they prepared for that day's methods class, such as how the three modes of the Communication standard are addressed, how authentic materials are incorporated, which of the three Ps of the Cultures standard are included, etc. The questions they ask and the comments they make in small groups and whole-class discussion, though, show that TCs quickly realize that the activities, lessons and units go beyond the sanitized curriculum of most textbooks where generic vocabulary based supposedly on one's everyday experience, grammar concepts, and 'windows' on culture reign (Ariew, 1982; Herman, 2007; Osborn, 2006).

As the TCs analyze sample activities, lessons and units from week to week, they begin to articulate that social justice pedagogy involves teachers and students dealing with real-life issues, focusing on diversity and questioning norms. They also see that the sample materials include and encourage multiple perspectives through the use of authentic materials and through discussion of students' own experiences. Without having yet read any scholarly texts about social justice, TCs have a basic understanding of what it is and what it looks like in some classrooms.

'My culture is not a costume': A sample lesson on cultural appropriation. One lesson that Jennifer has shared with TCs was created for intermediate-level students of Spanish during a chapter on food and celebrations. Activities in the Spanish textbook focused on students describing how they used to celebrate holidays with their families, thus combining vocabulary on celebrations and grammar forms to narrate and describe in the past. There was no consideration of why their families celebrated those holidays as they did, how others might celebrate those holidays or not, or how the celebration of those holidays might have changed over time. In addition to having students in her class consider these questions, Jennifer also created a lesson in response to a university news item that had gone viral. Prior to Halloween, a newsletter post encouraged students to think about their choice of Halloween costumes and to remind students that campus resources were available if they were troubled by anything they witnessed. Various news outlets picked up the post, and some readers' comments on those outlets' webpages applauded the reminders while others bemoaned the fragility of students and the extremism of PC culture. Recognizing the opportunity to link in-class discussion to what students were talking about – and how they were being talked about – outside of the classroom, she asked students to critique the issue of dressing up as a group of people.

She guided students in pre-, during and post-reading activities for the original newsletter post and an article from *CNN en español* (2013) about the 'My culture is not a costume' campaign that university students had created ('Una campaña contra los disfraces de estereotipos se viraliza con "memes"'). The first time TCs looked at the lesson in the methods course early in the semester, they analyzed how it allowed students to work with the interpretive mode via an authentic text and guided phases where students move from demonstrating comprehension, explaining inferences and using the text to consider others' points of view, to using information from the text to inform and justify their own opinions on the essential question (see high-leverage teaching practice #3 in Glisan & Donato, 2017).

After TCs had seen seven to eight sample activities, lessons and units that focused on textbook chapter themes viewed through the lenses of power relations and inequalities during the first six weeks of the methods class, TCs read selections from *Words and Actions: Teaching Languages through the Lens of Social Justice* (Glynn *et al.*, 2018). Jennifer often assigns this text as the first of at least four scholarly texts about teaching world languages for social justice, including selections from Osborn's (2006) *Teaching World Languages for Social Justice: A Sourcebook of Principles and Practices*, Kubota's (2003) 'Critical teaching of Japanese culture,' and selections from Cahnmann-Taylor and Souto-Manning's (2010) *Teachers Act Up! Creating Multicultural Learning Communities through Theatre*. Using these texts as frameworks for understanding, TCs return to analyze how the sample pedagogical materials they had analyzed previously enable instructors and students to engage critically with products, practices and perspectives, to question how power circulates (or not) and what are its effects on people, and to wonder how to advocate for change.

When TCs returned to the lesson on the issue of dressing up as a group of people after reading selections from *Words and Actions* (*Glynn et al.*, 2018), Jennifer asked them to analyze the sample by answering the following questions and to offer suggestions on improving the lesson:

(1) What is the social justice issue?
(2) How does the issue relate to and build on the chapter theme and goals in the textbook?
(3) How do the activities allow students to consider power relations and inequalities?
(4) What supports does the instructor provide to help students explore the issue?
(5) How does the instructor create a space where all students can contribute?
(6) Are there any points in the lesson where the instructor might anticipate discomfort or tension as students explore the issue? How might the instructor be proactive in addressing them?
(7) What are possible takeaways of this lesson?
(8) How does the lesson encourage students to think about actions they could take to improve the situation?

TCs identified that the social justice issue was cultural appropriation. The takeaway understandings (Glynn *et al.*, 2018) of the lesson were for students in the intermediate Spanish class to consider that Halloween costumes are not value-free, that representing others based on stereotypes reifies those stereotypes, and that representing stereotypes can be hurtful. The questions guiding the reading and in-class discussion of the article on the campaign allowed students to critically examine multiple points of view on dressing up as someone in a cultural or ethnic group (including who is represented in the costumes, who is wearing the costumes, and what that says about power).

TCs noted that the framing of the readings and the discussion saw students answer what Ekiaka-Oblazamengo (2018: 59) called 'tough questions'. Beyond the question of should people be able to dress up as anything/anyone they like for Halloween, students were also asked to name what norms might be put into place if people should not dress up as anything/anyone they like, who decides what those norms are, and why anyone should follow those norms.

As the instructor of the lesson, Jennifer then shared with TCs how her students responded to the lesson, including the range of responses they shared during the discussion, how she asked them to reflect individually on what they were taking away from the conversation, and how she and the students decided what the next step in their consideration of the issue would be (e.g. talk with friends about the campaign to get their opinions, notice costumes at any upcoming parties and think about their own reactions, ask people why they picked their costumes). She then shared her framework to brainstorm, investigate and begin to plan to work with a critical topic. The theme of the lesson – in this case, cultural appropriation – fills each blank.

1. What is _____?
2. Why does _____ function the way it does?
3. Who decides _____ is the way it is?
4. Who benefits from _____?
5. Who is left out of _____?
6. How could _____ be different / better / more equitable?

This framework allows the instructor to name the theme (#1), think about power relations and inequalities (#2–5) and wonder about ways to take action to address the theme (#6). In thinking about ways to take action, the instructor – or ideally the instructor and students together (like Jennifer and her students above) – might consider an extension activity to the lesson or unit that would help them gather more information on the issue, raise awareness about the issue in others and/or volunteer, collect items, raise funds, etc. Questions #1–6 are important questions instructors can answer when planning instruction, but they are also helpful to students in the classroom. TCs noted that several of the activities, lessons and units that they had analyzed explicitly asked students to consider these questions and that the questions were both appropriate for the learners' proficiency level and conceptually challenging.

'Try something!' TCs continue to go back to activities, lessons and units throughout the rest of the semester to analyze them vis-à-vis social justice principles and practices. This sustained engagement with classroom examples has demonstrably impacted TCs' planning and instruction. Recognizing the importance of avoiding the banking model (Freire, 1970/2000) where the instructor fills up the student with knowledge (here, teaching for social justice) and the importance of TCs finding their own voice as educators, Jennifer does not require TCs to implement social justice principles in work toward a letter grade. Still, TCs almost always include social justice themes and critical inquiry about those themes in the mini lessons they present in the methods class and in final portfolios to share what they have done in their own classes. TCs also share lessons that focus on social justice in the department's repository of classroom materials. Some of these materials relate to immigration, inclusive language, reproductive rights, child labor, and eating disorders.

Informal conversations and surveying of TCs reveal that they are generally confident not only in their understanding of what teaching world languages for social justice is, but also how they can or will do it. This more inductive approach of sharing numerous classroom examples first and returning to examples to make sense of them after reading scholarly texts helps create new pedagogical experiences for TCs that they can draw upon and adapt for their own classrooms. Both these outcomes are consistent with principles for maximizing adult learning (Knowles *et al.*, 2005). Importantly, this approach is proactive. It tells TCs, 'don't just sit there. Try something!' (Osborn, 2006: 18).

Revisiting course goals

In the previous examples, we explored the practice of asking TCs to reflect on the language-course content provided as samples in the methods course. In this section, TCs are asked to meta-analyze at the course level. This approach to reflection requires TCs to respond directly to the stated methods course goals. In order to structure this activity for success, Stacey formulated course goals that meet the requirements of her program and the accrediting body, while also speaking to social justice, critical perspectives and personal transformation in the course. For example, in Stacey's methods course, the course goals include the following statements:

(1) I can use my knowledge of L2 teaching methodology to plan instruction that promotes language acquisition and successful intercultural communication.

(2) I can gather and interpret information about learning and performance to promote the continuous intellectual, social and linguistic development of each learner.
(3) I can evaluate instruction based on my knowledge of language acquisition and critically engaged teaching.
(4) I can make a case for what constitutes excellent language teaching based on my own and others' experiences; principles of justice, equity and access; as well as theory, research and best practices.

On the first day of class when TCs see the syllabus for the first time, they read and do a brief class discussion about the four goals to make sure everyone understands the terminology and has had time to process the goals. Then, during the same day, the instructor asks TCs to do a free-write in which they have 20 minutes to write everything they know about the four course goals. This can be fairly challenging, and the instructor encourages TCs to ask questions or think out loud if it helps them feel more confident. The instructor then gathers up the free-writes and puts them away. It is useful to read all the essays at that point to get a sense of where TCs are starting and how they are approaching the course. However, Stacey does not respond to the essays, provide feedback or return them to the writers. In fact, the intention is that TCs will forget the contents of the free-write and maybe even forget that they wrote them at all. Then, in the last week of the course as preparation for the final exam, the instructor redistributes the free-writes from the first day of class with no feedback or marking at all and asks TCs to take about an hour to write a reflective essay responding to the course goals and their initial free-write. Once again, they are encouraged to ask questions, think out loud, and to use any notes or resources from the course to answer the questions:

(1) What have you learned since you first wrote this? List some of the ideas, theories, studies or examples from this class that have been most influential in your learning this semester.
(2) How would you answer differently now? Revise your answers to reflect your current knowledge.
(3) What else do you need to learn to be able to effectively teach language with communication and social justice in mind? How will you get the knowledge and experiences you need to progress?

For TCs, this activity has two distinct stages of benefits. The first is found at the initial free-write. If they struggled at all to make sense of how to respond to the course goals, which in Stacey's experience is universal, TCs will go into the rest of the course internally motivated to develop the expertise required to demonstrate mastery of the course goals and solve the 'problem' that the free-write set up. Recall that, within the andragogy framework (Knowles *et al.*, 2005), both internal motivation and immediate relevance to solving problems are essential for meaningful adult learning. This activity allows students to engage deeply, because it honors their experience and orientations as capable adults.

When TCs return to the assignment at the end of the semester, they experience the second stage of benefit. The process of learning often happens so slowly and imperceptibly that they are unaware of the depth and breadth of their growth. This activity helps TCs become aware of that growth, while also asking them to review core concepts from the course and surface the most important experiences. At the beginning of the course, TCs may focus their writing on what they feel more familiar: elements such as grammar and vocabulary and skills in classroom management. However, by the end of the semester, TCs are more acutely aware of the importance of critical engagement and are able to describe specific ways they can focus on equity and access in the classroom as well as social justice issues in the world outside of the classroom.

Self-assessing development

An essential part of teaching for social justice is recognizing one's own positionality and personal growth. TCs can do this through reflection on how they might place themselves on a model of diversity development such as Chávez et al.'s (2003) model. This model, which can be found in Chávez et al.'s essay and conveniently fits onto one single sheet of paper so students can refer to it as they write. The model describes how in every aspect of their lives, people move from a place of unawareness of difference to a dualistic perspective, and on to increasingly more nuanced and integrated views of difference. This model also clarifies the cognitive, affective and behavioral aspects of diversity development and emphasizes that individuals may find themselves at different levels of development in different contexts or different moments. For instance, one person may be at a high level of diversity development in the workplace but demonstrate lower levels of development while traveling in a new country. Teachers can be at a high level of development when interacting with speakers of the language they teach but be at a lower level of development when working with students in their own classroom.

Knowing the stages of diversity development can be invaluable for language teachers in their day-to-day teaching practice. When students react with disgust or make insensitive comments about the language and culture they are learning, informed teachers can plan instruction based on the stages of development they observe in their students. However, in addition to the external application of the diversity development model, it can also be successfully used as a tool for introspection and self-knowledge.

In Stacey's course, the instructor gives TCs the image from the Chávez et al. article (2003: 459) and, using a think-pair-share approach (see Brame

& Biel, 2015, for more description of this classroom technique), TCs individually work through where they fall on the model in their role as a language teacher. Then, in small groups, TCs share short stories of when they themselves or someone they know demonstrated the cognitive, affective or behavioral markers of a particular stage in some aspect of their lives. Finally, small groups share what they learned about the model and what questions they have, and the instructor leads the group in a discussion about what behaviors they would expect to see from students in different language learning contexts and why instructor development matters. For example, if a student is in a dualistic phase of diversity development in the language learning domain, what kinds of utterances would we expect to hear during a lesson? How would we expect that student to act during lessons on critical topics? How could two otherwise identical lessons play out differently if one instructor is in a dualistic stage of development and another is in an integrated stage?

This activity has two benefits for TCs. First, using the model for self-assessment helps TCs understand that it is possible to have different levels of personal development in different areas of their lives. If teachers want to promote social justice in their own classrooms, they have to be committed to developing as teachers and continuing to move forward on the diversity development scale whenever they are confronted with difference. Second, the process of deeply engaging with the diversity development tool forces TCs to develop deeper expertise in how people grow and evolve around questions of diversity and what kinds of attitudes and behaviors to expect from students. This activity not only puts TCs in touch with their own limitations and potential; it also prepares them for the reality of classrooms where students will all be at different places in their diversity development.

Conclusion

A social justice-oriented methods course gives teacher candidates access to theory and research on critical approaches to language teaching, models a variety of examples of critical language teaching practices, and guides TCs through essential reflective processes. TCs are often surprised when presented with lessons and units that include diverse representations of language speakers and that ask language students to critically analyze texts focusing on inequalities. These were not the lessons they experienced as students in K-16 language classes! Working from a framework where TCs question and reimagine the curriculum they experienced as students and the curriculum often prescribed to them as educators by administrators and textbook companies, they can see themselves as possible change agents who create spaces where their students can critically consider what they are learning in the classroom and beyond, how they value and judge what they see happening in the lives of others and their own lives, and how they can be a positive force in the world.

Recall the teacher candidate named Tasha whose student reflection we quoted at the beginning of this chapter. Tasha worked with the methods instructor and her partnership teacher to create a unit on identity for a novice Spanish language course. Part of the unit involved examining intersections of race and identity. Among other authentic resources, Tasha used video testimonials from individuals (including well-known celebrities) who identified as Black and Latinx and excerpts from a news article examining the lived experiences of adolescents who identified as 'Blaxican.' Through online discussion boards, students in Tasha's class discussed intersections of their own racial identities as well as the implications of those intersections. As a concluding activity, students discussed ways their unique identities could be used to combat injustice and enable them to be advocates/allies for other individuals in their communities who may or may not share the same identities. After experiencing modeling and reflection in her social justice-focused methods class, Tasha was able to facilitate a lesson in which students reported that they had never before discussed race in a multiracial setting.

One author finds that her conversations with TCs, like one shared briefly at the beginning of this chapter, often turn to the questions 'Why didn't I know?', 'Is it right?' and 'What can we do?' In one particular methods class, as TCs learned to understand the teaching of culture as descriptive, diverse, dynamic and discursive – drawing on Kubota's (2003) work – one of her teacher candidates in Spanish, a Black male, wondered why he didn't learn about the African diaspora in Latin America at least as much as the 'white guys in Spain who look nothing like me' during his K-16 studies. Class members discussed colonialism and racism (among other sociopolitical issues) as possible reasons, along with the textbook industry's penchant for sanitizing curriculum to avoid controversy and the pressures on teachers to 'get through' textbooks. The question then became 'Is it right?' for these issues (and, by extension, whole communities of language users) to be ignored in the world language classroom. With group consensus being that narrow treatments of language and culture are neither right nor appropriate for any student, TCs collectively brainstormed concrete ways that they could move forward with their students to widen who and what counts in the curriculum while also meeting local, state and national standards (thus answering the question 'What can we do?').

We see our work as teacher educators as a way to take action towards social justice within our contexts. That is, the way that we answer the question 'What can we do?' is by planning methods courses that create a space for TCs to reconsider the curriculum and to conceptualize themselves as possible change agents with their students. We agree with Osborn's (2006) declaration: 'Teaching world languages for social justice is not the end (in the sense of a goal) of education; it is the beginning. The world is changed by teaching world languages for social justice – that becoming the goal of teaching and learning' (Osborn, 2006: 31). Regardless of the setting in which the TCs will teach after leaving our courses, we strive to provide them with the tools to teach language, culture and critical engagement. Our courses also aim to help TCs develop the intellectual tools to continue growing and developing for the rest of their careers. While we cannot predict exactly what kinds of situations TCs will face 10 years or 30 years down the road, we are able to provide instruction within the structure of the methods course that can help prepare them to be critically engaged teachers, whom we described earlier in this chapter as those who start from students' lived experiences and explore issues of difference and power in their classrooms.

Social justice outcomes can be achieved alongside other curricular goals when teachers are strategic and reflective about their curricular design and instruction. The same holds true for methods courses. Although it can be difficult, and maybe even overwhelming, to consider social justice as a key component of the methods course curriculum, it can be achieved through perspective shifting and intentional instructional design. Additionally, when we design methods courses that value the experiences, motivations and classroom challenges of our adult teacher candidates (Knowles *et al.*, 2005), we increase the likelihood that they will move into the role of the transformative intellectual (Kumaradivelu, 2003) who teaches to transgress (hooks, 1994). Through empirical and theoretical research as well as our own experiences in the classroom, we are convinced of the transformative power of social justice-oriented instruction in the methods course.

Discussion Questions

(1) How might you adapt the learning activities in your methods course to be more consistent with adult learning principles?
(2) In what ways are you modeling critical pedagogy for your teacher candidates? How can you expand on those practices?
(3) Consider the sample activities presented in this chapter. What challenges would you anticipate with implementing them? How might you address these challenges in your own class? Or how might you guide teacher candidates to address such challenges?
(4) What are the current goals of your method course? How might they be modified to incorporate a more critical lens that pushes teacher candidates beyond the 'passive technician' and 'reflective practitioner' roles and into the 'transformative intellectual' role?

References

Ariew, R. (1982) The textbook as curriculum. In T.V. Higgs (ed.) *Curriculum, Competence, and the Foreign Language Teacher* (pp. 11–33). Lincolnwood, IL: National Textbook.

Brame, C.J. and Biel, R. (2015) Setting up and facilitating group work: Using cooperative learning groups effectively. See http://cft.vanderbilt.edu/guides-sub-pages/setting-up-and-facilitating-group-work-using-cooperative-learning-groups-effectively/

Cahnmann-Taylor, M. and Souto-Manning, M. (2010) *Teachers Act Up! Creating Multicultural Learning Communities through Theatre*. New York: Teachers College Press.

Chávez, A.F., Guido-DiBrito, F. and Mallory, S.L. (2003) Learning to value the 'Other': A framework of individual diversity development. *Journal of College Student Development* 44 (4), 453–469.

Chubbuck, S.M. and Zembylas, M. (2016) Social justice and teacher education: Context, theory, and practice. In J. Loughran and M.L. Hamilton (eds) *International Handbook of Teacher Education, Volume 2* (pp. 463–501). https://doi.org/10.1007/978-981-10-0369-1

CNN *en español* (2013) Una campaña contra los disfraces de estereotipos se viraliza con 'memes'. See https://cnnespanol.cnn.com/2013/10/28/una-campana-contra-los-disfraces-de-estereotipos-se-viraliza-con-memes/

Coda, J. (2018) Disrupting standard practice: Queering the world language classroom. *Dimension* 2018, 74–89.

Crane, C. (2015) Exploratory practice in the FL teaching methods course: A case study of three graduate student instructors' experiences. *L2 Journal* 7 (2), 1–23.

Crane, C. (2018) Making connections in beginning language instruction: Structured reflection and the World-Readiness Standards for Learning Languages. In P. Urlaub and J. Watzinger-Tharp (eds) *The Interconnected Language Curriculum: Critical Transitions and Interfaces in Articulated K-16 Contexts* (pp. 51–74). AAUSC Issues in Language Program Direction. Boston, MA: Heinle.

Ekiaka-Oblazamengo, J. (2018) Exploring social justice education in South Texas preservice bilingual teacher preparation programs (Publication No. 10973360). Doctoral dissertation, Texas A&M University. ProQuest Dissertation and Theses Global.

Emdin, C. (2016) *For White Folks Who Teach in the Hood...and the Rest of Y'all Too: Reality Pedagogy and Urban Education*. Boston, MA: Beacon Press.

Ennser-Kananen, J. (2016) A pedagogy of pain: New directions for world language education. *The Modern Language Journal* 100 (2), 556–564.

Freire, P. (1970/2000) *Pedagogy of the Oppressed*. New York: Continuum.

Glisan, E.W. and Donato, R. (2017) *Enacting the Work of Language Instruction: High Leverage Teaching Practices*. Alexandria, VA: ACTFL.

Glynn, C. and Wassell, B. (2018) Who gets to play? Issues of access and social justice in world language study in the U.S. *Dimension* 2018, 18–32.

Glynn, C., Wesely, P. and Wassell, B. (2018) *Words and Actions: Teaching Languages through the Lens of Social Justice* (2nd edn). Alexandria, VA: ACTFL.

Goulah, J. (2011) Ecospirituality in public foreign language education: A critical discourse analysis of a transformative world language learning approach. *Critical Inquiry in Language Studies* 8 (1), 27–52.

Grosse, C. (1993) The foreign language methods course. *Modern Language Journal* 77 (3), 303–312.

Hawkins, M.R. (2011) Dialogic determination: Constructing a social justice discourse in language teacher education. In M.R. Hawkins (ed.) *Social Justice Language Teacher Education* (pp. 102–123). Bristol: Multilingual Matters.

Hawkins, M. and Norton, B. (2009) Critical language teacher education. In A. Burns and J. Richards (eds) *Cambridge Guide to Second Language Teacher Education* (pp. 30–39). Cambridge: Cambridge University Press.

Herman, D. (2007) It's a small world after all: From stereotypes to invented worlds in secondary school Spanish textbooks. *Critical Inquiry in Language Studies* 4 (2–3), 117–150.

hooks, b. (1994) *Teaching to Transgress: Education as the Practice of Freedom*. New York: Routledge.

Johnson, S.M. and Randolph, L.J., Jr. (2015) Critical pedagogy for intercultural communicative competence: Getting started. *The Language Educator* 10 (3), 36–39.

Knowles, M.S. (1968) Andragogy, not pedagogy! *Adult Leadership* 16, 350–352, 386.

Knowles, M., Holton, E. and Swanson, R. (2005) *The Adult Learner* (6th edn). Burlington, MA: Elsevier.

Kubota, R. (2003) Critical teaching of Japanese culture. *Japanese Language and Literature* 37 (1), 67–87.

Kumaravadivelu, B. (2003) *Beyond Methods: Macrostrategies for Language Teaching*. New Haven, CT: Yale University Press.

Lee, Y.A. (2011) What does teaching for social justice mean to teacher candidates? *The Professional Educator* 35 (2), 1–20.

Meredith, B., Geyer, M. and Wagner, M. (2018) Social justice in beginning language instruction: Interpreting fairy tales. *Dimension* 2018, 90–112.

Merriam, S. (2002) Andragogy and self-directed learning: Pillars of adult learning theory. *New Directions for Adult and Continuing Education* 89, 3–13.

Mills, C. and Ballantyne, J. (2016) Social justice and teacher education: A systematic review of empirical work in the field. *Journal of Teacher Education* 67 (4), 263–276.

Olson, M.R. and Craig, C.J. (2012) Social justice in preservice and graduate education: A reflective narrative analysis. *Action in Teacher Education* 34 (5), 433–446.

Osborn, T. (2006) *Teaching World Languages for Social Justice: A Sourcebook of Principles and Practices*. Mahwah, NJ: Lawrence Erlbaum Associates.

Pennycook, A. (2001) *Critical Applied Linguistics: A Critical Introduction*. Mahwah, NJ: Lawrence Erlbaum Associates.

Rachal, J.R. (2002) Andragogy's detectives: A critique of the present and a proposal for the future. *Adult Education Quarterly* 52 (3), 210–227.

Randolph, L.J., Jr. and Johnson, S.M. (2017) Social justice in the language classroom: A call to action. *Dimension* 2017, 9–31.

Schwartz, A. (2014) Third border talk: Intersubjectivity, power negotiation and the making of race in Spanish language classrooms. *International Journal of the Sociology of Language* 227, 157–173.

Shaull, R. (1970/2000) Foreword. In P. Freire *Pedagogy of the Oppressed* (pp. 29–34). New York: Continuum.

Sheared, V. (1994) Giving voice: An inclusive model of instruction – a womanist perspective. In E. Hayes and S.A.J. Colin III (eds) *Confronting Racism and Sexism* (pp. 27–38). San Francisco: Jossey-Bass.

Sheared, V. (1996) An Africentric feminist perspective on the role of adult education for diverse communities [Paper presentation]. International Adult and Continuing Education Conference. (ERIC Document Reproduction Service No. ED401417).

Stout, C. and LeMee, G.L. (2021) Efforts to restrict teaching about racism and bias have multiplied across the US. *Chalkbeat*. See https://www.chalkbeat.org/22525983/map-critical-race-theory-legislation-teaching-racism

Tisdell, E.J. (1998) Poststructural feminist pedagogies: The possibilities and limitations of feminist emancipatory adult learning theory and practice. *Adult Education Quarterly* 48 (3), 139–156.

US Department of Education (2016) *The State of Racial Diversity in the Educator Workforce*. See https://www2.ed.gov/rschstat/eval/highered/racial-diversity/state-racial-diversity-workforce.pdf

Vázquez, K. and Wright, M. (2018) Making visible the invisible: Social justice and inclusion through the collaboration of museums and Spanish community-based learning projects. *Dimension* 2018, 113–129.

Velez-Rendon, G. (2002) Second language teacher education: A review of literature. *Foreign Language Annals* 35 (4), 457–467.

Wilbur, M. (2007) How foreign language teachers get taught: Methods of teaching the methods course. *Foreign Language Annals* 40 (1), 79–101.

Wooten, J. and Cahnmann-Taylor, M. (2014) Black, white, and rainbow [of desire]: The colour of race-talk of pre-service world language educators in Boalian theatre workshops. *Pedagogies: An International Journal* 9 (3), 179–195.

Wright, T. (2010) Second language teacher education: Review of recent research on practice. *Language Teaching* 43 (3), 259–296.

Index

CPSIA information can be obtained
at www.ICGtesting.com
Printed in the USA
JSHW021809090522
25754JS00003B/205